GAME OVER

THE INSIDE STORY OF THE GREEK CRISIS

GEORGE PAPACONSTANTINOU

GAME OVER

THE INSIDE STORY OF THE GREEK CRISIS

GAME OVER

Author: George Papaconstantinou
Contact: gpapak@gpapak.gr

Editor-Proofreading: Paul Johnston
Back cover photo: Polyhronis Tsichlakis

First edition: May 2016

ISBN: 978-1530703265
ISBN-10: 1530703263

To Jacoline

CONTENTS

PROLOGUE

You are about to read a political thriller. It is not a work of fiction, not even a dramatized version of real events – it firmly belongs in the "non-fiction" category. The events it describes all took place; the people are real; and identities have not been changed "to protect the innocent". There are very few of those in this story.

This is the story of the years in which the Greek drama has riveted the world. The story of a country whose mistakes caught up with her and forced unprecedented and painful actions. The story of an incredible period, told for the first time not by an outside observer, but by one of its protagonists.

Most of all, it is a story about the people who shaped events by trying to respond to rapidly evolving circumstances often beyond their control. About their decisions – good and bad, right and wrong – and about those who had to live with them. Decisions taken in official and behind-the-scenes gatherings in Brussels, Berlin, Frankfurt, Paris, London, New York, Washington and Athens; conversations with politicians and bankers in Luxembourg chateau courtyards, Davos kitchens and Bilderberg gatherings; in elegant offices and dreary basement meetings rooms.

This is a story about facing a harsh reality, coming to terms with long overdue changes, rewriting the rules of the game, jettisoning comfortable truths. About struggling to understand the new environment, rising to the challenge, and balancing what should be done with what populist sentiment and electoral timetables suggest be done. It is about politicians who tried in vain to understand and outsmart markets; and markets that proved how myopic they are, but also exposed failings in political systems.

Eight years after the shock revelation about the runaway fiscal deficit and the big lie which sustained it brought a whole way of life down, Greece is a broken country. And yet, while enormously painful, the road travelled in these years has been immense.

Meanwhile, in European capitals, the initial fire-brigade approach has slowly given way to a more determined attempt to fix what is broken. This means coming up with a delicate balance of what needs to be done with what can be done given the complex politics of different countries.

This book is about this momentous period; but it is also my own story.

Politics is not for the faint-hearted. Like life, it is "nasty, brutish, and short" – only more so. Most people think the world of politics is populated almost entirely of self-serving cynics. I am not one of those. I was never a career politician, rising through party ranks. I was from the beginning an outsider; I ran for elected office after a successful career, leaving behind a well-paid job and a pleasant life in Paris.

I was appointed Greek finance minister in October 2009, landing the post that some later called "the hardest job in Europe". I was the one to sign the biggest loan ever received by a country, the loan that came with such a tough austerity programme attached. I went on to achieve an unprecedented deficit reduction and put in place difficult reforms. I then saw my popularity plummet as wage cuts and tax hikes took their toll and was eventually reshuffled when it became apparent I had become a liability.

Today, I am no longer in politics. I am *persona non grata* in my own country, with many blaming me for the crisis we are in and for their personal difficulties. Rather than the man who took harsh but necessary decisions which avoided the worst possible outcome for Greece, I am the architect of the hated "memorandum", to many a traitor to the country.

Greek society is desperately worried about its present and its future, having been let down by its self-serving political system and its broken institutions, with its values adrift. A large part of society is also buried deep in denial. It is quick to blame the ones who stopped the party in which so many were participating, very angry and looking for the "fall guy", the convenient scapegoat. That turned out to be me. I was the one who, when the music stopped, turned on the lights and told everyone the party was over. Nobody likes that guy.

As a result, I have lived for years under a peculiar sort of a "house arrest". Walking the streets became a dangerous sport. When going out, it was always accompanied by security. You need a thick skin in politics, but I never developed one. Whatever the undeniable mistakes made when handling an unprecedented and impossible situation, the personal cost has been higher than I ever thought. It even got to the point of me facing a life sentence in court and almost landed me behind bars.

Adding insult to injury, the anger is directed not so much at those who created the mess in the first place, but at those who tried to do something about it. We rarely talk about the arsonists who set the place on fire; instead, all the discussion is directed at the fire-fighters. Did they do their job right, did they cause too much water damage, or did they use too little water and allow the house to burn?

Friends often ask whether it was worth it. Would you do it again? Would you have done something differently? Yes, it was worth it. Yes, I would do it again. And of course I would have done some things differently. But not the main decisions we took; they were right and the only ones possible in the circumstances.

After all this is what politics should be about: you don't get to choose the time, or the role assigned to you, and you shouldn't just try to protect yourself in the process. You do the job to the best of your abilities. And you take the hit; but at least you can live with yourself.

Despite the fact that many years have passed since the crisis erupted, there are still many questions. Did we miss opportunities and solutions that were to hand? Should Greece have threatened to default to get a better deal? Should there have been debt relief from the beginning? Would Greece have been better off if it had left the euro? Could someone else have handled it all better?

These are legitimate questions and they deserve answers. In this traumatic period everything has been called into question; everyone has been second-guessed. And if we want anger, disillusionment and distrust to give way to the kind of self-awareness that heralds a new beginning, we'd better have convincing answers.

In an early draft of the book, I came up with the subtitle "How Greece Saved the Euro". People I discussed this with were shocked with the audacity of the premise. But it seems increasingly to be the case. What started as a problem in a peripheral country at the edge of Europe is now recognised for what it really was: a wake-up call to the whole of Europe to defend one of its greatest achievements and repair its design faults. In a way, to fix the bicycle while riding it.

For my country, it was a unique opportunity to correct past mistakes and start anew, this time on a more solid footing. An opportunity it has so far missed. Europe may have averted disaster, but Greece has not been saved – at least not yet.

Chapter 1

VICTORY

It was a landslide.

The call came around 5pm. At the other end of the line was one of the more respected pollsters. "Are you sitting down?" No, and I was too nervous to do so. "The difference may be over 10 points. You will end up with around 160 seats."

As voting closed at 7pm I watched the TV exit polls give us a comfortable lead. We had won; we just did not know by how much. Would we have enough of a majority to be able to form a government or would we be forced into a coalition?

Our supporters were already out celebrating. I made my way to party headquarters, and had to get out of the car and walk the last two blocks. On this balmy October evening, hundreds of people were already blocking the entrance and side streets; flag-waving, chanting, jubilant. I was congratulated, hugged and kissed. Had we actually done it? I still needed to hear the official results.

Around 9pm, a roar from the street below brought us all to the balcony. George Papandreou, leader of PASOK, and prime minister-elect, was being mobbed by the crowd. People were reaching to grab his hand or kiss him as his security detail desperately tried to clear a way for him to enter the building. He paused briefly to address the crowds with a makeshift loudspeaker, his voice almost drowned out by the wild cheering.

This was his night.

By 10pm, the pollster was proven right. The final projections gave us almost 44% of the vote, more than ten points ahead of the conservative New Democracy party. This translated into a comfortable parliamentary majority of 160 seats in the 300-seat Greek parliament. We had won, and we had won big. George

Papandreou would be forming a PASOK government, without the need for coalition partners.

We were surprised and elated by the margin of our victory, and thought it meant we were embarking on a four-year term to make change a reality, as we had promised in the election campaign. What we did not know was that, in fact, we were entering the most troubled period in Greece's post-dictatorship history; a period in which past mistakes would catch up with her, bring her to the brink of catastrophe, lead to a rude awakening and some very tough decisions – with terrible social consequences and huge political fallout.

But for now, it was time for the acceptance speech.

The Zappeion Megaron is an imposing neoclassical building adorned with soaring Corinthian columns. Opened in 1888, it is the first building to be erected specifically for the modern Olympic Games – in this case the 1896 Athens Games, the first of our era. It is also the venue of choice for historic moments such as election night triumphs.

When we arrived, around 11pm, the building was already surrounded by PASOK supporters. Our motorcade could not get to the entrance and we had to walk. It took a while to push through the wild crowd and to access the press area, filled by now with Greek and international media. As the party's press spokesman, I was supposed to be organizing this and putting order to the chaos. But we were all overwhelmed; and frankly, it did not matter much. We were living a historic moment; logistics could take care of themselves.

Papandreou's acceptance speech was brief, even sobering – no more than five minutes. He talked of hope and of a new beginning; of unleashing the country's potential, which had been held back by corruption, a lack of meritocracy and disregard of the rule of law. It was a continuation of his campaign slogan "either we change or we drown"; very much a "Yes, we can" moment.

Sitting next to him as he spoke, I was barely listening. I was dominated – and divided – Greek politics for two decades.

George Andreas Papandreou (GAP to us) had a lot to live up to. Born in the US and educated in Ontario, Stockholm, the London School of Economics and Harvard, he was very different from the image of a typical Greek politician in terms both of personality and outlook. His core set of beliefs was a blend of American liberalism and Scandinavian social democracy. A sociologist by training, he liked trying to achieve consensus, which is not the first thought that comes to mind about Greek politics.

In many ways, Papandreou was a breath of fresh air in Greek politics. Very much at odds with cross-party established wisdom, he had been accused of many things, but nobody had ever doubted his integrity and willingness to change things and shake up the calcified political system. He brought with him a cosmopolitan approach to life and politics, and an unconventional style, not least in taking a chance with young people.

GAP became the president of PASOK in 2004 after outgoing prime minister Kostas Simitis in effect handed him the leadership. Rather than simply accepting the mantle, he asked for a popular mandate. One million people showed up to vote and to elect him leader; but he lost the national elections a few months later to Kostas Karamanlis, leader of the conservative New Democracy party.

As party leader, Papandreou introduced innovations (the direct election of party leader was widely copied) and experimented, not always successfully, with "changing everything" in a party that had lost its youth and vigour. As the son of the founder of PASOK, he united behind him the traditional wing of the party; as a modern unconventional politician, he spoke to the country's need for change.

In 2007, after again losing the elections to the incumbent prime minister, as a newly elected MP I sided with him when there was a challenge to his leadership. He won the leadership contest against the odds and with the mainstream media rooting for his opponent, and went on to win the 2009 election with the largest victory margin achieved in the last thirty years.

In a country desperate for renewal and bold decisions, I was with him because I believed he was the one who could pull it off. And in 2009 almost one in two Greeks who went to the polls shared this view.

People were asking for change. And we were that change.

After almost six years of conservative rule, Greece in 2009 was in much worse shape than in 2004 when Kostas Karamanlis became the country's youngest-ever prime minister. He took over at a time when its economy was the fastest-growing in the coveted Eurozone club, and with the Athens Olympics showcasing the country's new-found potential and capabilities.

Karamanlis completely missed the chance to capitalise on this momentum. He also failed to address the country's economic, social, and institutional problems, the roots of which were already deep and needed urgent treatment. He promised to "reinvent government"; he did nothing of the sort. Instead, he allowed corruption and cronyism to reach new levels. "Leave it for later" became his favourite response to calls for reforms in all areas.

By 2009, the wave the country had been riding up to 2004 finally crashed after prolonging its life for a few years by sheer momentum. The economy was already in recession and the government was battling to survive a spate of corruption scandals. The most notorious of those was a bizarre "land for water" real estate swap involving one of the monasteries on the Mount Athos peninsula.

Anyone who has been to Mount Athos, the northern leg of the Chalkidiki peninsula in the north of Greece, cannot but be awed by its sheer otherworldly beauty. Twenty centuries-old monasteries, huge part-castle part-fortress edifices, dot a pristine coastline or nestle in forests. The monastic communities have weathered wars and occupations for a thousand years and survive today as a self-governed enclave. It is men only – women are banned.

I had visited Mount Athos with Papandreou while in opposition and before the scandal broke. It was a short trip, but one vivid image has stayed with me: the ethereal light in one of the oldest cathedrals with dozens of huge chandeliers swinging in unison, to the sound of chanting by monks.

Spirituality is what the place is all about; but lately, it had been better known for some very questionable business practices. The entrepreneurial abbot of the 14th century Vatopaidi Monastery came up with the idea of parlaying a deed dating from Byzantine times that awarded his monastery ownership of a worthless lake in the north of Greece into the deeds for expensive state property, which was then turned into commercial development in various parts of Greece.

The truly "miraculous" multiplication of value which ensued was made possible with the help of people in various Greek ministries, who had control over state land and who expedited, in record time for the Greek public administration, the exchange of contracts. Crucially, the office of the prime minister also seemed to be somehow involved. When the scandal broke it was the last straw, and brought the government to its knees.

This was no big surprise. The Vatopaidi affair was the latest and most glaring of a string of scandals that discredited the Karamanlis government. Back in December 2008, the fatal shooting of a 16-year-old by a police officer provoked some of the largest demonstrations Athens had ever seen.

In one of those, student demonstrators were due to march past PASOK HQ in the centre of the city. Heavily armed riot police had surrounded the building. We were worried their presence would provoke a clash, so a number of us stood as a "human shield" between the demonstrators and the police. It was a foolish thing to do and we were lucky to escape unharmed. The hatred, combined with fear, in the faces of the students marching by – some as young as 15 – has stayed with me. There was something seriously broken in the country.

The election campaign was as much about corruption and

insecurity as about the economy. In an exchange in one of their televised debates, Papandreou pointedly asked Karamanlis if he would confirm the official public deficit figure of 6% of GDP projected for 2009 or whether the deficit would in fact be higher. An irate prime minister had dismissed the question, responding tersely, "you know the numbers".

Meanwhile, in line with other Eurozone countries with similar official public deficits, our election manifesto proposed a modest fiscal package of increases in public investment, spending on education and helping those hardest hit by the economic crisis, equivalent to about 1% of GDP. This would be accompanied by measures aimed at curbing waste and increasing revenues, thereby reducing the overall deficit. A few months later, as the disaster in the public accounts came fully into view, this fiscal package had to be abandoned.

The size of the problems we would be called to face were at the time known only to a few in the Karamanlis government. Nevertheless, what stuck in the public mind and was to haunt us later was a phrase used by Papandreou during the campaign. "There is money", he would say, trying to highlight the waste in public expenditures, as well as pervasive tax evasion. When, a few months later, we started cutting wages and pensions and hiking taxes, this phrase became the rallying cry of the opposition to make us look deceitful. Whatever the intention and its real meaning, it did us tremendous damage.

In the Greek political system there is no hiatus between elections and the swearing-in of the new government. The changeover is quick, almost brutal. Elections are on a Sunday; by Wednesday the new government is in place. Absolute parliamentary majorities are the norm, so there is no need for time-consuming cross-party negotiations about a government platform. The two days following the election are for the prime minister-elect to huddle with his closest aides, writing and rewriting names on a list. For all those who hope to be on that list, it is a time to hover over their mobile phones, waiting for that call offering them a seat in government.

On Tuesday afternoon after the election, Papandreou summoned a small group to his office. He was wearing his emblematic white shirt, sleeves rolled up, red tie, no jacket. "The Obama look", we had come to call it, after a newspaper had published side-by-side campaign pictures of President Obama and Papandreou looking remarkably similar. We had congratulated our communications team; they were flattered, but could not take the credit – this was not engineered by some clever PR guy; it had just happened. But since it worked, it became a trademark look.

There were about ten of us – the "war room" team that had run and helped win the election. Chief of staff, party secretary, press spokesman, communications director, some of his closest aides – we had all spent months working for this moment: the formation of the George Papandreou government. On this particular day, we were there to offer our advice and hear his decisions; and some of us expected to be offered cabinet posts.

The composition of the new government was bold – the new prime minister had decided on a hefty dose of renewal. Top cabinet posts went to some of his closest advisors. Half the people in cabinet had never held ministerial posts before. But there was also an attempt to maintain equilibrium with the more established generation of PASOK politicians – among other appointments, by giving the important defence portfolio to his 2007 rival in the party leadership contest.

Then there was the issue of the job of finance minister.

Papandreou decided to split the powerful Economy and Finance Ministry in two, reconstituting the original Finance Ministry with responsibility for the budget, and creating a new Economy and Competitiveness portfolio. And I became the man who would sit in the highly symbolic office of the "economy tsar", on the 6th floor of the finance ministry building overlooking parliament, with the best view of the demonstrations in the central square below. I was the man in the hot seat.

"Be careful what you wish for" – isn't that what they say? This was certainly my case. The finance job is in normal circumstances the hardest job in government; in the circumstances we were about to go through it would prove harder still. Even at that moment, I had enough sense to realize it was going to be the test of a lifetime. But I had no idea what an understatement that would prove to be.

The ceremony for swearing in the government is a solemn affair, which takes place in the Presidential Palace. To outside observers, the spectacle of ministers swearing allegiance to the Constitution on the Bible, with black-robed clergymen headed by the Archbishop officiating, may seem out of place in a modern and secular European country. It is yet another one of many Greek paradoxes.

Following the swearing-in, the entire cabinet walked to Parliament for the first cabinet meeting. The short distance was covered on foot, with a crowd cheering, cameras in tow, and journalists trying to extract statements as we walked. It was a beautiful autumn day, with a bright sun shining - Athens at its best. The parliament building, an impressive edifice that had been the main palace of the Greek king, was gleaming in shades of ochre.

This was to be our happiest day in government.

The cabinet meets in a dark, wood-panelled room in parliament, around a huge oval table that sits about 40 people. The prime minister is in the middle on one of the longer sides, and ministers are placed around him according to rank. The higher the ranking, the closer to the central seat. I was seated two places away, taking it all in, very much in awe.

The first cabinet meeting is normally a ceremonial affair, with a photo-op and then, behind closed doors, the new prime minister giving directions and encouragement to his new ministers. That was not good enough for us. Instead, Papandreou broke with tradition by having a televised speech, focusing on the need for deep institutional change. To make the point, this was followed by the presence in cabinet of the national ombudsman, the first of a series of outside figures called in to address ministers – another innovation, and a source of irritation to the old guard in the room.

Once the meeting was over, we all left to go to our ministries for the final part of the day's choreography, the official handover by each outgoing minister. In my case, this was Yannis Papathanasiou, who had been in the post for less than ten months. In January 2009, he had replaced George Alogoskoufis, who had held the post since Karamanlis came into power in 2004.

The meeting was cordial but brief. Papathanasiou was flanked by his deputies. "George, you will have a difficult time with Brussels. They are pressuring us to reduce the deficit." The outgoing minister's problems in Brussels were by then the stuff of folklore: his late-night phone calls to Karamanlis to convey in vain the pressure he was under at the Eurogroup; and the lighter moments revealed later, such as when he tried to explain deficit reduction plans to Christine Lagarde, then the French finance minister, by writing them on a paper napkin.

I had the distinct impression they were in a rush to leave.

Once they were gone, I looked around. The office was empty. No books in the library, no files on the desk. The hard disks on the computers had been physically removed. There was no trace of any correspondence archive. No files left behind with agreements and on-going negotiations with our European partners.

The slate had been wiped clean. It was as if we were taking over with no history, having to figure out and start everything from scratch.

I was soon to discover why.

Chapter 2

LIES, DAMNED LIES, AND STATISTICS

"Minister, there is one more thing..."

The small balding man speaking from the end of the long conference table was a senior official from the General Accounting Office, the part of the finance ministry dealing with the budget process. He sounded embarrassed.

"What do we do with the €770 million annual payment to the Public Power Corporation pension fund?"

We were in a conference room, close to my office, known as "the portrait room". Its walls are lined with portraits of all those who served as finance minister since the restoration of democracy in 1974 after the 7-year military dictatorship. It is a display which speaks volumes for the troubles of the country.

The first portrait is that of Xenofon Zolotas, a renowned economist and central banker who became finance minister after the junta was overthrown. It is followed by other political heavyweights. Some made it to prime minister; most, however, failed even to get re-elected to parliament. There were 20 portraits, so the average tenure was about a year and a half.

Not a good omen.

As I looked around and took in the illustrious company to which I now belonged, I could not suppress the thought that, under every name, next to the period that each served in the post, another important piece of information should be indicated: the size of the public deficit and debt when each took and left office.

For the past week, I had spent a good part of each day in this room, going through what a lawyer would call a "discovery process", running through budget numbers with all relevant departments and agencies: the Ministry's General Accounting Office, the tax people, the Bank of Greece, the statistics service.

I was trying to piece together a complete picture; to figure out where we were, what the projected deficit was for the year, and therefore what would be our starting point for next year.

October is budget month in Greece. There was no draft budget prepared and left behind by the previous government, so we were frantically trying to pull one together and submit it as soon as possible after the vote of confidence. It was clear from the beginning that the picture was much worse than what we were expecting.

On my second day in the office, I was visited by the governor of the Bank of Greece. George Provopoulos had been appointed to the job a year earlier. During the election campaign he had privately warned PM Karamanlis as well as the Papandreou that, on current trends, the deficit as a percentage of GDP could hit double digits. I wished many times afterwards that he had made these warnings public. But even those projections turned out to be overly optimistic.

The news he brought on that day was not good. I realized it would create a political storm in Greece and Europe, as well as rattle the markets. Hence the announcement should not come from the new finance minister, who could be seen as having an axe to grind against the previous government, but by the Bank of Greece. So we walked out of my office to the corridor where a large group of journalists, with cameras in abundance, had assembled. The scene was pretty chaotic, and the journalists knew that something important was about to be announced. I asked the Governor to speak.

"What I can say on the basis of cash data for the first three-quarters of the year is that unfortunately the deficit is already 10% of GDP. Given its dynamic and what can be done in the next few months, I would venture with a large degree of certainty that the deficit – unfortunately – will touch or even surpass 12%."

The news was out. The words were mild, but the message was clear. Greece was in huge trouble. Its public deficit was a runaway train, at least twice as large as that officially announced by the previous government only a week ago. What's more, the difference from the previous official figures raised uncomfortable questions about the reliability of Greek statistics and the candour of Greek politicians.

The numbers were quickly confirmed by other sources. The head of the General Accounting Office sheepishly brought the monthly bulletins on budget execution for July, August and September. Each should have been publicly released at the latest 20 days after the end of the month to which it referred. This had not happened. They had been duly prepared but, incredibly, had remained in the drawer of my predecessor, who never gave the green light for their publication.

The reason? They described, beyond any doubt, the fiscal derailment. According to the latest September bulletin, the situation was even worse than the Bank of Greece numbers suggested: by August the officially recorded fiscal deficit was already close to 9% of GDP. Despite this, on October 2nd, two days before the election, the previous government had notified Eurostat, the statistics agency of the European Union, that the projected deficit would be 6% of GDP for the entire year.

In short, they had lied.

Bad news comes in batches. Together with those "forgotten bulletins" came a list of expenditure overruns that were not included in the current budget. They added up to over €3 billion. Next arrived a letter from the minister for social security. The pension funds had run out of money; to pay pensions for the remaining three months they needed an additional cash injection of €2 billion. This amount was also not budgeted.

Then there were the unpaid hospital bills. All €6 billion worth of them, going back four to five years; owed to suppliers by public hospitals, but nowhere to be found in the yearly government budget. They were "phantom obligations" that the state had accepted, but had not bothered to account for fully in its books. The hospital suppliers were already threatening to interrupt the supply of essential items if they were not paid. So here we were, trying to add up the numbers and make sense of them. The meeting in the conference room had been going on for days. At the end of each day, the officials would come up with a deficit number. I would sigh and ask, "Is this all? Are we missing anything?" The next day there were more calculations, some forgotten expenditure identified, a more realistic projection of revenues by year-end produced, a skeleton found in some closet, and invariably the deficit number went up. It would usually start with a timid, "There is one more thing, minister". The issue of the €770 million annual payment to the Public Power Corporation pension fund was today's main problem. It was another of those expenditure items that, although paid every year, was not actually recorded as part of the deficit. It was not the only case - a similar situation occurred with the 2009 pension payments for OTE, the partly privatized telecoms company.

In this particular case, back in 2000 when the Public Power Corporation was partly privatized, the state had – as part of the deal with the union – taken upon itself the obligation to pay annually a large sum to the employee pension fund, and to do so forever. This sum was not recorded under pension obligations but instead in the "privatization account"; however, that normally only records revenues from privatizations, not current expenditures.

Privatization revenues reduce the debt, but typically are not counted in the yearly deficit. So this particular pension payment increased the debt, but not the deficit. Everyone was happy: the power company, since it had unloaded a liability on to the government; the unions, since the government had accepted an obligation; and the government, since this annual expenditure would not be visible and would not worsen the social security balance, and hence the fiscal deficit.

There were about 20 people around the conference table, most from the ministry, the rest from the Bank of Greece and the statistics service. These were dedicated, hard-working professionals, the best the Greek civil service had to offer. To my utter astonishment, I soon realized it was the first time they had ever been brought together. The people responsible for cross-checking data on expenditures and revenues and those formulating projections had never before cooperated on a budget or on the data submission to Eurostat.

To make matters worse, each of them could prove that there was no way the 6% of GDP annual deficit figure submitted to Eurostat on October 2nd could be anywhere near the truth. They were completely unable to explain how that figure had come about, instead pointing to all sorts of elements that were inexplicably left out of the submission.

I called the head of national statistics to my office. Professor Kontopyrakis had become a cult figure when, a few years earlier, in the context of an exercise to revise official GDP figures, he had argued that Greek GDP should be bumped up by 25% to take into account the black-market economy. The reason: proceeds from drugs and prostitution were not properly counted. This statement made the CNN "101 dumbest moments in business" list.

The meeting did not go well. Kontopyrakis claimed his service never cross checked or attempted to validate data received from the ministry; they just added them up and forwarded them to Eurostat, no questions asked. So he had no idea where the 6% deficit projection for the year came from; after all, his office did not do projections. But, he noted, it nevertheless seemed a "reasonable projection". And why on earth did I want to change the official notification sent to Eurostat anyway?

I told him that we would be sending a revised submission to account for the real picture – Eurostat had in any case already asked for explanations. I asked him some questions. What had his office done to validate the "official" 2008 deficit, the starting point for 2009? Why had he omitted to include hospital arrears? And how on earth could he seriously think an economy already in trouble by the end of 2008 could produce such high tax revenues in 2009? Then I asked for his resignation.

At about the same time, I discovered a European Commission note, which had been discussed at the July 2009 Eurogroup meeting but never made public. On the basis of first quarter data, the note warned, "Should these trends continue over the year the central government deficit would exceed 10% of GDP, which contrasts with the official annual target for the central government deficit of 5% of GDP".

So the previous Greek government were not the only ones who had known. The Commission also knew things were really off track. They had warned the government, which had responded with deficit-reducing measures that were judged as inadequate. The Commission had not made these warnings public. They had relied on promises more measures would be taken. And as Greece was heading towards elections, it was perhaps decided not to make too much of a fuss.

Eurogroup President Jean-Claude Juncker had put his concerns in a letter to the previous Greek finance minister. He had indicated that measures to date were inadequate and that he was expecting proposals to reduce the 2010 deficit at the October 2nd Eurogroup meeting. The Greek finance minister never showed up for that meeting. Instead, two days before elections, he instructed the statistics service to submit to Eurostat a projected deficit figure of 6% for the year, when his own ministry was already putting the deficit at 9% for the first eight months. And then he jumped ship.

During the summer, under the weight of scandals and in view of the impending economic collapse, Karamanlis had called snap elections. In the campaign, heading for defeat, he played the responsibility card: he talked of the need to control the deficit, and pledged measures to that effect, such as a public sector wage freeze. It was too little and way too late. Had he actually implemented what he announced, the measures would have made barely a dent in a situation already out of control.

In reality, the fiscal deficit had by that time already reached proportions that required the kind of drastic measures no Greek political party was prepared to stomach; and which Greek society – lulled for years into the false security of a continuously expanding economy and a state happy to fund expenditures by borrowing – would soon find out were necessary and very painful indeed.

The final numbers calculated at the end of those interminable budget meetings in October 2009 tallied to a deficit of 12.7% of GDP, or €31 billion. But this was not the end of the story. Some months later, in April 2010, the number was revised up further to 13.6% of GDP. And in October 2010, after almost a year of investigation, and an exhaustive audit of Greek deficit and debt statistics by Eurostat, the final tally was an incredible 15.4% of GDP.

From a targeted 2009 deficit of 2% of GDP set in the December 2008 budget to an actual deficit outcome of over 15% of GDP. In absolute numbers, from a projected €5 billion deficit to an actual realized deficit of over €36 billion. How can someone miss a deficit target by €31 billion in one year in a €240 billion economy?

The answer is in the numbers themselves. The deficit is the difference between what a government spends and its revenues. With everything properly counted, in 2009 the state in all its manifestations – ministries, social security funds, universities, hospitals, local authorities – had spent about €15 billion more than originally budgeted. To pay for that, the government had collected about €16 billion less than originally envisaged. Hence the gigantic shortfall, which the previous government had desperately tried to sweep under the carpet.

These figures hide an infinite number of stories about waste and mismanagement: the €35,000 spent every month by the finance ministry to buy newspapers; public relation budgets gone wild, or outrageous remodelling budgets for ministerial offices that ended up like gaudy Middle Eastern hotel suites;

extravagant gifts, like the dozens of Hermes ties bought by one minister to give away; and crazy salaries – in excess of €300,000 annually – paid to some public sector "golden boys".

Wherever we looked, there was evidence of a system gone mad: hospital supplies, for which the state was charged ten times more than private hospitals; tens of thousands of pensions fraudulently collected, long after the pensioner had passed away; millions distributed to obscure sports or cultural associations, which happened to operate in the electoral district of the minister approving the funds. And all this without going into the serious waste and corruption issues in areas such as defence procurement and major public works. Without looking at the cost of the non-viable pension system, or of the bloated public sector wage bill.

We brought these numbers to parliament on the occasion of the government's vote of confidence, two weeks after election day. Papandreou talked of "an explosive situation", and of the increase in the public debt during the conservative tenure: from €160 billion in 2004 to €300 billion in 2009, nearly double in only six years.

But he also talked of another deficit, one that was turning out to be more important and more corrosive than the fiscal deficit or the competitiveness deficit: a deficit of values and institutions. The fiscal derailment was the result of a crisis of governance, of non-functioning institutions, of people failing to act or making the wrong decisions.

I followed the prime minister with my own speech. I was genuinely angry at what we had discovered, at the complete lack of any procedures to control expenditures, at the extent of the deception. It was not a case simply of laying the blame on my immediate predecessors. They were responsible for the situation over the past few years; but I knew the roots of the problem went back much longer. My own party in its previous stints in government was also to blame for this monster public administration that was incapable of even knowing how much it spent.

In our speeches, both the prime minister and I reiterated our campaign pledge to restart the economy and help the most vulnerable citizens. We promised to honour this commitment, while simultaneously embarking on a serious fiscal consolidation exercise to bring the deficit down to single digits in 2010, and below the 3% threshold in the next three years.

We believed at the time that the two could co-exist; that our European partners would give the benefit of the doubt to a new government openly willing "to come clean" with the country's past and to face problems head-on; and that the markets would continue to lend to Greece and give it time to get its act together.

We were proved wrong.

Chapter 3

LUXEMBOURG

The VIP arrival hall at Luxembourg airport is a small, private affair, very much like the Grand Duchy itself. A one-storey dedicated building away from the main passenger terminal welcomes passengers arriving on private planes and swiftly processes them on to the city.

Alongside Brussels, Luxembourg is host to Council of the European Union formations. Ministers responsible for different areas of government meet there a few times a year. Hence my first European Union meeting as Greek finance minister on this damp October day was in the Grand Duchy.

We arrived at the VIP terminal on a plane proudly wearing its *Hellenic Republic* insignia. There are few direct commercial flights from EU capitals, so the terminal of Luxembourg's Findel airport was packed with government jets. *Republica Italiana, République Française, Swedish Air Force...* Larger jets for the big countries, smaller for the small ones. The delegations were arriving one after another, quickly getting off to be greeted according to protocol and shuttled to their hotels before joining the meeting.

We were a small delegation. I was joined by deputy finance minister, Philippos Sachinidis, a newly elected MP with responsibility for the budget; my two closest advisors, and an assistant. Of our group, I was the only one with experience of such gatherings. Back in 2003, as an aide to the then Greek finance minister I had participated in a number of EU meetings.

As a protest by farmers had blocked the city centre, the meeting had been rescheduled to take place in a château outside the city. It started late, to make sure everyone was notified of the changed venue and had a chance to get there. Presiding – in his hometown – was Jean-Claude Juncker, then prime minister of Luxembourg, as well as president of the meeting of Eurozone ministers, the Eurogroup.

Jean-Claude Juncker is an original. He was at the time the longest-serving head of government in the EU – in fact, the longest serving democratically elected head of any government in the world. A dedicated European, he was one of the architects of the Maastricht Treaty, which created the fiscal framework for EU member states. He had been chairing the Eurogroup since its creation in 2005 and was about to guide it in its most difficult period. A realist and a fan of "constructive compromise", he would end up playing a crucial and very positive role in the unfolding Greek and broader European drama.

Juncker presided over Eurogroup ministers speaking in English, French and German, chairing in a haze of smoke, making the life of those sitting next to him miserable. Nobody dared remind him he was in a non-smoking building. His country, his town, his meeting, his rules. He liked to give bear hugs and kiss you in public; and conveyed affection, appreciation or gentle reprimand by vigorously patting you on the back or hitting you on the head with a newspaper, all in front of the cameras. They don't make them like this anymore.

This particular meeting was focused on what in euro-speak was called "credible exit strategies": phasing out the expansionary fiscal policies in place to combat the recession associated with the 2008 global financial crisis. While it was still considered too early to step on the brakes, it was felt important to be ready to do so at the earliest opportunity, for fear of rising deficit and debt levels.

The texts on the table referred primarily to fiscal measures, but also to the need for central banks to gradually "mop up" additional liquidity provided to commercial banks during the recession by lending to them at low interest rates. They also talked of "strengthening national budgetary frameworks to underpin credibility of consolidation strategies" – code for permanent mechanisms to be institutionally embedded in each country so that politicians would have a hard time running deficits in the future. A bit like tying Odysseus to the mast as he was going past the island of the Sirens.

Against this background, as the recently appointed Greek finance minister I was given the floor for the customary statement of an incoming minister from a new government. This is an occasion to outline priorities, and for the people around the table to size up the new kid on the bloc. Juncker introduced me by referring to "our friend George", a nod to the fact that I had sat around this table before as an aide to a minister and knew a number of officials. I was nervous, both about being there in my new role and about what I had to say.

I took a deep breath and started.

"President, dear colleagues, it is a pleasure to be here representing the new Greek government which was elected two weeks ago and yesterday night received a vote of confidence from parliament".

I spoke at length – longer than is customary in such introductory statements. I talked of the repercussions of the global financial crisis on the Greek economy. The recession was deeper than previously thought. Investment had taken a big hit, and private consumption had turned negative, for the first time in 16 years. Banks were hit by the lack of confidence, and this translated into reduced liquidity for the real economy. The recession exacerbated our chronic weaknesses – the high public deficit and associated large stock of debt, and weak international competitiveness.

But what everyone wanted to hear were the deficit numbers. So I dropped the bombshell and repeated what I had said to the Greek Parliament the night before: the deficit was currently projected to be around 12.5% of GDP for the year, more than double what was previously reported.

There were loud gasps in the room.

I gave three explanations for the situation. The first was an "economic cycle" effect. With a bigger than expected fall in GDP, tax revenues were much lower than projected, and expenditures (such as those for unemployment insurance) higher. As revenues were overestimated and expenditures underestimated to begin with, the difference on the deficit was significant.

The second was an "electoral cycle" effect. Greece had gone through two election campaigns – for the European Parliament in June, and national elections in October. In a country with insufficient control over expenditure outlays and poor revenue collection, ministers before elections tend to spend more than is budgeted, while tax revenues suffer. Unfortunate, unacceptable, but true – and not new, of course; but this time round, things had got out of hand.

Finally, my third explanation - and the most damning: the deficit figures also included what I euphemistically called a "non-reporting" effect, due to the previous omission of certain expenditure items. They ranged from obligations to suppliers, as in the case of debts incurred by hospitals, to the transfers made by the state to the pension funds of public companies that were never recorded. Including these bumped up the figures.

I underscored our commitment to face up to all this by bringing the deficit down to single digits by next year, while at the same time honouring our campaign pledge to help restart the economy and support the most vulnerable. I pointed out that this targeted short-term stimulus, combined with consolidation, was in the spirit of the European Recovery Plan that all EU countries were following. But we needed time – there was no way we could bring the deficit down to 3% of GDP in two or three years, given our starting point.

I also addressed the thorny issue of the credibility of Greek numbers. We planned to immediately legislate the independence of the National Statistics Service to rid it of political interference, and to address the institutional and procedural failings in the systems of expenditure control and tax collection. We knew that until the data issue was addressed, no-one would believe any of our policy announcements.

There was silence as the news was digested. EU Commissioner Almunia took the floor. He informed everyone that in its regular reporting of deficit data due out the following week, Eurostat would put an asterisk next to Greece's name until the mess was sorted out and light was shed on the large discrepancy. He suggested that Greece could be given more time to get its deficit under control, but to agree to this he invited me to produce a blueprint on how we would address the situation.

Next came Jean-Claude Trichet, the president of the European Central Bank. He warned that the problem with the figures would have a wider repercussion on the entire European institutional framework. The extent of the misreporting was "hard to believe". He focused on an element to which he would come back, again and again, in the months to follow: the evolution of wage costs in Greece. They had been growing much faster than in other EU countries, making the economy increasingly uncompetitive.

The other ministers were guarded and did not say much; they had no brief on this from their advisors, and needed time to process the information and figure out how to handle it. But outside the meeting, the mood was not good.

In the press conference, Juncker announced to journalists that the new Greek government had presented a significantly higher public deficit estimate and declared tersely: "The game is over. We need serious statistics." Almunia added: "I am seriously concerned about the significant statistical discrepancies. These discrepancies will require an open and deep investigation."

This would probably be the shortest honeymoon period afforded to any new finance minister up to that point.

It was obvious to everyone that the whole sorry affair was not the fault of the new government or mine; we had come clean and said it like it was. But the sign in front of me read "Greece", not "the new Greek government that is not to blame". So while there was sympathy with our plight and with me personally, what dominated was a feeling of frustration and even exasperation.

But there was more than that. As the Financial Times aptly put it the following morning, the news of the much higher deficit "came as an unpleasant but not entirely unexpected surprise to Greece's 15 Eurozone partners". Well, of course. They had known – or at least suspected – that the deficit was higher than officially reported. After all, wasn't the July note by the Commission saying that on current trends the Greek deficit would hit 10% – the one not divulged to the public by the Greek government at the time – discussed at the Eurogroup?

However much the Greeks were to blame – and no doubt we were – there was also a massive institutional failure of supervision and reporting. So the countries were asking the Commission why they had not been told this was coming. The Commission asked Eurostat exactly the same question. Eurostat responded, "because you never gave us the tools to do my job properly". And the Commission reminded the countries that a few years back it had asked for audit powers for Eurostat, but they were denied. Who had blocked them? France and Germany, among others.

The underlying problem was the blatant breach of confidence. The Eurogroup is a closed club, and clubs have rules. One of these is that, in general, you are above board with your numbers. Everyone tries to take advantage of the grey zones that exist in Eurostat rules to make numbers look a little better than they truly are; but overall it is presumed there is no blatant attempt to conceal a big – in this case, huge – hole in your public finances.

What made the situation worse was that in the minds of many, the whole story had a strong sense of *déjà vu*. Back in 2004, the incoming New Democracy government had announced an "audit" of the deficit data, which led to upward deficit revisions. Part of the revisions was due to a change in the way military expenditures were recorded: rather than at delivery, the new government recorded the expenditures when the commitment was made, conveniently inflating past deficits and deflating future ones. However, Eurostat had concluded that other irregularities were also present and the final figures climbed up.

The affair had caused an acrimonious debate, with the opposition (PASOK at the time) accusing the government of playing politics with the numbers. The worst part was that for the first time it put into question the Holy Grail itself: the reduction of the deficit level in 1999 to below the 3% of GDP threshold, which had been the ticket for Greek entry into the Eurozone and the adoption of the euro in 2001. "Greek statistics" became the shortest joke around European capitals, and the joke stuck.

Following the 2004 Greek "audit", Eurostat proceeded to a series of changes in its rules, intended to close loopholes and lead to more accurate deficit measurement. After all, Greece was not alone in using all the rules in the book – and then inventing some. France and Belgium had used privatization receipts to reduce their deficits; Germany kept the deficits run by Treuhand, the agency that privatized East German enterprises, outside official figures; and Italy and the Netherlands used revenues from the sale of central bank gold reserves to reduce their deficits – all not allowed under current rules.

So the recent data revision brought back memories, and they were not pleasant. Many people remembered it was not the first time Greek statistics had been called into question. But this time round the problem was of a different order and magnitude; it was big, very serious, and it came at a very delicate point for the whole of the Eurozone. Deficits and debt levels were on the rise, and markets were worried about their exposure to sovereign debt in general.

The next day I met with Commissioner Almunia to discuss how to move forward. We agreed on a battle plan to deal with the situation. The Greek government would send its best estimate for the 2008 and 2009 deficits to be included – with that asterisk – in the Eurostat publication, due out in a couple of days. At next month's Eurogroup I would present plans to bring the deficit down to single digits in 2010.

The Commission would propose a Council Decision stating that Greece had showed "lack of effective action" to deal with its deficit – a euphemism if there ever was one. Also, in November we would announce a plan to fully overhaul the process for assembling, preparing and publishing statistics. And early in 2010, we would present a three-year plan to bring the deficit under the 3% of GDP threshold.

On my way back to Athens, I reflected on what I had just experienced, and even more on what was to come. While apprehensive about the future, at the same time I felt a sense of relief; the problem was now out in the open, and we would have to deal with it. Going forward would be tricky; I just did not know how much.

We had reached a critical point as a country, where mistakes, omissions and the lack of political will to face up to decade-old problems had caught up with us. The catalyst was the fiscal derailment of 2009 and the blatant attempt to hide it. The Greek state had for a long time been spending more than it collected in taxes, borrowing the difference. With this borrowed money, Greek consumers mostly bought imports. It was a wild party, but it had come to an abrupt end.

When the music stopped, we were the ones who switched on the lights and told everyone the party was over.

For some time, there would be a deafening silence. Then there would be a rumble coming from afar and getting louder by the moment: the sound of the stampede by investors as they dumped Greek government bonds and ran for cover.

Chapter 4

BRUSSELS

The first reaction to the new deficit figures came only two days after the "game is over" announcement. Fitch Ratings, one of the three main credit rating agencies, downgraded the debt of the Hellenic Republic, signifying it had now become more risky to buy or hold Greek government bonds. This was followed a week later by Moody's, another of the agencies, putting Greece on "negative watch", thereby opening up a series of downgrades.

Perhaps surprisingly, the markets initially seemed to take this in their stride. The spread on ten-year government securities (the difference in risk between investing in a ten-year Greek bond and a similar German government bond) barely blipped, staying put at around 140 basis points (1.4%). By year-end, spreads had edged up to between 200 and 250 basis points, but were still lower than the 300 points they had reached in early 2009 – when all was thought to be under control.

Looking back, it seems markets, and the credit rating agencies that were supposed to warn of impending dangers and reflect these in their ratings, had fallen asleep at the wheel since the creation of the euro. They had blithely subscribed to the belief that in the Eurozone, member states all faced a similar level of risk, give or take some basis points. The markets had grossly under-priced Greek risk – and would later overprice it in a belated effort to compensate.

It was an accident waiting to happen.

The numbers for the last decade in Greece told a worrying story. Government expenditures in 2000 were 47% of GDP; after 2005 they started climbing to peak just under an unprecedented 54% of GDP in 2009. At the same time, revenues were down, from 43% in 2000 to 38% in 2009. As a result, the difference between what the state spent and what it took in as revenues eventually ballooned to almost 16 points of national income – a record.

Such differences year after year add up to a serious impact on the national debt. Even by 2000, the state owed in total an amount equivalent to that year's national income. In the years that followed, high growth rates managed to keep the situation in check. Persistent deficits added to the debt stock, but the expanding economy steadied the debt to GDP ratio at around 100% of GDP. This "knife-edge" situation eventually collapsed. After the economy ground to a halt in 2008, the debt climbed to 130% in 2009.

Things looked equally bad in terms of international competitiveness. Greece has always imported more than it exported; when it entered the Eurozone it had a current account deficit of almost 8% of GDP. Then things unravelled: the economy expanded, credit became cheap, and everyone started buying foreign cars, flat screen TVs, and laptops. Banks would send salespeople round to your house to peddle credit cards at a staggering 18% interest rate, and people nonchalantly accepted them.

The result was that in 2008, the external deficit had reached a record 15% of GDP. The country lived on imports, but could not find export markets for its own products. Outside a currency union, this imbalance would be swiftly dealt with by a steady depreciation or devaluation of the currency; within a currency union such as the euro, something had to give. Eventually it did.

Against this background, it is very surprising that credit rating agencies were so relaxed until the beginning of 2009. Then again, these are the same people that were giving Lehman Brothers top-notch ratings until a few days before it collapsed, taking the rest of the US financial system with it – and who never convincingly explained the failings in that assessment.

Similarly, markets were up to that point content to continue lending at relatively low rates. The basic premise in finance of *caveat emptor* (let the buyer beware) was thrown out the window. Everyone was lulled into a false sense of security. In February 2009, when Greek spreads suddenly spiked, Peer Steinbrück, then German finance minister, quickly doused the fire by saying that the Eurozone would act if any country got into trouble. This worked, for a while. The storm passed, but the problems remained, and nobody acted on the warning signs.

As we were navigating our first few months in office, with the revelation of the true fiscal picture behind us and tough decisions ahead, spreads and downgrades were worrying but not an immediate concern. The 2009 borrowing programme had almost been completed before we took office; rather than the planned €44 billion, the New Democracy government had by September 2009 already borrowed a record 66 billion – 50% more than initially planned!

The only large loan subscribed since we took office was a 15-year bond for €7 billion in early November 2009, at a 5.3% rate. This was expensive, but still lower than the 6% rate of the 10-year bonds issued by the previous government in March and June. There were no more financing needs for the year, so on the advice of our debt management agency, we issued no more debt. Any borrowing for next year would send a sign of alarm. In any event, in December the market is thin; investors are counting their gains and planning Christmas skiing holidays.

Meanwhile, the big international banks had begun to circle and check out the prey. The spreads made returns for those willing to take the risk very attractive, and made for handsome returns for the banks acting as agents.

Enter Goldman Sachs. With its smart people and aggressive moves, it was known in Greece for a 2001 mega-swap intended to propel some debt obligations into the distant future, but at a price. The deal involved so-called cross-currency swaps in which debt in dollars and yen was swapped for euro debt for a period, to be exchanged back into the original currencies at a later date – providing hidden credit in the process. It was a perfectly legal operation at the time, though a very expensive one.

Greece was not alone in using such fancy financial engineering with so-called "off market" transactions to hide the debt. Everyone was doing it. Until, that is, Eurostat changed the rules and in 2008 asked every EU member state to divulge such operations and add them to their stock of debt. Of all countries, Greece chose not to do so. The swap was therefore left unaccounted for until 2010, when the new government provided all the relevant information and, following an audit by Eurostat, some two percentage points were added to the debt to account for it. The correction to the debt figures was small; but the loss in credibility due to this "omission" by the previous government was very large.

The boys from Goldman Sachs were now back and offering to put their substantive firepower at the service of our struggling economy – for a fee. A dinner was organized in November with the prime minister and Gary Cohn, Goldman Sachs chairman. It was hosted in the private dining room of the historic Pentelikon hotel in the northern suburbs of Athens, so we could talk while avoiding prying eyes.

Papandreou had just come back from his first European Council in Brussels. He had done his best to reassure his peers that, while the fiscal situation was indeed alarming, the government was determined to face up to it. He had been honest, laying out all the troubles bedevilling the country: a patronage system in politics, corruption in the public sector, endemic tax cheating. His candour had taken everyone by surprise and blunted the criticism. He had bought the country some time.

At the dinner the Goldman Sachs team offered all sorts of ideas. They wanted to help with the €6 billion of overdue – and, until recently, unaccounted – hospital bills, and explore whether we were open to "private placements" for Greek debt. We were, in principle – it all depended on price. We still had access to markets, and a private placement is usually not cheap, never mind private. It can end up spooking markets into believing you no longer have market access.

In the weeks and months that followed, every international investment bank worth its salt showed up at my office, with suggestions on private debt placements. The numbers thrown about were large – €10 billion, €20 billion – but in the end not a single significant private placement came through.

George Soros also came to town. The legendary financier who made his name by forcing the British government to withdraw sterling from the European Exchange Rate Mechanism in 1992, was being hosted at another private dinner. Soros believed in the euro, but thought its design faults had come back with a vengeance and required urgent action. If there was to be no action – and here he pointed to Germany – the future looked grim. I got the distinct sense he believed we were embarking on a "mission impossible".

Meanwhile, my main preoccupation was to prepare a credible budget. Until now, Greek finance ministers simply negotiated the rate of increase in appropriations. I was to be the first to actually ask for cuts. So the conversations with my fellow ministers were testy. Everything was mission critical; apparently, nothing could be cut. Closing down some of the abandoned army bases around the country? Very difficult. Putting a cap on overtime pay in public hospitals or reducing the guaranteed profit margins of pharmacists? Impossible. Telling public companies to shape up and reduce costs or else? Not really. Reducing the yearly intake into police and army academies? Are you serious?

In the end most ministries saw a decline in their annual appropriations, and we managed an actual reduction in primary state expenditures (i.e. excluding interest payments). And in this first round of budget negotiations I realized it would be extremely difficult to bring the deficit down from its double-digit heights without a serious break from business as usual. We would have to venture where others had not dared to go.

One of the difficulties I faced was finding money to pay for our emblematic campaign promise: a one-off "solidarity subsidy" for those hurt most by the recession, estimated at €1 billion. The money was not there, but no-one was ready to give up on our promise so soon after the election. Given the situation, clearly it would have to be budget-neutral, financed by a one-off tax on the most profitable firms.

So off I went to the Federation of Greek Industries to break the news. I painted an honest, unadorned picture of the state of public finances, outlined an ambitious reform programme to free up the economy as well as put the budget back on track, and then asked for €1 billion. They took it rather well. They were actually relieved we were prepared to attack problems festering for decades. Had they known however this was to be the first of many such 'solidarity taxes', they would have been less obliging.

We did collect over €1billion from the tax, but ended up spending only half of that. By the time the second instalment of the solidarity allowance was due to be paid early in 2010, the difficult situation in the international financial markets meant we had to look for further savings and hence we had to scrap it.

Budget aside, it was critical to address our "credibility problem" – the euphemism used for the Big Lie – with the fiscal statistics. I had already asked and accepted the resignations of the head of the statistics service and the general secretary of the finance ministry, who were evidently both involved in sending shady data. But we needed to know exactly what had happened and what needed to change. So I set up a Statistics Commission, formed by a group of independent experts.

Their verdict– delivered after collaboration with Eurostat – was clear: the numbers had been cooked. The difference between the submission to Eurostat of October 2nd (the last before the election) and the one of October 21st (sent by the new government) was that, unlike in the first case, in the second, as their report put it, "the real data of the various services were actually recorded".

The question now was how to repair the mess. So in addition to this inquiry on what had happened, the Statistics Commission put forward a number of proposals for overhauling the processes of preparation and reporting of fiscal data. These were the basis for the legislation granting independence to the statistics service and safeguarding the integrity of the data that was subsequently enacted in 2010.

I was now ready for my second Eurogroup, this time in Brussels.

The Eurogroup is the "high table" of ministerial meetings – a case apart. It was set up as an informal group for Eurozone members and was only formalized with the Lisbon Treaty in 2009. Unlike in most other meetings, here you have a genuine debate, not a series of prepared statements. There is little legislative work, and most of the discussion focuses on economic developments and prospects. The debate is open, often adversarial, and sometimes brutal.

The meetings are prepared by the Euro Working Group, composed of senior finance ministry officials, who then sit next to their minister at the Eurogroup. They are the real guardians of the temple. They meet often, are a close-knit bunch and do the technical work, as well as a large part of any negotiations. I had just appointed as the new Greek representative to the EWG George Zanias, who over the next two years spent more time in Brussels than in Athens. The bruises were almost visible on him – it was gloves off, without the niceties of the ministers' table.

The 17-member Eurogroup meets the night before the Ecofin meeting of all 27 EU member states. The fact that important decisions are taken at the Eurogroup and not Ecofin frustrates EU countries such as the UK and Sweden, which are not in the euro. They complain they are not privy to discussions that affect them. Well, you can't have your cake and eat it - they have opted not to be part of the Eurozone club (or of the EU now for the UK).

There is a ritual to each Eurogroup. Cameras and photo-reporters are allowed into the room until the meeting is called to order. As ministers walk in, they are followed around as they greet each other, chat and find their seat. Everyone knows this, and everyone acts up to it. The facial expressions, who you greet and talk to, are all captured. Microphones are sensitive, and on more than one occasion snippets meant only for two people have ended up on the news.

In general there are two types of finance ministers – the stars and the rest. To be a star typically you need to be finance minister of a big country – but you can also be the minister of a small country in big trouble. That was me. So on my entrance there were lots of flashbulbs, and a stampede as photo reporters and cameramen followed me around while I was going around greeting others in the room.

Unlike in the October meeting, this time Greece was actually on the agenda. The procedure normally involves giving the floor first to the Commission and the European Central Bank, then to the minister of the country concerned, before finally opening the floor to all. But I was asked to speak first – not a good sign.

I started off with the most difficult item, the data. We had already fired the head of statistics and the top official in the ministry who were implicated, created the Statistics Commission, we were welcoming Eurostat to come and audit the books, and we were about to bring to parliament the bill for the independence of the statistics service. So far so good. Some credibility was being clawed back.

On the budget I announced we would be submitting to parliament in the next few days a proposal with a fiscal correction of 3.3% of GDP (eventually raised to 4%) for 2010. This would be achieved through tax hikes, a public sector wage freeze and a reduction in public service employees through non-replacement of retirees and the cutting of short-term contracts. For the first time, we would be reducing primary expenditures, the hard core of the state's obligations. We had to; from 2005-2009 these had risen by an incredible nine percentage points of GDP.

I asked for a realistic and non-punitive timetable, both for the fiscal consolidation and for structural reforms. I rattled off a list: opening up closed professions, making it easier to set up a company, market liberalization in utilities. I outlined a timetable: the budget to be discussed and passed by parliament in November and December, the three-year Stability and Growth Programme scheduled for January to bring the deficit below 3%, and the roll-out of a privatization agenda.

But above all I asked for a suspension of disbelief.

I got one – sort of. But not before listening to some harsh words. Commissioner Almunia talked of a "terrible record" in the previous years. It was not just a question of the quality of measures adopted – it was more an issue of lack of credibility in implementation. On the issue of statistics he wondered aloud, "What happened to the implementation of the conclusions after the 2004-5 review?" For him, this was about public management and accountability – both of which had been conspicuous by their absence.

ECB president Trichet welcomed the "bold way" put forward by the new government – but also zeroed in on the credibility issue. He waved a set of tables and graphs with which I was to become very familiar in the months to come, as they would appear in every single Eurogroup meeting: "exhibit number one" in the case against Greece.

The main table the ECB president was holding showed that over the last decade, while for the EU as a whole wages per employee had increased by 30% (12% in Germany), in Greece they had increased by 85%. Worse for public sector wages: a 40% increase in the EU (17% in Germany), an astonishing 117% in Greece. The resulting massive loss in competitiveness simply meant that "you have managed the euro as if it were the drachma", as he put it. And a final warning: "Greece is one step before non-eligibility for ECB cash."

The floor was then given to Thomas Wieser, the president of the Euro Working Group. He is an Austrian who vacations in Greece, loves the country, and played a very constructive role throughout the crisis. He reminded everyone that the Greek credibility issue had been around for some time; but also that the Greek problem showed a lack of credibility in the European monitoring framework. Some countries in the EWG were calling for extreme measures, such as withholding EU funds from Greece.

Then came Wouter Bos, the Dutch finance minister, leader of the Labour Party and coalition partner in the Dutch government. He was worried about the wider implications for the Eurozone of the combination of the high deficit ("Is it really 12.5%? Or higher?") and the statistics fraud. He was not in a forgiving mood. "We know it is not your fault, George. But shouldn't someone go to jail for this?"

With those words, the discussion finally came to a conclusion. The Commission would suggest measures and prepare messages. Eurostat would send a complete team to Athens to figure out exactly what was going on. Greece would send a letter to the Commission and the Eurogroup outlining in detail the measures to bring the deficit to single digits in 2010 and to jump-start reforms.

The Eurogroup was beginning to realize it had a very big problem in its hands.

It was a problem that started in Athens but could affect the entire Eurozone; one for which there were no precedents and no off-the-shelf tools that could be used to deal with it.

The bomb was already ticking, and no one had a clue how much time we had.

Chapter 5

BERLIN AND PARIS

My second visit to Luxembourg came sooner than I'd thought. A few days after the November Eurogroup, I got a call from Jean-Claude Juncker. I was being summoned to a small meeting in Luxembourg the next Sunday – the kind of invitation you do not refuse. It would be an unofficial meeting with him, Jean-Claude Trichet, ECB deputy chief Lucas Papademos (who later became economic advisor to Papandreou and eventually replaced him as prime minister), and Commissioner Almunia. There would be no publicity, no announcements; just a meeting between friends.

The meeting had a specific purpose: to rattle the Greek government and push us to take more fiscal measures for 2010. Alarms were already ringing and repercussions from the Greek problem were beginning to preoccupy European institutions. Nobody wanted at that point to face the fact that there would have to be some support mechanism, so the onus was on Greece to put its house in order, do it fast, and convincingly enough to keep the markets at bay.

Juncker started off the meeting with a stiff warning: the Treaty has a no-bail out clause; "you are on your own." Almunia followed: "we had warned the previous government and they did not listen." Trichet was next: "the debt dynamics are very alarming." They insisted that more effort to reduce the deficit was required. They wanted us to announce additional measures and aim for a 2010 deficit of 7.5% of GDP, a 5% reduction in one year.

And there was a refrain: we have heard many political pledges before from Greek governments who promised but did not deliver; why believe them now?

I was not happy with the meeting itself, with its tone and with the arm-twisting. Their frustration from past commitments that were not honoured was understandable; but I thought that the criticism of our efforts did not give sufficient credit to what we were trying to do. More than that, the idea that, if only we took more measures, the problem would go away and confidence would return was flawed – naïve even.

It seemed to me they were not willing to draw the conclusions for the rest of the Eurozone. The problem was not just Greece. It was systemic; whatever Greece did, there needed to be a coordinated and credible European response that no Eurozone country would be left to default.

So I made a simple point: the only person in the room who bore no responsibility for the situation we were in was me – and that went for the government I represented as well. We had inherited a terrible situation and were trying to deal with it. Everyone else was around when the tragedy occurred and should have been paying more attention – and that included the European institutions. We had committed to reducing the deficit by more than three percentage points and I could not offer more; but I promised to go back and explore options.

When I got back, I informed the prime minister. Juncker was also on the phone to him to impress the seriousness of the situation. We agreed to make an additional effort in the final budget to parliament a few days later, on November 20th, and to prepare further measures to announce if the situation deteriorated. We would aim for a deficit of 9% of GDP in 2010 – a significant reduction from the 12.7% deficit we were projecting for 2009.

The difficulties we would face became evident in the cabinet meeting that took place a couple of days later to approve the final budget. Ministers grumbled about additional deficit reduction. Some claimed that the size of the adjustment was too large; others called for a longer adjustment period. There was no full realization of the seriousness of the situation; it was still too early, and no government before had dared to venture where we were about to go.

Much later, there would be a number of voices who criticized ex post and with the benefit of hindsight the fact that we did not move earlier and more aggressively to reduce the deficit. But at that point, there was absolutely nobody in the cabinet recommending more measures – quite the contrary.

The fault line between two completely different approaches to the situation was already apparent. A minority understood the need to reduce the deficit immediately; but a majority questioned every expenditure reduction and tax increase. In the middle was the prime minister, arbitrating. He stood behind his finance minister and was willing to go the extra mile in announcing additional measures if necessary; but he was not yet ready to rupture with our past and slay some of the holy cows of the party's beliefs.

Compared with what was to come, this was nothing. At that point we did not know that we would soon start cutting public sector salaries outright, ending up with salaries at nominal levels in some cases 30%-40% lower than in 2009.

On November 20th, I submitted my first budget to parliament. Protocol called for a pile of books – the budget in all its gruesome details – to be handed over to the speaker in a short public ceremony. Instead, I handed it over in an electronic form, in a symbolic gesture about cutting costs.

The budget passed in December with a comfortable majority. The conservative opposition accused us simultaneously of having artificially inflated the 2009 deficit (i.e. you don't need so many measures) and of having made a U-turn from our pre-election rhetoric. Public sector unions also lambasted us for freezing wages and reducing the public sector intake of employees. But most people understood that something needed to be done with the deficit, and that the public sector was a big part of the problem.

This understanding was, however, in large part theoretical.

There was no majority in the government, the party or in society willing to back more extreme measures. I tried to force that debate and provided Papandreou with some ideas of more radical cuts. He asked me "to test the waters" with some senior cabinet members. I did so, arguing that we should announce we could not in the circumstances honour our pre-election pledges, and instead immediately cut wages and other expenditures in the public sector. It was a no-go.

The month of December opened with yet another Eurogroup meeting. This one inaugurated a series of informal notes elegantly entitled "elements of external communication on the fiscal situation in Greece". They were meant to reduce the cacophony coming out of Eurogroup, as it was already clear that discordant leaks and even actual statements were rattling the markets and making a difficult situation impossible to handle.

The Eurogroup communication was a hot-cold affair. It acknowledged that "the draft budget is one important step in the right direction", but added that "additional correction is needed". This refrain of "more measures" would dog us in the months and years to come. Whatever we did, however much we tried, piling additional deficit reduction on to an already weak economy, either the European institutions or the markets (often the former reflecting the latter) would proclaim that more was needed. The impact on confidence was disastrous.

We were not alone in facing a difficult fiscal situation. Ireland, Spain, and the UK also had double-digit deficits; Italy was flirting with debt at 120% of GDP, Belgium was above 100%, and even France and Germany were around 80%. And our borrowing spreads were about the same as Ireland's. But taking all indicators together, Greece was by far the weakest link in the Eurozone – in a league of its own. And it had an additional characteristic no-one else had: lack of credibility.

December was the month when all the rating agencies decided that it was time to jack up their risk assessment for lending to Greece; it was time for downgrades. First came Fitch.

As is the custom, they warned us of the impending revision and asked for a comment. We requested an appeal hearing and tried to convince them in a teleconference that they were jumping the gun. It was in vain – they had decided to compensate for their past inertia when they had ignored signs of trouble.

Then came Standard and Poor's. They argued that what we were doing was not enough, and that even if it were, there was a long hard road ahead and we were unlikely to succeed. This type of double argument became increasingly prevalent as the crisis deepened. Analysts said we were not taking enough measures, and then argued that because of all the measures taken, growth would be lower and the government would not survive the social protests. We couldn't win.

Moody's closed this round of downgrades a few days before the budget was voted on in parliament. They argued that the problem was long-term solvency, not short-term liquidity. Their concern was the deterioration in debt metrics; hence, a warning that the rating could remain on a downward trajectory over the long term.

This shift from liquidity concerns to solvency issues was slowly gaining traction amongst analysts. Yet nobody in official Europe was willing even to open that discussion. The debt trajectory was an issue of concern, especially in Frankfurt, but the response was to lean on Greece for front-loaded fiscal consolidation in order to begin checking the debt dynamics. The big elephant in the room, the size and evolution of the debt, would not be faced until much later.

Throughout November and December, the markets were particularly volatile. Spreads on Greek bonds as well as the price of credit default swaps, the infamous CDSs that act as insurance for holders of government debt, both had significant ups and downs. They fluctuated however around median levels that a few months down the road would seem in retrospect positively northern European.

In the December European Council meeting, Papandreou

found himself under intense pressure. The other leaders were worried about the markets and convinced that the only way to avert catastrophe was for Greece to adopt more measures, both fiscal and structural. Papandreou responded by defending our budget and reiterating our commitments. He insisted the problem was not just fiscal; it was about changing governance, rooting out corruption, rebuilding institutions. This required time and the support of society.

His insistence on the need to look at the deeper causes of the fiscal derailment and the associated collapse in the country's competitiveness was correct and well placed. The other leaders sympathized, but at the same time wanted to hear more concrete fiscal measures with immediate impact.

Following the Brussels summit and in view of the worrisome market reactions, it was evident that there would have to be a major policy statement, reinforcing the government's commitment to fiscal consolidation and reform, and outlining the measures we were about to take. In a speech to the organisations representing the social partners, the prime minister would impress on them the need for a "social pact" to move the country forward.

We were back in the Zappeion for that event, only two months since the victory speech on election night, but already in very different circumstances. As I was waiting for the speech to start, I could not but think of our jubilation then; of the first days of hope and innocence as we seemed to be doing everything right; the days when I would walk from my office the few short blocks to parliament and have people shout encouragement and support. Things were changing so quickly.

In his speech, Papandreou talked of the danger to our sovereignty if we did not address the crisis head-on. He warned that in the next three months we would need to implement changes that had not been undertaken in the last three decades. He outlined a "road map" of fiscal consolidation and sweeping reforms in areas such as pensions and freeing up of the business environment. He raised the deficit reduction target for 2010 to 4% of GDP and outlined concrete measures to back this up, while also throwing in measures aimed at giving a sense of social justice to the process, such as taxing the bonuses of senior bank executives at 90%.

The speech got a mixed reception. In Greece it was widely considered to signal a break with the past, but it did not generate the kind of follow-up that we were hoping for. The social partners camped in their entrenched positions and the rest of the political system repeated its mantra-like opposition.

Outside the country the speech was well received by the European institutions, with the Commission acknowledging that it represented a significant step in the right direction. The news coverage presented the glass half-full rather than half-empty; some focused on the determination and the measures, while others claimed the speech was thin on detail about how to achieve the stated goals. But one thing was sure: despite some positive feedback from analysts, the markets as a whole did not buy it and spreads continued to go up.

It was now time for some serious PR abroad.

The next day, I set off on a trip to Berlin, Paris, London and Frankfurt. I needed to have one-on-one conversations with the two most powerful finance ministers in the Eurozone, and I combined this with "road shows" for investors.

The first stop was Berlin, for a meeting with Wolfgang Schäuble.

The Bundesministerium der Finanzen is housed in an imposing and grand building which has been uncharitably described by an architect as "a typical example of Nazi intimidation architecture". When erected in 1935, it was the largest office building in Europe, boasting 2,800 rooms, with seven kilometres of corridors. It is best known as the Air Ministry building as it housed the Luftwaffe in the war and, according to legend, you could actually land a plane on its roof.

Wolfgang Schäuble's office is more in line with the quiet

understated austerity that characterizes the whole of modern-day German government. The most powerful finance minister in Europe took up his post in late October 2009, a few weeks after I took up mine, and quickly became the figure to watch in the Eurogroup. A dedicated European and a strong figure in German politics, his voice carried even more resonance than his country naturally commands. His confinement to a wheelchair following an assassination attempt in 1990 in no way blunted his political instincts or his capacity to dominate the proceedings.

From the beginning, we had established a relationship based on trust and a solid mutual understanding of how difficult the situation was. After, that is, I got over his question to me on our first meeting: "Are you a real finance minister?" By that he meant, could I take the tough decisions necessary, ignoring the sirens of the political system and going against cabinet colleagues, even my own prime minister?

I was already being tested on that.

This good working relationship was helped by his deputy, Jörg Asmussen, who played a positive and constructive role in the EWG, and with whom I built a good personal relationship. Schäuble was himself sceptical of Greece's capacity to change, could be very sharp in his criticism but was appreciative of what we were trying to do as a government in general, and of how I was doing my job in particular. So on that day, I felt I could say bluntly, "Wolfgang, we need to be preparing a Plan B". The response was direct. "George, there is no Plan B. Markets will respond if you show you can reduce the deficit." It was the official line.

It's not that he had not thought about the necessity of a Plan B if our efforts at deficit reduction did not prove enough to convince the markets; it's just that he was not yet ready to discuss such an eventuality, even though he realized we would get there soon. He knew what a bailout would mean and how hard it would be to sell to the German people, starting with his own chancellor. So he stuck to the safe party line: do your job, and all will be fine. Unfortunately, the new German government under Angela Merkel and with Wolfgang Schaüble was not willing to act preventively, as had the previous coalition government, with the statement by then Finance Minister Steinbrück that the Eurozone would act if any country got into trouble.

The second stop was Paris and Christine Lagarde – in the Ministère de l'Economie et des Finances. Unlike most official buildings that trace their ancestry back hundreds of years, this one was built in the late 1980s as a giant *paquebot*, like a huge ocean liner with its bow plunging into the river Seine. No doubt, its size and grandeur were meant to express the idea the French state wants to project about the country's economy and its administration. I was driven to the ministry from the airport in a motorcade and greeted by a porter in the traditional *livrée* – no other country does pomp and circumstance like the French.

In the world of finance Christine Lagarde is a star. Tall, silver-haired and elegant, she stands out in any meeting of men in grey suits. As finance minister of the second largest Eurozone economy, her views obviously mattered. In her case, she had also managed to establish herself as a respected voice, a deft negotiator looking to push the ball forwards. And – *quel horreur!* – she would choose to speak in meetings in impeccable English, honed at the time she worked for a New York law firm, rather than her native French – no doubt making some bureaucrats back home very unhappy.

I put to her the same issue: "we need a Plan B." I got the same kind of response, but with more of a nuance. France was one step ahead of Germany; they understood the systemic repercussions of Greece failing at some point to access markets, and had fewer misgivings about coming to our help. It was still too early in their mind to discuss specifics, and they would in any case have to speak first with the Germans, but they were less worried about internal political ramifications. There was no "anti-bailout hysteria" in France; a package to provide emergency funding to Greece if it became necessary would easily pass parliament.

I left slightly more reassured. However, it was obvious that the strategy around European capitals was one of buying time. On the other side of the Channel, the reading of the situation was very different. A breakfast meeting the next day with the full editorial team of the Financial Times showed deep scepticism of Greece's capacity to overcome its problems and of the Eurozone's capacity to defend the Euro. Martin Wolf, the chief economic commentator of the paper, was asking pointed questions on debt sustainability and on whether there would be a bailout if needed. On my way out, in typical British understatement, he wished me luck "on this very challenging assignment".

I found the same mood at the headquarters of The Economist that afternoon. The staff and editors of the influential magazine had done the maths and it looked tricky; more to the point, their analysis started – correctly – from the inherently incomplete, even flawed, characteristics of the Euro construction and continued – incorrectly to my mind – to challenge the willingness of the Eurozone to defend its creation politically and economically.

A meeting with investors organized by British banks in London and a similar one organized by Deutsche Bank in Frankfurt the next day showed the need to give investors first-hand information on what exactly was going on in Greece. They wanted to be close enough to be able to see the whites of our eyes.

Both meetings were packed. I spent hours in each one fielding questions on the true fiscal situation, how we were planning to reform budget and tax systems, the planned pensions reform, our cash reserves, when and how we were planning to access the market. All the people in the room had positions on Greece and wanted to get a sense on whether they were about to lose their money, or whether they should instead double down, buying more government debt for a higher return.

With the budget passed before Christmas and this incredible year coming to a close, it was time for some days off with the family, away from everything.

Jacoline, my Dutch wife, is a travel writer and has written some wonderful books on small hotels with character all over Greece. By now she knows her adopted country better than I do. She picked a great place in north-western Greece in one of the Zagori villages in Epirus for us to spend a few days over New Year's Eve. Nicolas, aged 14 at the time, and Stefanos, aged 11, had barely seen their father in many months and so were very happy about this short family vacation.

So we set off in our faithful family Subaru to make the 500-kilometre trip up north. No security tailing us, no accompanying vehicle, no warning of who was coming, no formalities. Just us.

We got there in the evening and I was delighted to discover a small stone house in a complex of only seven such houses that together comprised our charming hotel. Absolute privacy, a roaring fireplace, my favourite people in the world around me, and a few days where the phone was hopefully not going to be constantly ringing.

In the evening, we all went for dinner to the hotel restaurant – a café cum *taverna* which, because of its food and friendly atmosphere, attracted vacationers from nearby villages as well. It was packed – families and groups of friends huddled around large tables to welcome the New Year with loads of great food and people they loved. As we entered, there was a murmur of recognition. And then, to my utter surprise, spontaneous applause.

This was totally unexpected; I was embarrassed and moved at the same time. Despite the austerity budget we had just passed, despite the accumulation of bad news, we still continued to have the people's confidence. They knew things were broken and needed fixing; their instinct told them to trust us and believe in what we were trying to do. They were worried about the future, knew it was not going to be easy, but still believed that somehow, we could find a way out of this mess.

Some probably believed that there was a magical path which would enable everyone to more or less continue living as they used to.

Unfortunately, this path did not exist. And as this gradually became evident, the applause turned to criticism and then to outright rejection.

Chapter 6

DAVOS

At the beginning of 2010, as we were bracing for what was about to come, we were increasingly attacked over our first three months in office. The more the reality of what needed to be done became clear, the harsher the criticism.

The last few months of 2009 have been debated and second-guessed ever since. Did we "jump the gun" and shock the markets by announcing a deficit figure double what was previously believed? Did we allow the 2009 deficit to balloon in these months – or worse, cook the figures to make it bigger – in order to make the previous government look bad? Did we delay in taking appropriate measures?

The idea that we should or could have somehow avoided "shocking" the markets smacks of the desire to continue the deceit over the country's accounts. How could we "ease in" the truth when the Bank of Greece announced figures that showed the deficit to be at least double what was previously reported? How could we submit a budget based on false figures, only to admit to the reality a few months later and lose all credibility? Continuing a policy of deception was never an option.

Could we have controlled the deficit more in the last quarter of 2009? Would it have been possible to close the year with 9.9% of GDP deficit – at single rather than double digits? That magical figure – reminiscent of the dime shop attempt to fool customers about a product's true price – has captured many an imagination.

Both logic and maths can help here. First, logic: why exactly would the government want to show the deficit so much higher than it truly was? To have to announce even more measures and make sure its popularity fell even faster? In order to be beaten up some more at the Eurogroup? A 10% deficit (no, make that 9.9%) would have been enough to make the previous guys look bad. No need to push it further. Masochism has its limits.

Maybe there was a way to keep the 2009 deficit lower in the last quarter of the year? Simple maths helps: the cash deficit over the first three quarters as recorded by the Bank of Greece was already 10% of GDP. There is therefore no way 2009 could have ended with a deficit below 13-14%. It was growing by over 1% of GDP a month. Salaries and pensions had to be paid in the last quarter and, as the recession deepened, revenues were weaker. Hence even our initial 12.5% estimate turned out to be optimistic.

Did we at least try to limit the damage? Yes, we did. We curtailed operational expenditures and cancelled some programmes – such as an extravagant "bangers-for-cash" policy of the previous government, nonsensical in a country which imports all its cars. But with most of public expenditure made up of wages, pensions and social programmes, our margin of manoeuvre was small.

A simple back-of-the-envelope calculation tells us that to keep the deficit 3% of GDP lower we would have needed over the October-December period measures with an immediate impact of about €7 billion. With a total €30 billion annual bill for public sector wages and pensions, this would have meant not paying wages and pensions at all in the last quarter; not defer them, just cancel them altogether. And having done that, take the next plane out of the country.

You cannot stop a runaway train in a short space or in a short period of time. If you want to reduce the deficit you take measures in the beginning of the year. You don't wait until October. By the time you are in the fourth quarter, the end-year situation is pretty much determined; you can influence it, but not by much.

Did we delay in announcing robust measures to reduce the 2010 deficit? In the budget we committed to the biggest fiscal consolidation announced by any Greek government. Unlike in the past, it was backed by specific measures. Nevertheless, some were not robust enough; we shied away from "shock and awe" measures such as outright wage cuts – this was to come later. We were over-optimistic about our ability to deliver a 4% of GDP deficit reduction with the kind of measures we were proposing, and the markets saw that.

This hesitation also reflected a belief best encapsulated by the great François Mitterrand, when he said, "*il faut donner du temps au temps*" – you need to give time the time to do its work. Radical change cannot happen overnight; it takes time for the understanding of what needs to be done to sink in and be accepted.

One thing is certain: whatever delays there were in those last months of 2009 in getting fully to grips with the situation and announcing the kind of deficit-reducing measures which were adopted later, it would not have made a difference to the final outcome. By late 2009 it was already too late.

Markets were by then not just looking for a convincing deficit-reduction strategy; they were increasingly looking for a "financial backstop" at EU level, an iron-clad guarantee that the Eurozone would rally in support of one of its struggling members and not let it go belly-up; and that was not yet forthcoming.

Our focus in the early months of 2010 was on outlining a credible medium-term plan to bring the deficit below 3% in the near future. This was to be described in the country's so-called Stability and Growth Programme (SGP), to be delivered to the European Commission in January. Preparing it, with all its macroeconomic and fiscal scenarios and associated measures, was the job of the Finance Ministry.

To help this process, a brainstorming session was organized, focusing on the successful Swedish experience of radical fiscal consolidation in the 1990s. Leif Pagrotsky, a Swedish minister at the time, and Jens Henriksson, who worked for the Swedish government before joining the International Monetary Fund, went over some do's and don'ts: make sure the sacrifices are borne by everybody; develop a positive story; accept that it takes time; and understand that it is very hard. They pointed to some obvious difficulties in our case: lack of credibility; no functioning social contract; and the inability to devalue, as Sweden had done.

At the end of that meeting, they handed me a very useful booklet entitled "Ten Lessons in Budget Consolidation" ("Lesson #3: The one responsible must put his job on the line"). I was reminded that in the Swedish case, the Social Democratic Party which took the hard decisions actually also won the elections in the end.

I had a strong suspicion this was not going to be the case with us.

The completed SGP presented a plan to bring the deficit down to below 3% of GDP by 2012, with a four percentage point adjustment foreseen for 2010, and three points in each ensuing year (the "4-3-3" plan). At the Eurogroup discussion a few days after it was submitted, Commissioner Almunia was broadly positive: "The Greek government should count on our support for the implementation of this programme." So was ECB President Trichet: "The ambition is right."

Both, however, identified a number of risks: an overly optimistic growth scenario; too much reliance on measures which experience suggested would not deliver the desired results in time (such as the fight against tax evasion); and the need to spell out more the measures that would reduce the deficit beyond 2010. The refrain was: above all, we needed to convince the markets and the rating agencies.

The markets had indeed become jittery since the beginning of the year. Spreads went up when, at the beginning of January, Eurostat released its damning report on Greek statistics, stating that the problem was not technical, but rather institutional and political (translation: you lied to us), and warning there could be more data revisions to come once it had finished its in-depth audit of all Greek accounts.

Spreads rose further when Trichet announced Greece would not receive special ECB treatment in terms of easier rules for banks posting collateral to borrow from it. The same happened when the Wall Street Journal reported that the ECB had prepared a confidential paper exploring the legal and logistical issues of a country withdrawing from the EU. It seemed the market was increasingly sensitive to the difficulties ahead, as well as to the risks inherent in a massive fiscal correction such as ours.

Against this background, the Hellenic Republic attempted its first foray into the debt market for 2010. On January 25th, we issued a 5-year bond, aiming to raise €5 billion. The response was good, with an offer book of €25 billion, and a final €8 billion accepted and raised at a rate of 6.2%. Even though we had prepared the bond issue well and were confident it would be a success, I was still relieved when my phone rang with the news from our Public Debt Management Agency (PDMA).

This successful though expensive issue eased concerns and showed that Greece was still able to tap the markets. It also later generated yet another conspiracy theory about an "easy fix" to Greece's problem: "if only you had taken all €25 billion offered, we would not need to go to the IMF."

Except this is not how markets work. Every bond offer is oversubscribed; investors bid more than they are willing to buy, knowing they will only get a fraction; the €25 billion was simply not there to be taken. Also, a move to go much higher than our original €5 billion target would have sent a signal of desperation and immediately shut Greece out of the market, at a time when the Eurozone bail-out mechanism was still a twinkle in the eye.

Nevertheless, to this day, there are those who insist that if only we had taken that €25 billion when it was offered, and also borrowed from the Russians, the Arabs and the Chinese, we could have avoided everything that followed. I wish.

The lull in the market was short-lived. Two days after the

successful bond issue, spreads went up as the Financial Times reported we had mandated Goldman Sachs to seek Chinese money ("Athens hopes that Beijing will buy €25bn in government debt"). We issued a strong denial. The initial market reaction of "they can't access the EU and US markets and are turning to China" then became "not even the Chinese are willing to lend to them". Spreads hit 400 basis points. It was very frustrating.

What had happened was that a number of investment banks had approached us with proposals to diversify our investment pool by tapping the cash-rich Chinese and Asian markets. We were generally positive; a road-show in Asia was even envisaged. There were however no official talks with China, and no mandate; we simply paid the price for someone's bragging rights in order to get ahead in the competition amongst big international banks to tap Chinese financial markets.

For the moment, it was a waiting game. Investors were looking in the direction of Athens, and towards Brussels and Frankfurt, waiting for signals from all sides. Athens kept signalling it was getting on top of the problem, announcing measures to reduce the deficit; but there was no corresponding action from its partners. It was the EU delay in showing that no default would be allowed to happen which eventually locked Greece out of financial markets. A self-fulfilling prophecy.

January is Davos time, when that sleepy Swiss alpine village is transformed into the only place to be seen if you count for anything on the global stage. Starting in 1971, Klaus Schwab built the World Economic Forum (motto: "Committed to Improving the State of the World") into a multi-million dollar operation whose annual centrepiece is this meeting of presidents and prime ministers, chairmen and CEOs, academics and civil society leaders. It is three days of intense networking – no time to ski, despite the magical setting.

Unlike business people, politicians don't have to pay the hefty fee to participate – they get invited. The invitee in this case was Papandreou, not me. But as the event was a unique opportunity to explain to the world what the situation was in Greece and what we were trying to do, I was asked to come along. This was all last-minute, so I actually had to initially travel and register as a member of the PM's security detail, recovering my finance minister identity later.

We arrived in the dead of night in a small motorcade provided by the organizers, only to discover what it means to pack thousands of people in a small Swiss village, even a famous one. Our rooms were about the size of a shoebox. Never mind – we were here, eager to face the world. And face the world we did. We were inundated with requests for interviews, participations in discussions and bilateral meetings. The Greek crisis had hijacked the proceedings. Papandreou participated in a roundtable ("Rethinking the Eurozone" – "Re" was this year's 'it' prefix) with the prime ministers of Spain, Belgium and the Netherlands, and the ECB chief. After the discussion, Trichet took him aside to deliver a warning: the Eurozone was in danger; the Greek government needed to implement more austerity; and no, there would be nobody coming to our rescue.

In a series of TV interviews with global media, most of which were broadcast in true Davos spirit from makeshift open-air studios in the freezing cold, we stayed on message: yes, Greece had problems, but we were confronting them; there was no default scenario for the country, but we needed time to get the job done.

We repeated the same message to a packed press conference, and to anyone else willing to listen. Papandreou went to the point of publicly telling off "prophet of doom" economist Nouriel Roubini, when he bumped into him in one of the corridors of the main conference hall. Roubini had written that Greece was so desperate it was trying to borrow from the Chinese. It was not true; we asked him to retract, and he did.

Davos was also the venue for another meeting. This one was kept secret. It was with Dominique Strauss-Kahn, widely referred to as DSK, the managing director of the International Monetary Fund.

The IMF is to most people the devil incarnate. Its popular image is that of men in black, coming in and slashing wages and pensions, administering untold pain and suffering on people with their dogmatic, "neo-liberal" prescriptions. This was pretty much the image of the IMF in Greece as well – and we were very much aware of that when, as the new government, we started our dialogue with them.

As a member of the IMF, Greece had been regularly examined by a team from the Fund in the context of what are called "Article IV" consultations. The Fund economists were getting increasingly worried about what had been happening over the last few years. In fact, as Bank of Greece Governor Provopoulos has revealed, the Karamanlis government persuaded in 2008 the IMF to delay releasing a damning report on the Greek economy (it was eventually released mid-summer 2009). We had started talking to them in December, and kept an open and frank dialogue going, even asking for their view on our budget and SGP. Their position – offered unofficially – was that they could not see how we could avoid cutting wages and pensions and increasing VAT at some point soon.

Papandreou appreciated and trusted Strauss-Kahn, whom he had known for many years, and often sought his view and advice. He felt comfortable with the political positions and European sensibilities of the French socialist. He subscribed to the view that the IMF under Strauss-Kahn was becoming less dogmatic, more open to learn from its mistakes in the past and more attuned to taking into account the social impact of its economic prescriptions.

As the crisis unfolded the two men regularly spoke on the phone. Not in the sense that the conspiracy theorists would want people to believe ("he was planning to take us to the IMF from the very beginning"). The Greek PM was simply examining options with someone who was European and who believed Europe needed to address the crisis, but was at the same time not constrained by electoral calendars and parliamentary difficulties as European leaders were.

I had met DSK a few years back when he was in the political wilderness. Out of office, in opposition, very much looking like his career was over. We had invited him for a seminar at PASOK's think-tank, a small affair which assembled barely 50 people. I remember thinking it was a shame this obviously gifted politician was out of politics for good. And then he was appointed to lead the IMF with the support of President Sarkozy, who thought this was a perfect way to get him out of his way and kill any presidential ambitions the French socialist may have had.

Instead, the sharp and charming ex-finance minister quickly used the US and global economic crisis to reposition the IMF at the centre of the discussion and himself as interlocutor of choice. For a while, he was a shoe-in to be the next French president. His political ambitions crashed in a hotel room in New York, when he was accused of sexual assault.

In those early discussions with the IMF our position was simple: we wanted a European solution, without the Fund's involvement. But our European partners refused to accept the need for a rescue mechanism. They kept repeating the "no bail-out rule" mantra and were not willing to consider a "Plan B". So if Greece was shut out of international markets, the only mechanism that could lend to us was the IMF. We were not crazy; we knew what going to the IMF would mean in Athens. But no responsible government could ignore the option, even if it was one we wanted to avoid.

We had been in telephone contact with DSK before Davos and had arranged to meet up. We knew that any official meeting held in one of the designated conference rooms, or even a less formal meeting in a hotel, would make the front pages the following day ("Greek leader asks the IMF for help"). This was a place crawling with media. There was no way to meet without being noticed.

So we met in a kitchen.

Just behind the main meeting area of the conference hall,

there was a large space acting as a makeshift kitchen. This was where the outside catering was brought in before being served in the main meeting area for participants to nibble between events. Waiters were busily coming in and out of revolving doors holding trays and glasses, but there were no journalists or other prying eyes. That's where we met, the IMF managing director, the Greek prime minister and his finance minister, standing awkwardly – there was nowhere to sit – with security keeping an eye on who came through those revolving doors.

"How can the IMF help?" Strauss-Kahn's opening phrase led to a discussion of the situation and of our options. We repeated our position: we wanted to continue borrowing on the market. If that failed, we wanted a European solution. Ideally a European lending facility needed to be announced, thereby convincing everyone that we would not default under any circumstances. But the Europeans were not there yet. What if they refused to come to our rescue? Could the IMF step in if needed?

DSK was clear: lending money to countries which had lost access to markets was the Fund's mission; if Greece asked, it would have to help. But as long as other EU countries did not want the IMF involved in the Eurozone, they could block such a decision at the IMF board of directors. Nothing could be done without the agreement of the other European states and of the ECB. In any case, the IMF by itself would not be able to put up all the money needed for Greece.

So he agreed with us it would have to be a European affair, and the Europeans needed to be persuaded to create a mechanism. He promised to use his weight to help convince the main country which needed to be on board – Germany.

Nobody noticed the IMF managing director sneaking out of a Davos kitchen, followed a few minutes later by the Greek prime minister and his finance minister. Our meeting never came to light, but in the months that followed DSK played an important part in pushing the Europeans to face up to the reality of the situation.

In Greece, however, Davos was encapsulated in another moment. It was the scene in which Papandreou was on his way to a scheduled TV interview in the basement of the conference hall. He was hurriedly walking down the steps and going through a dark corridor, with a British journalist, camera in tow, in hot pursuit. The journalist was running behind him, microphone extended, trying to interview him: "What do you mean when you say it is the fault of the speculators? Will you borrow from the Arabs? How deep will the cuts be?" Polite man that he is, Papandreou continued answering the journalist as he walked faster to get away.

The scene was played over and over on Greek TV. It produced a very uncomfortable feeling in the millions of Greeks that saw it; that of a leader under duress, trying to deal with an impossible situation; and of a country being watched critically by the whole world.

Davos was a turning point.

Chapter 7

CROSSING THE RUBICON

Death and taxes. As the saying has it, they're the only two things you cannot escape. Well, in Greece we have been working on immortality for the last couple of thousand years, but as far as tax avoidance is concerned, we have nailed it down. Only one in three euros owed as VAT to the state actually collected. Less than 100 people in the country declaring annual income above €1 million, and only around 20,000 people officially earning over 100,000 euros. Three out of four people in liberal professions paying no income tax. Over 150,000 tax cases pending in the courts, with seven to twelve years for such cases to be adjudicated. This was pretty much the situation we inherited in 2009: a system with endemic tax cheating; with large tax evasion by a few taxpayers, and small tax evasion by many taxpayers; with a tax administration rife in corruption; a system in which the chances of being caught cheating are very low; a grotesquely unfair system.

The tax system was indicative of a broader problem – a broken social contract. Education, supposed to be free, as guaranteed under the constitution, is anything but. Greek families routinely pay for private tutoring to get their kids into university. Health is a public service in name only. Surgery in a public hospital often involves paying the infamous *fakelaki* ("little envelope") under the table. So people pretend to pay taxes – and the state pretends to give services in return.

Tax evasion and tax avoidance permeated the entire economic fabric. It started at the top, as in the case of a prominent newspaper publisher caught with millions in undeclared cash, who had managed for years to avoid punishment; or in the numerous tax exemptions, as in shipping, enshrined in the constitution. It continued with high-end professionals – doctors and lawyers prominent amongst them – whose declared income could not justify their lifestyles. And it was widespread in every small shop and service provider in the country.

Early on in our effort, I asked for the tax profile of doctors practicing in Kolonaki, the most expensive district of Athens. Around one-third of them were declaring incomes below the tax-free threshold. They typically did not issue receipts – and patients felt too vulnerable to insist on getting them. We went after them, raiding their offices and outing them in the media. But our success was limited; not issuing receipts for services and underreporting income has continued and is widespread.

It was the same story with our crack down on bars and nightclubs, also widely known never to issue receipts. It was hard enough to find tax inspectors that were both honest (i.e. would not phone ahead that a raid was coming) and willing to endanger themselves, as bouncers would physically threaten them when they confronted owners with the infraction. We shut down dozens of these places, only to see them reopen – and then continue not to issue receipts.

This was going to be a Sisyphean task. And it would later prove to be much more dangerous for me personally than I ever imagined.

From the very beginning we knew that doing something about the tax system and tax evasion would be crucial if we were to have any hope in restoring a sense of social justice, especially in the midst of a severe economic crisis. We enthusiastically set out on broad tax reform in late 2009, inviting social partners to participate in a dialogue aimed at creating a "just and effective" tax system.

To get some firepower on board in our reform effort, we asked the IMF for help.

The first meeting with the IMF technical assistance people on tax matters was in January 2010. The Fund brought in a large team with experience in tax reform from countries around the globe (and another team to work on budget reform). The team leader assured us they would put all the Fund's knowledge and expertise at our disposal. He then slid a report bearing the IMF logo across the table.

The title was: "Greece – A Plan for Improving Tax Compliance."

I was taken aback. "When did you have the time to examine the Greek tax system and arrive at a plan with recommendations?"

"Minister", came the reply. "Please look at the date."

I did: "April 2005." It had been commissioned by the previous government at the start of their time in office. Signed and delivered – but the report had been shelved. It was too politically sensitive to touch. I soon discovered a similar report had been commissioned from and prepared by the IMF on the budget side ("A Strategy for Modernizing Budget Management"). It had been shelved as well.

I was embarrassed.

I assured them this time was different. This government was determined to address the problems of the tax system. We saw it not just as an issue of revenues and deficit-reduction, but as a question of social justice. We were prepared to do whatever it took – change the legal framework, overhaul the tax administration, fire corrupt officials and go after tax cheats, no matter how important they were.

The Fund officials were sceptical, but polite. Over the next year, they provided us with much-needed advice, practically all incorporated into changes in law or administrative practice. And yet we made a mistake up front. In our early discussions, I put on the table two options: incremental change; or a more radical approach, by which we would create an independent tax agency from scratch, modelled after the US Internal Revenue Service, the IRS. They thought it was too risky – revenues would collapse while we made the transition. They were probably right; but in hindsight, given the resistance we faced with more moderate incremental changes, I wish we had gone for the radical solution.

The diagnosis of the original 2005 report was still valid in 2010: low effectiveness of operations, weaknesses in tax compliance, widespread corruption; a fragmented and outmoded tax administration, with hundreds of small tax offices around the country and weak headquarters; no risk-based compliance strategy; numerous unresolved disputes; a very high stock of tax arrears; and extensive abuse of offshore tax havens.

We set out to overhaul the system, and instituted a number of key changes. These included incentives for consumers to insist on receipts from vendors and the mandatory use of tamper-proof cash registers to combat VAT fraud; the mandatory use of bank accounts for business-to-business transactions; and risk-based audits, supported by a centralized and automated selection system.

We put in place stiffer penalties for tax evasion, allowing for immediate arrests and minimum mandatory jail sentences, as well as the seizure of property. We facilitated this by a complete lifting of banking secrecy laws, made it easier for tax officials to use bank account information, and created the function of economic prosecutor. A fully-fledged tax anti-evasion operational plan was prepared, complete with timetables, quantitative targets and administrative structures to support them.

These changes faced fierce opposition, including in the cabinet. A number of ministers objected that stiff penalties for white-collar crime were not "in the spirit of the Greek justice system". The same was the case in parliament, where every opposition party voted against the measures to combat tax evasion. Stiffer penalties, arrests, economic prosecutor: they said no to everything. Everyone was against tax evasion, but when it came down to doing something about it, they simply played politics.

Given our parliamentary majority, the measures passed. And they made a difference. It is because of them that today prominent and previously untouchable people (including some of Greece's "oligarchs") are being prosecuted for tax evasion.

But the problem was by no means resolved; that will take generations. And in the process I realized that some of our measures, while well-intentioned, produced perverse side-effects. Additional powers in the hands of a corrupt and inefficient tax administration in many cases have led to abuse of power.

Upon our return from Davos at the end of January 2010, Papandreou assembled the cabinet. The mood was sombre. He conveyed his conviction that speculative games were being played against Greece in the markets, with the euro itself the ultimate target. He warned that if the markets shut us out and the Europeans continued to refuse to help us, the IMF was the only available avenue – politically disastrous, but our last resort. Meanwhile, we needed to send a strong signal of determination to reduce the deficit – in other words, announce more austerity.

The cabinet was split. Many wanted to avoid additional measures at all costs. Some suggested we borrow from China and the Middle East. But an increasing number argued that if we were going to take additional measures, better sooner rather than later. For the first time, public sector wage cuts were no longer taboo. We talked of the IMF option; everyone thought it would be politically equivalent to declaring default.

Two days later, on February 2nd, the prime minister addressed the nation and declared that deficit reduction was the "absolute priority" – the only way to continue to have access to markets. He announced increased tax rates for high incomes, property taxes and excise taxes, as well as further cuts in expenditures, a complete freeze on hiring, a reduction in wages in the narrow and broader public sector, a freeze on pensions and an increase in the statutory retirement age.

These measures had already been communicated to the European Commission and helped the approval of Greece's Stability and Growth Programme the next day. The SGP was praised as ambitious, but did not resolve the concerns expressed by the markets.

On February 9th, the cabinet endorsed the two major tax and budget bills that we had prepared, but not without problems. Many ministers asked for some existing tax exemptions to be retained: for the army, diplomats, nurses, for those working in jails. I argued that if we made one exception, either on the expenditure or the revenue side, we were doomed. The prime minister agreed, and in the end both bills were approved as they stood.

Armed with these decisions, I participated in a Eurogroup teleconference call the next day to prepare for the European Council emergency meeting on Greece on February 11th. This was Olli Rehn's first official participation as the new EU Commissioner for Economic and Monetary Affairs. He had officially assumed his function the previous day, replacing Joaquín Almunia.

Olli Rehn is Finnish. You couldn't really mistake him for anything else. Stoic, quiet in demeanour, resilient and straight-forward. He came to the job after serving as EU Commissioner for Enlargement; one of his biggest headaches had been the delicate entry of Cyprus into the EU without the resolution of the status of the Turkish-occupied part, an issue in which Greece had an intense interest. When I called to congratulate him, I had joked: "You just can't get away from us, can you?" He had chuckled – as far as a respectable Finn could go.

On his first day on the job, the new commissioner raised the bar for Greece. Barely a week after the Commission had approved the Greek SGP, he asked for more austerity. He acknowledged the SGP was an important step, but argued that since the markets were not convinced, we needed to do more – and do it now. This was necessary in order for the European Council to send a strong message of support. If Greece was ready to undertake new measures, the EU would be ready to help.

ECB President Trichet followed suit. His warning was dire: "We are in the midst of a speculative exercise; an exceptional situation, where treasuries could be touched." He thought observers did not consider the Greek plan credible. He asked for specific additional measures: an increase in VAT by two points; further increases in fuel taxes; a cut in the 14th public sector salary (employees in Greece had been traditionally granted a 13th and 14th salary, meaning that their annual income was paid in 14 instalments, the extra payments coming at Christmas and Easter). After all, he said, public sector personnel outlays had increased 30% in the last three years.

The message was repeated by all the ministers who took the floor. However, there was also good news: for the first time, the door to EU help was opened, a direct result of the measures we had adopted and the credibility we were slowly regaining. It was finally sinking in that whatever we did, the markets would still be looking for an EU "backstop". Ministers approached this gingerly. After all, the EU Treaty was very specific: there was a firm "no bail-out" provision. EU members could not assume the debts of a member state in trouble.

Christine Lagarde was the first to make the big move: she talked of "help", which "should be bilateral, voluntary, with as many countries involved as possible". The same message then came from Berlin: Wolfgang Schäuble said the legal basis for any help should be "bilateral and coordinated by as many as possible". He ruled out IMF funding: "No IMF – but yes for technical assistance and implementation help." France and Germany had coordinated their positions. Financial aid for Greece was on the table and it was put there by the largest Eurozone economies.

This ad hoc approach to helping Greece was echoed by Finland, the Netherlands and Belgium. But others wanted a more collective commitment. Giulio Tremonti, the Italian finance minister, insisted, "it's time to show a European framework. The casual voluntary bilateral framework is not convincing". Elena Salgado from Spain seconded this: "We are all respectful of what George has done. We are ready to help with bilateral loans, but even a small part must come from the EU as a whole."

At the end of the discussion, Rehn summed up. The

Commission had endorsed the SGP, but its approval mentioned additional measures if needed; they were indeed needed, and were estimated at 1.25% of GDP. Based on this, there would be a declaration of support for Greece from the summit, with a combined EU and ECB mechanism, without yet spelling out the instrument. As for the IMF, only its technical assistance would be required. Involving it in designing and implementing any support package "would be an end to the Eurozone".

Analysts had already been speculating that this was where we were heading. Reuters and Financial Times Deutschland were quoting unnamed German government sources that there was a decision "in principle" to help Greece, based on bilateral loans and strict conditionality, going so far as to claim Schäuble had briefed the CDU parliamentary group. Spreads took a dive as markets saw the risk of default receding.

I had mixed feelings after the teleconference. I was frustrated that, only days after the approval of our SGP, we were asked to do more. But I was also relieved our insistence that a European support mechanism was necessary for Greece – even as a deterrent towards the markets, never to be actually used – was finally getting traction. It was a major breakthrough.

I also knew Papandreou would have a hard time in the summit the next day.

Before the start of the meeting, a restricted gathering was organized, with Commission President Barroso, the ECB's Trichet, Angela Merkel, Nicolas Sarkozy, Spanish PM José Luis Zapatero (holding the rotating Council presidency) and Papandreou. The intention was to put pressure on the Greek prime minister. Barroso opened by telling Papandreou that the austerity measures in the SGP and those already announced were not enough, and that Greece would have to take yet more measures.

Papandreou is a calm man – more Nordic than Greek in his demeanour. But this time he exploded. He was absolutely livid. He told Barroso that the Commission was not doing its job; if they thought more measures were necessary, why did they approve the SGP only a week ago? When were they right – this week or last? And how did they expect a government to keep public support for a very difficult austerity programme when the goalposts kept shifting? He accused Barroso that he had looked away when the conservative Karamanlis government was derailing Greek public finances. He then asked everyone to agree that these would be the last measures his government would be forced to take – after that, Europe would come to Greece's help. If they were not willing to make that commitment, he would take the plane back to Greece and tell the people that Europe had abandoned Greece.

After a difficult Council meeting, the leaders issued a statement saying they supported the efforts of the Greek government which was committed to doing whatever was necessary, "including adopting additional measures". But the phrase, the major commitment, that everyone was looking for, was at the very end: "Euro area member states will take determined and coordinated action, if needed, to safeguard financial stability in the euro area as a whole." And it added, "The Greek government has not requested any financial support".

The Rubicon had been crossed; the Eurozone had effectively ditched the "no bail-out" principle and would – under certain conditions – help one of its members if need be. Now all that remained was to agree on the how, when and how much.

These questions were supposed to be answered at the Eurogroup meeting scheduled a few days later. When I arrived in Brussels I was met at the airport by Maria Assimakopoulou, the head of our Brussels Permanent Delegation's economic department. Maria was an old Brussels hand and had a good sense of the mood, the views and the likely outcomes. She painted a bleak picture: countries were frustrated; they did not agree with each other about what to do, so we would be under tremendous pressure. Everyone would pretend that the only problem was Greece not taking enough measures.

Indeed, in the meeting countries pushed us mercilessly for more austerity to show that Greece was being punished for its sins. It was a very difficult discussion, held against the background of the markets' disappointment at the lack of detail in the summit statement. There was a whiff of panic in the air, as ministers realized the situation could spin out of control, even prompting Jean-Claude Juncker at some point to ask rhetorically: "why are we surrendering to the markets?"

Germany took the floor first. While acknowledging our efforts by saying, "I would not swap my job with George", Schäuble refused to go any further than the "wise" decision of the European Council a few days earlier. "The decision holds", he said, "but it is sufficient to repeat what they said. 'Determined and coordinated action'. No need to say anything more." He added: "it's up to Greece to convince markets."

The Italian finance minister followed. He was in lyrical mood, invoking "fate and destiny." Tremonti was clearly worried: "We ought to be discussing crisis management – all the warning lights are on." He insisted this was not just a Greek issue: "There are enormous financial flows between countries from core to non-core Europe. We need to look seriously at counter-party risk."

Practically every country took the floor. There was confusion and divergence of opinion: How far should we go in preparing the support mechanism? Should we announce details? The Irish finance minister, Brian Lenihan, who has since sadly passed away, understood better than most the pressure of the financial markets. He had been critical in the past of the failure of Greek governments to take measures, while Ireland was doing exactly that. He noted, "the new government has far greater determination" and urged everyone "to behave like a currency".

The pressure on us was intense. In an unusual exchange, Trichet interrupted me while I was explaining the measures already announced by a terse, "we need more measures *now!*" My polite but annoyed, "please don't interrupt me, Jean-Claude," marked the palpable tension in the room. We were not about to announce yet more measures a few days after the last ones, and before knowing how far our partners were willing to go in creating a "safety net". And yet there was no detail of the kind of support that would be forthcoming if we had trouble accessing the markets.

IMF involvement was a hotly debated issue that night, and at the Ecofin meeting the next morning. The Eurogroup president, the Commission, and the ECB chief all thought this would mean that the Fund, in Trichet's words, "would substitute for the Eurogroup". This was also at that point the position of the large countries, with Schäuble saying that IMF funding, "would prove the Eurosceptics right". But important non-Eurozone Ecofin members (Sweden, Denmark, the UK) saw a role for the IMF.

Juncker insisted, "it must be clear that Greece will not go to the IMF without agreement of the Eurozone". I was certainly not planning to do anything of the sort. But I was also very much aware that because the prime minister and I had openly discussed the IMF as a last resort, our partners had finally been forced to accept that the stability of the Eurozone involved creating a European support mechanism.

In the end, it was agreed that to convince the markets Greece did indeed need to announce more "concrete measures that are credible", and do so by mid-March. In terms of financial support, a technical subgroup would discreetly examine the modalities of potential assistance. And we would all do our best to communicate a consistent message to the markets. Of course we would.

On the margins of the meeting I was invited to speak at a packed gathering organized by the European Policy Centre, one of the leading Brussels think-tanks. I talked about what we had inherited, outlined what we had already done and what were planning to do. But – I pleaded – we needed time to get the job done. To make my point, I invoked the Titanic. "We are trying to change the course of the Titanic, and it cannot be done in a day", I said. I told the audience that while under the previous government Greece was headed straight for the iceberg, with the captain asleep in the cabin, now all hands were on deck, determined to avoid the collision.

I thought the Titanic metaphor was apt; but months and years later, I was still being accused in Greece of that phrase having single-handedly caused the spreads to shoot up. Too bad the numbers tell a different story: 10-year spreads on that day were around 300 basis points; two weeks after the speech, they were at about that level; one month later, the same again. What a shame to spoil a good conspiracy theory.

The Eurogroup decision did not go down well in Athens. In a cabinet meeting, ministers thought we should insist on what we had already announced – and not a step further. But denial was slowly giving way to looking at alternatives. How much further could we cut from the annual pharmaceuticals bill? How about pensions for those taking early retirement (sometimes at the age of 50)? Reality was setting in.

On February 16th, Papandreou visited Moscow and met with the Russian president and prime minister, Dmitry Medvedev and Vladimir Putin. Those who thought Greece could solve its problems by finding alternative funding were already speculating on a large Russian loan to Greece. The PM did indeed broach the subject of Russia purchasing some Greek debt. There was no enthusiasm; in fact, while meeting with the visiting World Bank President Robert Zoellick, Medvedev was asked about whether Greece had asked for help. He did not deny it, but added, "I told Papandreou that he should go to the IMF". So much for that.

Meanwhile, the German media were playing at provocation. Focus magazine produced a cover with the sculpture of Venus "giving the finger" – presumably to the rest of Europe. Bild ran incendiary articles about "lazy Greeks", who supposedly wanted to live off German tax payers' money. But others tried to inject common sense. Der Spiegel referred to the press coverage of

Greece as one of "increasing irrationality", while Süddeutsche Zeitung dismissed talk of "Greeks who work only when they have been bribed". The paper reminded its readers that the largest bribes in Greece had been paid by a German company, Siemens, and that Greeks continued to feel that the issue of war reparations was never seriously addressed by Germany.

It was in this climate that Joe Ackermann came to Athens. We spoke regularly on the phone to the genial Swiss head of Deutsche Bank, who was concerned about the implications of the Greek impasse on the European banking system. He remembered being woken up by Chancellor Merkel at one o'clock in the morning back in 2008 to help salvage German banks from collapse following the Lehman debacle. His was a simple calculation: the exposure of German banks to Greek, Portuguese and Spanish government bonds exceeded €500 billion. A big number concentrates the mind.

Ackermann brought with him an audacious idea: a €30 billion package to help Greece – half from the private sector (with his bank assembling the investors); and half from the German and French governments, possibly via federal and state agencies such as the KfW Development Bank in Germany and the Caisse des Dépôts et Consignations in France. It was a good idea, a large pre-emptive transaction, that would demonstrate private sector confidence in Greece and the willingness of the strongest economies to support the weakest.

Ackermann presented the idea to us, and we were positive. But there was a snag: the German government had not signed off on it. In fact, over the next few days as the news of the visit made the international press and some details of the proposal leaked, the German government went to great lengths to communicate that Ackerman was flying his own kite, and that they were not too happy with the initiative.

The idea quickly died.

The dramatic first two months of 2010 had a fitting end. On March 1ˢᵗ, Olli Rehn came to Athens. We presented to him additional measures we were about to announce in the next few days, and asked the Commission's support in pushing Eurozone countries to put the support mechanism in place. His assessment of the measures was positive, and he would be delivering this message to Brussels.

Afterwards, the two of us held a joint press conference, where Rehn reiterated his support of what we were doing, emphatically repeating the now famous EU pledge, "to take determined and coordinated action" if necessary. He insisted, "we have the ways and the means to safeguard the stability of the Euro".

At the end of the press conference, he summoned his best Greek: "*Kalo kouragio*", good luck. We were going to need it.

Chapter 8

THE WEST WING

It was time for the bitter medicine.

We had until mid-March to announce yet additional measures. But there was no point in waiting. The day after Olli Rehn left Athens, Prime Minister Papandreou addressed PASOK's parliamentary group. Before announcing anything as drastic as we had in mind, we needed to have the cabinet and our MPs behind us. This was not an easy task; the cabinet was split, and the members of our 160-strong parliamentary group would have a tough time explaining wage and pension cuts to their constituents.

The MPs assembled in parliament's senate chamber, an ornate room with walls of pale pink marble, leather armchairs, and a "sovereign's box" perched above, used at some point in the past by the king to follow proceedings. Papandreou was late – working on his text until the last minute, and even after that.

It was his most dramatic speech to date. The country was in "a state of war", he said. Tomorrow he would be convening the cabinet to take painful decisions. He drove home the severity of the problem: "Every year, we borrow about half of what we spend; and every year, we spend more while taking less in taxes. This is just not viable. It cannot go on." He continued: "This is truly the end of an era for Greece. We are better than this. We need to prove that if logic and measure were lost by some governments, they were not lost from the nation's conscience."

He had them.

The next day, the prime minister also had the full backing of his cabinet. Some of the same ministers, who had questioned the much milder budget measures two months ago, were now saying they thought all along we should have taken stronger measures earlier. I was amazed – I remembered well the positions everyone had taken in recent months. There were some dissenting voices, but most objections were a sort of "insurance policy" – to claim later that they had reservations if things went wrong.

The measures were the most drastic expenditure cuts and tax hikes announced by any Greek government. They involved a 30% cut in the 13th and 14th public sector salaries, a 10% cut in the contribution to pension funds by public sector companies, a freeze in all public and private sector pensions, and further cuts in public investment. We also increased all VAT rates, with the top rate rising to 21%, further increased excise taxes on alcohol and tobacco, introduced a hefty luxury tax on expensive cars and boats, as well as a 1% "solidarity levy" on incomes above €100,000.

The measures were well received abroad; the international markets were giving us the thumbs-up. In an analysis piece characteristic of the market mood, entitled "Greece does it", Bank of America Merrill Lynch stated "Greece may well have set a new record for the speed and efficiency of its policy response".

The reception in Greece was another matter. The opposition screamed we were doing the opposite of what we had promised before the elections. But the main enemy was within. In an exchange that was a prequel of things to come, my deputy minister, Philippos Sachinidis, faced a rough time in parliament. He was blasted by the secretary of PASOK's own parliamentary group: "Which government do you think you are part of? It's one thing to get out of the crisis and another to lose our soul." Nevertheless, the measures were voted through on March 5th, solely by PASOK MPs.

A day after the measures were announced, we issued a 10-year bond, aiming to raise €5 billion. The issue was oversubscribed with €15 billion offered, but we decided to raise the original amount. It was an expensive exercise, with an interest rate at

6.3%; it was, however, 50 basis points lower than the previous issue, which also had a shorter duration. More importantly, we proved that we still had market access.

Armed with the result of the vote and the bond issue, on the afternoon of March 5th I accompanied Papandreou on a quick visit to Angela Merkel in Berlin. The two of them had interacted at various European Council meetings and had spoken on the phone a number of times, but it was his first official visit to the Federal Chancellery.

The Bundeskanzleramt in Berlin is a huge, stark, concrete and glass postmodern building, a symbol of the reunified Germany, eight times the size of the White House in Washington DC. Merkel greeted us warmly at the entrance as our convoy pulled up; she was very much the lady of the house, welcoming her guests for dinner. We walked together to the first-floor conference room where the meeting was to be held.

Once we sat down for the first part of the highly choreographed visit (meeting, press conference, working dinner), the chancellor was efficiency embodied. The press was waiting downstairs for the press conference, she said. We would have plenty of time to discuss things at length over dinner; so let's just agree on what we will say to the press. We will say Greece is making a great effort and should continue, and Germany supports this effort. But, above all, we will not mention anything about a potential financial support package. Agreed?

Well, not quite. Papandreou insisted that, in order to calm the markets, a statement should be made that the EU and Germany would stand by Greece if it became necessary.

In the press conference the chancellor had lots of good words about our recent measures, and about the bond issue, which proved that we maintained market support. There were references to Greeks living and working in Germany, Germans vacationing in Greece, the strong ties between the two peoples, and the need for further cooperation. There was also the obligatory swipe at speculators, whom "we shall fight together". When it came to the recent European Council decision, she stated categorically that "Greece has not requested financial help".

In the question and answer session that followed the official statements, Merkel was pointedly asked about financial help. She deftly avoided answering. Papandreou was asked – yet again – the "why don't you sell your islands?" question that had become the rallying cry of the populist German press in recent months. He retorted, "why don't you visit them instead?" and with that we went to dinner.

This was where the real work took place. The chancellor was accompanied by Wolfgang Schäuble and some of her closest advisors, including Jens Weidmann who would later head the Bundesbank. Having dispensed with the press, everyone was eager for a real discussion. It was obvious the German side was in the process of doing a lot of thinking about how to help Greece, but also that it did not speak entirely in one voice.

Astonishingly Merkel openly said, "Wolfgang and I do not agree on this issue", referring to the willingness to commit Germany in an active way to a support package, or to authorise the ECB to take steps in the secondary bond markets to keep spreads low. The finance ministry was pushing for a resolution, but the chancellor had not yet made up her mind.

Over coffee the two leaders and their finance ministers huddled in a corner, away from advisors. Merkel wanted to know how much longer we could last without official help. No doubt the May 9th election in the North Rhine-Westphalia Länder was on her mind, and wanted to avoid decisions before that. We answered that it depended on whether the markets believed the Eurozone pledge to come to our rescue or not; if they did not, we did not have that kind of time. We asked for a short-term financing facility from the treasuries of the largest countries as back-up until a full-fledged mechanism was put in place. They promised to think about it, but made no commitment.

After dinner, we said our goodbyes and set off for the airport. We arrived at the government plane waiting to take us back to Athens to find a red carpet leading all the way to the plane's steps and ranks of military guards lined up on each side. After the protocol people left, Papandreou – seasoned ex-foreign minister that he was – gave a wry smile: "They always pull out the stops with the ceremonial stuff when they have nothing else to give you…"

Next was Paris for a visit to the French president on March 7th. France had been more positive than Germany, even though the French did not want to be seen publicly taking a different line from the Germans. Christine Lagarde was the first to speak openly in the February Eurogroup teleconference, of the need for a European mechanism "to be used if necessary" in the case of Greece. So we were hoping to make our case and get some visible support.

We were not disappointed.

The meeting was held in a small elegant room at the Elysée Palace, with a beautiful pale blue *tapisserie* on the walls and comfortable embroidered armchairs. It was a stark contrast with the sober Chancellery in Berlin. The French president was flanked by his finance minister, chief of staff, and some advisers. But he was the only one doing the talking, in rapid-fire French, with an interpreter struggling to keep up.

Nicolas Sarkozy was restless, constantly moving in his armchair and impatient with the proceedings. He gave the impression of a man who could never relax. He was obviously someone who did not tolerate objections from the people around him. He opened bluntly: "*Nous ne sommes pas d'accord avec Merkel*" – "We do not agree with Merkel." To France, "supporting Greece is supporting the euro. If Greece needs our help, we will be there". He was on a roll as he addressed Papandreou: "Georges, we asked you to take more measures and you did. We can't now just stay at the level of the European Council statement."

He wanted to make it clear he was pushing the Germans to make the leap, and that he was the man who could deliver the goods. "Merkel says that she will help only if all else fails. But how? *Elle refuse de le dire*" – she refuses to say. "I do not want a crisis with Germany, but nor do I want a European crisis." He continued: "Trichet agrees with me, and so does Barroso. Juncker too," adding, "although he keeps smoking in those European Council meetings!" I tried hard to stop myself from smiling at this outburst.

There was a lot of bravado as the president gave instructions. Christine Lagarde was to work on the modalities of an eventual scheme. Any final decision on a bailout would have to be made at the level of European leaders. Meanwhile the Trésor Public should make €5 billion available to Greece as a short-term loan if necessary, and France would work towards other countries doing the same. The message was: Greece cannot be allowed to go bankrupt. In his word, accompanied by expressive gestures: "*il faut mettre la digue!*" We need to put up a dam!

The bravado extended to France's position on whether the IMF should be involved. The French president had a strong view. We needed its technical expertise, not its money. "Forget the IMF. The IMF is not for Europe. It's for Africa – it's for Burkina Faso!" This time I did not manage to suppress a smile. A clear position, but one that would be reversed only a few weeks later when the German government informed everyone that, without the IMF participation, it would not sign off on the European rescue mechanism.

As the meeting was coming to a close we turned briefly to other issues – Turkey was one. Sarkozy repeated his well-known position: it was out of the question that the country would ever join Europe. And almost as an afterthought, as we were wrapping up, came a gentle reminder: "About those fighter planes: if you take our Rafale, we will take back the old Mirage planes you have. But there is no rush – only when you can…" As we were walking down the steps to the entrance of the Elysée

Palace after the meeting, I whispered to Christine Lagarde: "Is he always like this?" She just smiled.

It was what the French would call a *tour de force*. The president of the second largest EU country was taking matters into his own hands, handling the situation, setting out his plan to solve the crisis. The strong words spoken and commitments made at the meeting were pretty much repeated in the press conference that followed – a far cry from the cautious approach in Berlin. "We will do what it takes – we will not let Greece down" was the message.

In practice this bravado and the noble intentions were not going to be a match for the real power in the EU, Germany. The lesson we learned to our cost in the weeks and months that followed was that nothing mattered much until Berlin made up its mind; and until it convinced everyone else to follow suit – on its terms.

We flew out that same evening from Paris to Washington for a planned three-day visit. President Obama had invited Papandreou and I was to accompany the prime minister. The Eurozone crisis was firmly on the US radar; hence the invitation from the US President. I had used the opportunity to plan meetings of my own, notably at the IMF, and both of us had scheduled media appearances to explain to a US audience what the Greek government was doing to address the crisis.

On the first day I visited the IMF headquarters. The meetings there were meant to discuss technical assistance from the Fund on fiscal and tax issues. But we also exchanged views on the situation on the ground and the economic prospects. The IMF staff were worried about the fiscal path in our SGP, thought we needed more time to bring the deficit under control, and that resumption of growth in 2011 was not realistic.

Olivier Blanchard, the IMF chief economist, believed the situation was worse than anyone was admitting: the debt dynamics were alarming; and Europeans were underestimating the systemic repercussions of letting the situation get out of control. I left with mixed feelings: a combination of gloom because of the severity of the situation but, at the same time, hope that everyone was working towards finding a solution.

But would we find the solution in time?

The visit to Washington was also an occasion to meet with the Greek-American business community and enlist their help. In an evening event organized for this purpose, the guest star was Bill Clinton; as an old acquaintance of Papandreou, he wanted to help. The former president glided effortlessly around a room full of rich Greek-Americans, exuding his trademark charm. The man simply owns whatever room he walks into.

Before the main event, there was a private meeting to exchange views on what should be done. I arrived late to find the prime minister with the ex-president and some others. I was greeted by Clinton as an old friend, with a thunderous "come in and join us, George". He listened carefully, told us he believed we all needed to push the Europeans to move faster to produce a "backstop", and promised to do his part.

March 9th was a crisp and sunny Washington spring day, and the White House gleamed. The most famous building in the world is quite unassuming. Anywhere in Europe it would hardly make an impression. This one, however, is different. This is where "the leader of the free world" lives and works. The man we were here to see.

Except that, in my case, the polite but firm policewoman at the security entrance for visitors did not seem to agree. Her computer screen had my last name spelled with a 'c'. My passport spelled it with a 'k'. Not the same person. We had a problem. With a growing sense of panic I tried to explain that I absolutely needed to accompany my prime minister to the meeting in the Oval Office with the president. Meanwhile, the rest of our delegation was waved through and the prime minister's car had gone through the gates (he was the only one allowed to be driven in).

I was already imagining the embarrassment of being left out

of the meeting because of a misspelt name. Then, miraculously, the problem was solved and I was issued a pass. To my delight the young policewoman, who almost caused me a heart attack earlier, waved me through in broken Greek. She was a second-generation Greek-American, her family hailing from the Peloponnese.

To people like me who have not missed a single episode of *The West Wing*, the actual place is a bit of a let-down. Forget the TV series' long corridors and high ceilings. The real thing is a low one-story building on the side of the White House, with a separate entrance to the main building. We were greeted at the entrance, asked to surrender our mobile phones and other tech devices, then shown into a conference room lined with bookcases, to sign the visitors book. I was expecting for us to be taken to the Oval Office somewhere else in the building. Instead, a door opened behind us. A familiar figure was standing there, beckoning us in.

Barack Obama is a tall man, towering above Papandreou, who is not exactly short himself. A warm handshake and the cool demeanour you expect. We were ushered into the Oval Office and introductions were made. The president had summoned treasury secretary, Tim Geithner, with whom I was already in contact; his chief of staff, Rahm Emmanuel, who glanced up from his Blackberry and said, "so you are the guy with the toughest job in Europe!" ("Thank you, yes, so they tell me."); and Larry Summers, then director of the US National Economic Council.

These meetings are heavily choreographed. The president and his visitor sat side by side in armchairs slightly angled towards each other in front of the Oval Office fireplace, with the George Washington portrait hanging above. Our delegation sat on a yellow couch beside Papandreou, with the president's team on the couch facing.

President Obama barely glanced at the cue cards prepared for him as he fluidly moved from one topic to another: Greece's economic crisis, relations with Turkey, Cyprus, the Middle East. But the discussion centred on the financial crisis. The conversation was mostly between president and prime minister. Papandreou asked me to elaborate on the state of play and I did. Tim Geithner also joined in.

For some time now, the US had been worried about the events in the Eurozone. The aftermath of the 2008 financial crisis was still very much present, and the administration feared an uncontrolled eruption caused by a Greek default would have far-reaching repercussions and deepen the recession on a global scale. From the beginning they understood well that the problem was systemic and not just confined to Greece. They did not need us to tell them.

Obama said as much: "We cannot have another Lehman [Brothers' bankruptcy]." He was concerned that a resolution to the problem was not shaping up fast enough. He had been briefed about the measures we had taken – "courageous" was the word he used – and thought it was the turn of the rest of Europe to show its determination to safeguard the integrity of the euro.

It was obvious to everyone in that room that Germany had to be persuaded to commit to a bailout. The president indicated he would speak to the chancellor. He also made it clear that the US – which provides almost a fifth of IMF funds – would support IMF involvement in a rescue package if the Europeans chose that path. In the weeks that followed, the role of the US in pushing its European partners to commit to a bailout mechanism was indeed instrumental, both through bilateral talks between Obama and Merkel, and via US influence on the IMF.

As the meeting was drawing to a close, Papandreou reminded Obama that, apart from being Greek prime minister, he was also president of the Socialist International, an organization embracing over 100 like-minded political parties from around the world. Half-seriously he said, "We should think of initiatives we could work on together". "Well," came the smiling reply from the president, "amongst us socialists, maybe it's not the best moment right now!" Obama then mused about visiting Greece and his kids riding a donkey on a Greek island, "when I get out of here".

As we were leaving, the president shook our hands. "Good luck" were his parting words to me. I was beginning to hear those words a lot.

Chapter 9

ULTIMA RATIO

What always struck me during my time as finance minister was the incredible "disconnect" between home and abroad. Coming home from Eurogroup meetings or after high-level meetings with prime ministers or presidents, meant landing in a harsh reality with other priorities, where even the language of political discourse was different. While the rest of Europe was abuzz with discussions about the form and timing of a Greek bailout, in Greece the problems were of a very different nature.

The genuine hardship of a growing part of the Greek population as a result of the recession and continuing austerity was one side of the coin. It was real, increasingly acute and made worse by the sorry state of public services. It was made worse by the fact that the social safety net in Greece was full of glaring holes, unable to target resources where they were needed most. And it hit particularly hard outsiders, such as young people without a job or a prospect of eventually getting one.

The other side, however, was the grievances of special interest groups, which now felt threatened. Olympic Air, the debt-laden state airline privatized by the previous government, was a case in point. The unions had fought the privatization tooth and nail, and in the process, extracted exorbitant redundancy payments, coupled with re-hiring of staff in the public sector. To claim these they now occupied the General Accounting Office and stopped traffic on one of the central Athens boulevards. Such occupations were a protest tactic used often in 2010 and 2011. I regularly had to move to another office because the main finance ministry building was occupied.

In an emergency meeting with the ministers involved, we tried to inject some sanity into the deal that had been brokered by the previous government. The end result was a compromise that left no-one satisfied. As far as I was concerned, it was still too expensive, as well as grossly unfair to people in the private sector losing their jobs that could not extract such generous concessions; for the unions, it was going back on things previously agreed. But at least we reclaimed the building. I worried this was just the first of a series of similar confrontations, and that we were not showing real resolve.

Outside Greece events were accelerating; decision time was here. In expectation of an impending bailout scheme, spreads continued to remain around 300 basis points and the price of credit default swaps (CDSs) was falling.

CDS trading in government securities was not responsible for the crisis, but was making it worse. Criticism particularly focused on "naked CDSs", which enabled holders to trade bonds they did not own: a bit like taking out insurance on your neighbour's house and then setting it on fire to collect. So, on March 10th, Merkel, Sarkozy, Juncker and Papandreou signed a joint letter asking the European Commission and the European Council to address the issue. The letter argued for minimum holding periods for CDS trading and a ban on speculative CDS trading.

As we were preparing for the March Eurogroup, and despite public denials, the European institutional machinery was hard at work behind the scenes to prepare the ground for a possible intervention in Greece. A detailed non-paper was drafted by a Euro Working Group task force and was circulating amongst European capitals.

The non-paper made the point that an external intervention would not only help fill Greece's liquidity gap but also, crucially, reinforce the credibility of the euro itself. It suggested the mechanism used should be rapidly operational, transparent and flexible so as to maximise the positive impact on confidence. It should also minimise moral hazard, with strong conditionality and pricing set to provide an incentive for Greece to go back to the markets as soon as possible.

In terms of practical arrangements, an intergovernmental agreement would create a stability facility and entrust its management to the Commission. This could then be funded either directly by bilateral loans of member states, or indirectly by borrowing in the market with the guarantee of Eurozone countries.

In the March 15th Eurogroup, the fault lines around the different funding approaches became evident. The Commission preferred indirect funding but could live with either method, and most countries agreed; but not Germany, for which the Commission borrowing in financial markets was a non-starter. Given that without Germany there was no bail-out, the other countries one by one ended up agreeing to voluntary coordinated bilateral loans.

What was gratifying to me at that meeting was the general acknowledgment that the Greek government had done its job; in fact, had done all it could.

Following a report we prepared outlining the measures taken to date, there were, finally, good words around the table. Jean-Claude Trichet, a vocal critic in the past, said it was, "disappointing that these courageous decisions have not stabilized markets more". This was echoed by Christine Lagarde: "Greece has done its job and exceeded expectations, but markets have only limited acknowledgement." Wolfgang Schäuble spoke of his "respect for what Greece has done"; as did Finland's Jyrki Katainen ("Greece has done an excellent job"); and Austria's Josef Pröll ("my admiration for the measures taken").

More importantly, everybody now realized we had reached the point where, however many measures we took, they would not be enough. The markets required a "backstop" in case Greece stopped having market access. Not just a general promise but specific details of how, when and, especially, how much. I made that point by pleading for a "loaded gun on the table". If we had such a weapon and it were visible and credible to all, then maybe – just maybe – we might not have to use it.

Yet Germany was still not ready to commit. Wolfgang Schäuble had gone to the limit of his mandate. He wanted no decisions on the day; the matter should be referred to the summit in ten days. So the Eurogroup noted that, "it clarified the technical modalities enabling a decision on coordinated action and which could be activated swiftly in the case of need". (Translation: we are not ready yet to announce decisions, but we are getting there). And it underlined again, "the Greek authorities have not asked for financial support". Not yet anyway.

The days that followed were ones of intense speculation and brinkmanship. The press was frantically reporting on any pronouncement from German officials, trying to gauge which way Germany was going. One day, they hinted there would be a European financial package; the next, the German government spokesman was saying Germany was open to the possibility of Greece going to the IMF.

The confusion came to a head on March 18th when Dow Jones reported that Greece had lost hope for an EU solution and had instead decided "to go to the IMF". The story claimed this would be announced over the long weekend of April 2-4th. It sent spreads up, the Athens stock market down, and the Euro took a plunge against the dollar and the yen. Our frustration was immense: how do you issue a denial of something like that? So we told our beleaguered press officer, who was inundated with requests for comment: "Tell them that April 2-4th is Easter weekend, and on Greek Easter all we do is roast lamb!"

Such rumours had the potential to create enormous damage. We were constantly worried that the "bank jog" of the first months of 2010 – the steady bleeding as depositors withdrew money for safety reasons or sent it abroad – could become a fully fledged "bank run". Once that happened, there would be no way back and it would be necessary to close the banks and impose capital controls. We did not live through that in 2010 – unfortunately, we did five years later.

I spent that weekend on the phone to the heads of the major

Greek banks to ensure that ATMs were operational and fully loaded with cash. They understood the problem and were on top of it. The last thing any of us wanted was a string of empty or broken ATMs creating a rumour that "something is wrong", and the rumour spreading like wildfire with the result that, come opening time, there would be long lines of people in front of the banks.

As we got closer to the March 25th summit discussions between countries became more intense. We were edging towards a solution, and one of the sticking points remained the role of the IMF. Germany had by now done an about-face and was insisting the Fund needed to participate in any support mechanism. They did not trust the Commission to design and oversee a support programme – nor, crucially, to convince markets; and Merkel needed to be able to brandish the "tough IMF" for the discussion in the German parliament and for her internal audience.

On the eve of the summit, Fitch cut Portugal's credit rating, creating further pressure for a solution. But there was also good news. Trichet announced that the ECB would continue to accept our low-rated bonds as collateral, reversing his January refusal to give Greece special treatment. And white smoke seemed to be rising at last: Bloomberg cited unnamed German government sources saying that Berlin and Paris had finally agreed on a rescue package for Greece "as a last resort", on condition it also involved the IMF. Berlin had won.

The next day, as Chancellor Merkel arrived for the summit, she gave the game away to the throngs of waiting cameras and press: "I suggest we examine the idea of a combination of IMF assistance with European bilateral loans. This would be a last resort solution, if Greece no longer has access to international markets".

This would be a classic Merkel tactic, used time and again before crucial meetings. Send out signals for days and weeks showing reluctance to agree; then, just before the meeting, announce a position, commit to it publicly, thus pre-empting the discussion. She would typically appear in the Bundestag the day before or even the morning of a summit, and commit herself to a specific outcome. Or she would announce her position as she would arrive at the meeting. She would leave herself room for manoeuvre and compromise, but everyone would know she could not back down.

I accompanied Papandreou to Brussels for this crucial summit. Ministers were not allowed in the main room, but my presence was required for negotiations before the meeting. Indeed, we were summoned by Herman van Rompuy, newly chosen president of the European Council, to a meeting with the main players. We arrived to find Merkel, Sarkozy and Trichet, together with their aides, haggling over a draft statement the presidency would propose to leaders.

We spent some time arguing over the text. We wanted stronger language to recognize our efforts, and weaker language on the *ultima ratio* ("last resort") doctrine and the interest rates charged. Merkel liked the text as it was, but was willing to give in on some points. Sarkozy was impatient and wanted to get on with it. We got some changes into the text and then the leaders joined the summit.

In the European Council meeting, Papandreou presented what his government had done to get a grip on public finances. He did not paint a pretty picture, insisted reforms take time, and a country willing to go through what Greece was in a hostile financial environment deserved the support of its peers. He repeated that we wanted to succeed on our own; but to have any hope of doing so, the Eurozone had to make clear that it would never let one of its members down.

He made an impression. His was the image of an honest prime minister, heading a government fighting hard, having taken difficult decisions, but facing an impossible task. It was time for Europe to help with actions, not just words. And the European Council was ready to take decisions.

The statement issued spoke of "shared responsibility" for

economic and financial stability and recognized the "ambitious and decisive action" taken by Greece. It reiterated the mantra that we had not requested any financial support, but then announced a joint EU/IMF financing mechanism, in which "Euro area member states are ready to contribute to coordinated bilateral loans". This had to be "*ultima ratio*, meaning in particular that market financing is insufficient". A financing of last resort. With strings attached, as "disbursement would be decided subject to strong conditionality". And at explicitly punitive interest rates: "Interest rates will be non-concessional."

So there it was. At last, a European solution of sorts. Not completely European, as the IMF would also be involved. Only as a last resort, so there would be no pre-emptive use in order to calm the markets. On punitive terms, so as to avoid problems of "moral hazard". And still no mention of how much money would be on the table. The finance ministers would have to come up with that. But it was still a step forward.

It had taken four packages of measures (in the December budget, the January SGP, again in February, and finally in early March), together accounting for over 6% of GDP, for Greece to be able finally to claw back some of its lost credibility and convince the Eurozone to help. In record time by EU standards, navigating in completely uncharted waters, a new mechanism was created from scratch. Unfortunately, it had come too late. The loaded gun was on the table, but being there was no longer enough.

We were going to have to use it.

I have often wondered whether the leaders at the time actually believed their decision to set up a support mechanism for Greece would constitute "a credible threat". Whether, in other words, it would convince the markets Greece had a safety net if all else failed, leading to lower risk expectations and lower spreads, allowing the country to continue borrowing at viable rates in international markets.

As far as analysts were concerned, the March 25th decision

was yet another step towards the inevitable: official support for Greece to replace market financing. For them, it was just a matter of time to get there. But for the leaders? I think many of them genuinely thought – or at least still hoped – that what they decided on that day would be sufficient to stem the tide.

On the back of the summit decision we ventured into the markets with a 7-year syndicated bond issue for €5 billion. With a 310 spread, the rate was a shade below 6%, lower than the March issue, which was reasonable in the circumstances. But the market response was lukewarm; we received only half the offers that were made for the 10-year bond earlier that month. This would be our last long-term issue. We were now left with €12 billion in the till, enough to cover bonds maturing in April but no more after that.

At the end of the month, Ireland announced that its banks needed to raise an additional €32 billion of capital: another reminder that the problem we were experiencing went far beyond past Greek profligacy. Ireland had been a good pupil: time and again, it had pursued tough austerity. The Commission and the ECB would point to the Irish example when asking us to do more. Yet Ireland was also in trouble, and not because it had failed to curtail its deficit or because of lack of competitiveness.

On March 30th, Papandreou summoned me and the Bank of Greece governor to a meeting to examine the state of the Greek banking system. Since January, the system had lost €14 billion, about 2% of deposits every month. Liquidity was trickling to a stop, despite state guarantees to commercial banks and the ECB's decision to continue extending credit to Greek banks, effectively overruling the rating downgrades which made Greek collateral not acceptable.

The Governor was pessimistic, and this pessimism extended to developments on the debt front. With the economy tanking and spreads as high as they were, our public debt dynamics were alarming. The situation was quickly becoming unmanageable, and the markets knew that. Governor Provopoulos was of the opinion that there was no other solution to accepting the EU support package; and the sooner the better.

About this time, I started receiving frequent late-night phone calls from the other side of the Atlantic. On the line was Lael Brainard, US Under Secretary of the Treasury, Tim Geithner's No.2 with responsibility for international affairs. She wanted to know how we were holding up; what the developments with our Eurozone partners were; and how the US could help. My response was the same every time: talk to Germany and get them to move; time is running out.

On April 8th, Greece's 10-year bond yield reached 7.4%, following reports claiming the country was seeking renegotiation of the recent agreement to avoid the harsh terms the IMF would impose. On April 9th, Fitch downgraded us, and the market rumour was that Standard and Poor's was about to follow. Meanwhile, a Financial Times report on massive capital flight from Greek banks sent the Athens stock market crashing. In this environment, the budget numbers we released showing that in the first quarter of 2010 we had actually reduced the deficit by 40% compared with the same period the previous year, made absolutely no impact.

There was no more time. It was now obvious that a concrete and convincing financial support package had to be put on the table for all to see. So Jean-Claude Juncker convened a teleconference of Eurogroup ministers for Sunday April 11th.

A note was circulated beforehand summarizing the main elements of the proposed agreement. The funding would be through bilateral loans, centrally pooled by the Commission, and would include IMF financing. Activation would be decided unanimously, following a request by Greece. A "Troika" of the Commission, the ECB and the IMF would negotiate the loan agreement and the accompanying conditionality with Greece, for final approval by the Eurogroup.

The teleconference itself was a pretty dramatic affair. We all felt the significance of the moment; I more than most. The discussion centred on two issues: how much money, and on what terms.

The amount on the table was €30 billion for the first year of a three-year programme, and we had assurances that the IMF would add €15 billion. There were disagreements on whether the statement would refer to those yearly figures or to a total figure for the whole period, or omit figures altogether. The IMF was pushing for a large figure such as €80 billion to be announced, but several countries wanted no explicit overall figures mentioned. The latter was understood to be suicidal, and the final statement referred explicitly to €30 billion for the first year.

Next was the cost of financing. This was where things got tough. Germany was no longer insisting on "market rates" (nobody knew what that meant anymore); however, they did want rates that would look high enough to avoid the criticism of being too soft on Greece. The formula gave a lending rate of around 5%; certainly lower than the current 7.5% in the market, but still high. France and other countries were open to a lower rate, but the punitive element prevailed.

Then we got to the proposal of a 50 basis point "service fee". I objected strongly – a service fee charged by a Eurozone country to another? Practically everyone agreed it made no sense. In the end, the discussion was abruptly cut by Schäuble: "We have already told the Bundestag about the service fee." So he could not agree on scrapping it.

The next question was when we were going to activate the mechanism. To prepare the ground, I would send a letter to Rehn, Trichet and Strauss-Kahn requesting "discussions" with the Troika on a multi-year programme that could be supported with financial assistance from Eurozone countries and the IMF, if we decided to request such assistance. We agreed that technical discussions would start on Monday April 19th, following the informal Ecofin, to be held in Madrid over the weekend.

The so-called "informal" Ecofin meetings are occasions for

the country holding the rotating EU presidency to play host and invite ministers to its city of choice. Spouses are also invited, and the Presidency organizes social events and dinners around the meetings – in this case, at the Reina Sofia Museum. The discussions are informal, no decisions are taken and central bank governors are also present.

The Madrid Ecofin meeting was memorable for a different reason. The volcanic eruption in Iceland had produced an enormous ash cloud, rapidly expanding in all directions. Aside from jokes about "volcano revenge" for the Icelandic bank meltdown, the ash cloud was disrupting air travel throughout Europe. We cut the visit to Madrid short and managed to catch the last commercial flight back to Athens. The EU delegation due in Athens on Monday was not as lucky. Flights had been grounded and they spent the next couple of days crossing half of Europe by rented van before managing to board a flight from Vienna to Athens.

Meanwhile the IMF delegation had already arrived and we took some of them out for dinner. It was important to get to know better the people who would have such a central role in our lives. Heading the delegation was Poul Thomsen, a tall Dane, soon to become a household name in Greece. He was to be the person sitting opposite me at the negotiating table. He was an accomplished professional with a keen political sense and would turn out to be a tough negotiator. With him was the Dutchman Bob Traa, the IMF's local representative, an economist with an uncanny ability to see through complicated budget figures.

During dinner, I received a call informing me that on April 22nd Eurostat would announce a higher revised figure for the 2009 Greek fiscal deficit. Following work by our now independent Statistics Authority and Eurostat, the figure was 13.6% of GDP, over a point more than that previously announced. This was very bad news, and it was made worse by the fact that Eurostat had reservations even about this higher number, meaning that the final tally could be higher still.

I understood immediately this was the final straw. We would now have to activate the mechanism. There was no way we could continue borrowing in the markets once this figure became public. It reinforced investors' fears that the Greek problem was worse than they had thought. I immediately called Olli Rehn in Brussels. He was also worried – the timing was delicate. We agreed to ensure that in the next few days everything would be in place for the potential activation of the support mechanism.

On the drive home from the restaurant, my wife, Jacoline, could see how preoccupied I was. She had been following closely the events of the last few months: the interminable hours in the office, my anger about the mess we had inherited, the anxiety about whether we were going to make it, my frustration things were not moving in Europe, and my exasperation with those who did not realize how serious the situation was. And tonight she was not reassured. At one point during the dinner Bob Traa, a veteran of IMF bailouts around the world, had said to her in their mother tongue: "Your husband has no idea what is coming..." Prophetic words.

On April 20th, I called a meeting of my Council of Economic Advisors, together with the chief economists of the main banks and of Greece's main economic think tanks. The discussion ranged from the macro situation (bad, getting worse), to fiscal issues (do more on expenditures) and reforms (be aggressive on privatizations). Everyone was in favour of immediately activating the mechanism. In the words of Yannis Stournaras, then head of the think-tank of the employers' federation, and finance minister after the June 2012 elections, "why haven't we done it yet?"

The new Eurostat figures were announced April 22nd. Surprisingly Greece was no longer the EU country with the highest deficit: Ireland had overtaken us, its deficit revised up to 14.3% of GDP. Nevertheless Moody's immediately cut our credit rating. Greek spreads shot up and broke the 600 point barrier, meaning the country would be borrowing at above 9% – assuming it could still find takers for its debt, which was becoming increasingly unlikely.

During the morning, I got a phone call from Wolfgang Schäuble. Until then Germany had been reluctant for us to activate the mechanism; both publicly and privately they had been saying it was too early. However, that morning, he wanted to tell me that if Greece decided to ask for activation, Germany would not object. We had reached *ultima ratio*. I talked with a number of my colleagues in various European capitals, as well as with Commissioner Rehn. Everyone felt we were at the point where any further delay risked making matters worse.

In the afternoon, Papandreou assembled his cabinet at the Maximou Mansion. He and I described the situation and made the case that the "loaded gun on the table" had not worked. Greece needed to ask for activation of the support mechanism.

The discussion lasted late into the night. The consensus was that there was no other option left, but the cabinet was split on the timing. Most were in favour of immediate activation; some wanted to wait until we knew more details on terms and conditions. The EU-IMF support mechanism was seen as a "safe harbour" for Greece, but there was anxiety about additional measures that might be required by our creditors.

One of the secretaries came into the room and slipped me a piece of paper. Tim Geithner was on the line and wanted to speak to me. I excused myself from the meeting and took the call. Geithner wanted to convey the full support of the US of any decision we would take. They had talked to Germany and other European countries and everything was ready for us if we decided to make the move. The IMF was also on board and believed we should activate the support mechanism.

The message was simple and it was coming from all quarters: "It's time."

After the meeting ended, I followed Papandreou to his office. We stood by the door. "We should activate tomorrow", I said. "We can't wait any longer." He agreed. We stood silent for a while. This was a historic moment and we both felt it. He then stayed alone in his office to make a round of calls to other European leaders.

The next day, Papandreou had scheduled an official visit to Kastellorizo, a gem of an island in the Aegean Sea at the eastern edge of Greek territory, a stone's throw from Turkey. He discussed with his aides whether he should cancel and make the statement from Athens. In the end he decided against it. He wanted the symbolism of making the momentous announcement from the remotest of Greek islands.

What has since become known as "the Kastellorizo statement" had a surreal ring to it. On a beautiful spring day, against a backdrop of picture-perfect island houses hugging a miniature harbour, and with a fisherman – oblivious to the momentous event taking place – passing in a colorful wooden boat behind him as he spoke, Papandreou announced to the world that Greece was asking its Eurozone partners and the IMF to help it avoid default.

He briefly recounted how we had got to this point: the mistakes of the past, the efforts of the last months, the battle for the creation of the support mechanism, the hope its existence would by itself prove sufficient, and the need today to activate it in order to safeguard the interests of the country and of the Greek people.

He talked of "our final goal, our destination: to unleash the potential of every Greek man and woman, to overcome practices and systems that have held us back for generations, to bring justice and rules where today there is injustice, transparency where today we have darkness and corruption, security where today there is insecurity, and growth and prosperity for all. I am sure we can succeed. All we need to do is believe in ourselves, our values and in our capabilities".

In the meantime, on a more mundane note, I drafted a brief letter to Rehn, Trichet and Strauss-Kahn. The text simply read: "In accordance to the Statement of the Heads of State and Government of 25 March 2010 to provide financial support to Greece, when needed, and the follow up Statement of the Eurogroup, Greece is hereby requesting the activation of the support mechanism."

In his statement, the prime minister had called the occasion "a new Odyssey for Greece". He added, "But we know the road to Ithaca" referring to the eventual return of the ancient hero to his island home.

Like Odysseus on his journey, we were entering uncharted seas.

Chapter 10

THE IMF

It was after midnight local time when the Gulfstream jet landed at Andrews Air Force base in Maryland. It had been a long flight after an equally long day. We had left Athens at 10pm at the end of the day which had started with Papandreou's Kastellorizo statement, only to continue with the first negotiations with the Troika.

Our initial meeting with the Troika was about ensuring the disbursement of funds before our €8.9 billion bond matured on May 19 – that is, before the country declared bankruptcy. For this we needed a loan agreement as well as agreement on the "strict conditionality" creditors demanded: the "Memorandum of Understanding on Economic and Financial Policies" (MoU in short), henceforth known in Greece as the *Mnimonio*.

The timetable was tight and the process complicated. For the first loan tranche to be disbursed in time, it was necessary to ensure the smooth functioning of an intergovernmental mechanism which had never operated before. This involved completing a number of administrative steps after a Eurogroup teleconference had given the green light on May 3rd. And for that, we first needed to agree on a programme to reduce the deficit and to implement reforms, and then have it approved by the Greek parliament.

In other words, to avoid declaring bankruptcy we had little more than a week to draft and negotiate the kind of agreement that would change everyone's life in Greece for the next three years at the very least – more likely, the next decade.

That is why the Troika team in Athens was not keen to see me leave to attend the IMF spring meetings in Washington. I would only be away for 48 hours, but they wanted to maintain the momentum of the negotiations. For my part however, I could not negotiate an agreement without first having talked to the people giving the Troika their marching orders: the EU Commissioner, the ECB chief, and the IMF managing director, who were all in Washington for the IMF meetings.

More importantly I needed to know the size of the envelope: we still had not agreed on how much money would be available to Greece.

At Andrews, we were greeted by US immigration officials in a deserted VIP lounge, processed efficiently and whisked to our hotel in Washington. It was 2am when we got there, so I was very surprised to be met in the hotel lobby by an obviously tired journalist from a wire service, asking for a comment on whether Greece would declare default. My brief remark that no, we would not, made it to the media the next day, together with a dramatic – if inaccurate – description of "the Greek finance minister arriving from Athens at dawn at his Washington hotel, haggard and in a track suit". Jeans. I never wear track suits.

There was not much sleep that night. The meeting with the IMF managing director was at 7am. Olli Rehn and Jean-Claude Trichet had joined Dominique Strauss-Kahn in his spacious 12th floor office at IMF headquarters, which that morning was bathed in beautiful spring light. I was greeted warmly. Despite the difficulties there was relief that decisions had finally been taken and a sense of expediency to move things along. Over coffee we spent the next hour on three basic issues: the timeline ahead; the size of the financial support; and the measures to be taken.

Dates were agreed. Everyone was aware of the need to stick to a very tight schedule. We needed a draft agreement by May 3rd in order for the necessary actions to be completed for disbursement before May 19th. Parallel to the process in European capitals and in the Commission, the IMF board of directors would have to give its approval for the Fund's contribution; this was slated for May 10th.

Olli Rehn worried about the two-week period the German parliament needed in order to approve the German loan. I was worried about securing approval from the Greek parliament for a harsh set of measures, before foreign parliaments gave the green light for the loan. DSK suggested that, if push came to shove, we could look into some "bridge financing" to avoid outright catastrophe and buy ourselves some extra days until all the political processes were complete, as long as there was agreement on a robust programme.

On the size of the financial envelope, DSK pledged €30 billion from the IMF, which would be an extraordinary 30 times Greece's quota contribution to the Fund – a first. To get IMF board approval for such a number required not only the solid backing of the US and of EU countries, but also deft persuasion of the largest developing countries; they would not see this in a positive light.

The level of the Eurozone countries' contribution remained still undefined; a figure of €45 billion was being discussed, but we all felt that would not be anywhere close to sufficient, either to support Greece while we were out of the market or as a large enough "backstop" for the markets. A higher figure would be necessary. But on that, we would have to wait for white smoke from Berlin. Olli Rehn was due to speak to Schäuble and DSK to Merkel.

On the specific fiscal and structural measures to take, the trio did not want to go into details – not while a negotiating team was hard at work in Athens. But, in a comment emblematic of the realistic line the IMF would often take, Strauss-Kahn suggested that the three-year horizon for the deficit to fall below 3% of GDP was too short; we should move the goalposts from 2012 to 2013 or even further back. I couldn't have agreed more.

We ended the meeting with decisions on what to communicate to the world. The message was simple: "we are working on a programme; we will be successful; there will be no debt financing problem". And debt restructuring was not on the table. They were all adamant: we should all be absolutely clear on that point.

I spent the rest of Saturday in bilateral meetings. My first stop was Tim Geithner, who assured me the US would ensure there would be no problems at the IMF board. Geithner also repeated that as far as the US (and therefore the IMF) was concerned, debt restructuring was completely off the table. Then came Guido Mantega, finance minister of Brazil, a country that had expressed misgivings over such a large loan going to a Eurozone member. I argued our case and told him Papandreou would be speaking to President Lula da Silva. There was an affinity there and we were going to need it. Alexei Kudrin, the Russian finance minister, asked many questions but did not openly commit to supporting our demand. Equally inscrutable was Xie Xuren, the finance minister of China. They were all waiting for DSK's proposal to the IMF board, and for the positions taken by the US and the EU countries – there were larger geopolitical issues in play.

On Sunday morning, there was a follow-up meeting with Strauss-Kahn. This time I was accompanied by George Zanias and Panayiotis Roumeliotis, our representative on the IMF board, a former finance minister and longstanding DSK acquaintance. Some years later, Roumeliotis would argue that we should have insisted on debt restructuring from the start. However, that option did not exist in April 2010 – it was a "deal breaker" for the ECB and the major EU countries. Within the IMF some were expressing doubts about whether a Greek programme could succeed without debt relief, but the IMF leadership was completely in line with its European partners.

Before leaving Washington, I held a press conference. If we had any doubt that Greece was the only game in town that day, the sight of a packed IMF press conference room dispelled them. Before going on stage, I was told by Caroline Atkinson, director of IMF external relations at the time, that this was the biggest press gathering she could remember. There must have been about 150 print and electronic media journalists from all over the world in there.

I made a short statement and opened the floor to questions. "Are you bothered at all by a statement attributed to Schäuble this morning that Germany has not yet decided whether it will agree to Greece's request for financial aid?" *Hmm...how does one answer this without actually answering?* "We have full confidence that when the framework is completed and the negotiations are done, we will have a framework of conditionality and financing conditions attached to it to which all European partners will be able to subscribe."

"Would Greece fare better outside the euro zone, or inside?" *An easy one.* "Greece is a member of the Eurozone, will always remain a member of the Eurozone, will always remain within the European Union, full stop."

"Do you think it would have been better if you had gone directly to the IMF on day one and ignored the rest of the EU?" *Or not go to the IMF at all, I could have added.* "There was never an option or desire for Greece to go to the IMF. Greece is a member of the EU, and we are implementing the decisions by Ecofin. The decision to associate the IMF was taken by our European partners."

"Has a restructuring of the Greek debt been an issue in your negotiations at any time?" *Ok, let's try to kill this once more.* "Any notion of restructuring is off the table for the government, has never been put on the table in the negotiations, and has never been part of any suggestions or proposals made by the IMF to Greece."

And the clincher: "Do you have a message to investors who are betting on default?"

A deep breath, crossing my fingers. "All I can say is, they will lose their shirts."

And then we were on our way home.

We flew overnight and landed in Athens early on Monday morning, ready to start my toughest week in office, and a defining one for the future of Greece. There were non-stop meetings with the prime minister and the cabinet; hours spent in parliamentary committees explaining the support mechanism; and interminable hours in negotiations with the Troika.

The week started very badly. The markets were not convinced that Greece would make it in time to avoid defaulting on May 19th, so spreads on Monday 26th April climbed over 660 basis points. Had Greece tapped the markets that day, it would have had to pay a clearly unsustainable interest rate of close to 10%.

Ambivalence emanating from Berlin made markets nervous: Schäuble was having a hard time in his discussions with parliamentary group leaders in Berlin, and refused to commit publicly that everything would be ready by May 19th. This was echoed by Merkel, who – sticking to her "tough love" approach – repeated that Germany was ready to help Greece, but on condition that Greece came up with an appropriate austerity programme. We knew that; we just did not need to be reminded of it every day.

On Tuesday April 27th, spreads exceeded 700 basis points. The Athens stock market was in free fall. The market was abuzz with rumours of imminent Greek debt restructuring and you could almost hear investors dumping Greek bonds. A poll in Germany showed a 57% majority against the bailout, while Greece rose to first place in a world ranking of countries "most likely to default", surpassing Venezuela, Argentina, Pakistan and Iraq.

The mood in Athens was no better. In a poll released that day 60% of those asked were against the support mechanism and 70% thought the IMF's involvement was not a good thing. And in the midst of a surge of bank deposit outflows, which for April alone would be close to €6 billion, rumours of an impending "ceiling" on cash withdrawals from accounts prompted angry denials from the main Greek banks.

Standard and Poor's became the first credit rating company to cut Greece's debt rating to "junk". Market analysts were also raising the bar for the rescue package, some putting the necessary figure for the next three years at €150 billion, more than triple the publicly discussed combined EU/IMF figure of €45 billion. On Tuesday, Papandreou addressed the PASOK parliamentary group. In an emotional speech he thanked the 160 PASOK MPs for their support over the last six months; he confessed to the "loneliness of power" that he had felt during the period as he had grappled with historic decisions for the country, saying that he needed them behind him in "this moment of truth".

I followed with my own speech. I felt drained physically and emotionally after the recent days, weeks and months. This was not the time for analysis, numbers or playing the blame game. There was no sense in trying to embellish the situation: we were looking at very tough years ahead, during which we would all be severely tested. However, I was sure of one thing: "if we do our job right, we will be able to look Greeks in the eye and be proud of our decisions, however difficult."

On Wednesday, with Greek spreads hitting 1000 basis points, Strauss-Kahn met Merkel in Berlin. The meeting was meant to impress on the Germans how serious the situation was. Rather than sounding reassuring, the chancellor continued to pile on the pressure, saying negotiations needed to accelerate: "On that basis, Germany will then make its own decision." And she added: "In the year 2000, the issue was whether Greece could or could not join the Eurozone. It turns out that the decision made then was not examined thoroughly enough."

Despite these words, the German government had finally given the green light to a large package for Greece. There were rumours to this effect; and, for the first time, leaks that the overall package would be between €100 and €120 billion, enough to allow Greece to stay out of financial markets for three years. The change in tone was soon clear: a number of officials made statements aimed at preparing public opinion that "we are talking about a loan, not a grant, and it will be fully repaid".

In the evening, President Obama weighed in with a call to Chancellor Merkel. The US cavalry was coming to the rescue, making it very clear that there could be no more wavering or mixed messages; too much was at stake. The day finished better than it started, with spreads on Greek bonds dropping below 800 points. But, at the same time, Standard and Poor's announced it was cutting Spain's credit rating for the second time since January 2009, pushing the Euro to a one-year low.

In a meeting with key ministers on the programme, the consensus was that we should front-load all the tough measures. Better do the difficult things up front, in 2010, when the government still maintained popular support, and hope that by 2011 and 2012 the economy would show the first signs of a turnaround. The thinking was right, but the scale of the effort required was still not appreciated.

The next day, the prime minister called a meeting with social partners in an attempt to get them on board – or at least prepare them for what was to follow. He painted a bleak picture, asked them to help him and pleaded for a positive message to come out, a message of everyone doing their part to save the country. With few exceptions they did not move from their entrenched positions. The prevailing attitude was summarised by one of them: "I understand you have no other option; but I cannot support you." We would be alone in this.

On Friday April 30th we had a visitor. Ali Babacan, the young deputy prime minister of Turkey, was in town. The visit was to prepare the first Greek-Turkish meeting of councils of ministers, due to take place mid-May in Athens. This was to be an important symbol of improved relations between the two countries, but also an occasion to sign bilateral agreements in areas as diverse as transport, energy, construction, banking, education and culture.

The timing of the visit was deliberate. Turkey was proud of its achievements; reforms had borne fruit and its economy had prospered. It was no longer a supplicant for EU membership, having watched Greece and then Cyprus become members and eventually adopt the euro; it was now happy with its strong geopolitical position in the region. After many years of feeling inferior to Greece, there was now a thinly veiled sense of the tables being turned. We could all feel this, but chose to ignore it.

At the end of the meeting with the prime minister and myself, Babacan politely offered to help and asked if Greece needed a loan from Turkey. What are good friends and neighbours for if not to lend a helping hand in the hour of need? We thanked him and declined, equally politely.

Chapter 11

NEGOTIATING 110 BILLION

How exactly does one negotiate a €110 billion deal, the likes of which has never been seen before? Unfortunately, no such manual exists. The Troika team was in Athens, going through budget numbers. The work had started on April 23rd and had been going on all day, every day. The three institutions were in full force; their combined teams numbered over thirty people. They had fanned out across the General Accounting Office, the Bank of Greece, the Hellenic Statistics Authority and ministries to collect data, assess specific policy measures and make proposals.

We were outgunned.

The information gathered was discussed in interminable meetings with finance ministry civil servants, flanked by my young and competent team of advisors. The atmosphere was professional – staff on both sides discussed the description and costing of particular fiscal measures for hours. Our side argued every number when they thought the Troika was being unreasonable.

Once work on specific issues was advanced, I would convene a full negotiating session with the main Troika staff and the "principals" (Poul Thomsen from the IMF, Servaas Deroose from the European Commission and Klaus Masuch from the ECB). These were more formal in nature; we all felt the weight of what we were involved in. And they lasted well into the night, fuelled by sandwiches and pizza delivery.

In the last days of the negotiation, the meetings focused on line-by-line negotiation of the final texts, where the choice of words and nuances were capable of making headlines. When we had to find a difficult political compromise, I would suspend the meeting and invite the principals into my office for a closed session to thrash things out.

Until you've been through such a negotiation, it is hard to grasp its complexity. The programme was built on three pillars: deficit reduction; structural reforms; and policies to keep the financial sector stable. To formalize this into a final agreement, it was necessary to agree first on a macroeconomic scenario; then on all the fiscal, structural and financial measures to be taken over the next years in order to reach targets and fit the scenario; and finally to translate all this into binding texts.

And to do it all, we had barely a week.

The Greek government had never done this before. There was no expertise in medium-term programming or multi-year budgeting. Until the IMF came to town, the Greek state did not really know how to prepare and execute a robust annual budget, let alone a multi-year programme. And nobody in Greece had ever done deep deficit reduction before, and more so in a recessionary environment, where reducing the deficit while the economy is contracting requires greater effort and harsher cuts.

The Troika also had problems. The three institutions had never worked together before on such a programme. To make matters worse, they were operating in a fuzzy institutional environment. The Eurozone was putting up most of the money, so one should expect the Commission to be pre-eminent. Nevertheless, the nature of the financing arrangement meant that it had to ensure that the decisions to be taken would be palatable even to the most "difficult" of the Eurozone countries.

Bringing the IMF into the arrangement explicitly questioned the competence of the Commission and its ability to reassure the markets. This gave the Fund a weight in the negotiations larger than its one-third share in the financing. The IMF team was, in any case, not accustomed to being a silent observer in negotiations – its people were used to calling the shots. This did not go down well with the Commission.

The ECB was putting no money on the table. Their formal

association with the programme was awkward – the Commission was supposed to work "in liaison" with the ECB. But they wielded the ultimate weapon, control over the banking system; their rules on collateral for lending to commercial banks meant they had plenty of weight in the negotiations.

Each of the three brought different strengths to the table. The IMF had expertise and experience on fiscal issues; the Commission, knowledge on structural policies; and the ECB, veto power over the banking system. As a result, early on, a pattern emerged: the Commission team would formally lead, but would yield to the IMF on the assessment of fiscal measures; it was vice versa on structural issues, where the Commission team could draw on the combined competence of different EC directorates in Brussels. And the ECB position dominated when it came to the banks.

It was not hard to see why everyone yielded to the IMF on fiscal issues: they had done this before, and had a tool box with a clear methodology. Build your baseline scenario (i.e. "business as usual" without measures), identify the "fiscal gap" to close, find the measures to take, quantify them, run your model again to see what happens, and then pile up more measures as the original ones reduced GDP and did not bring down the deficit as much as originally targeted.

Despite the allocation of roles, there were tensions; on a number of occasions, negotiations had to be suspended until the three institutions could agree among each other. Underlying most of the tensions was the fact that, from the beginning, political considerations were very much present in the negotiating room. There was a strong moralistic and punitive element to the approach, especially from the Europeans.

After all, "ultima ratio" was the order of the day, and the Europeans were reluctant rescuers. They had decided to help Greece, but in a way that would inflict pain, act as a deterrent for other "errant countries", and show taxpayers at home that they were not being taken for a ride.

Politics aside, there were good analytical reasons for nervousness. The IMF felt it was being asked to design a programme for a country facing a combination of internal (fiscal) and external (competitiveness) imbalances, without two crucial policy levers: debt restructuring (if all else failed) and currency depreciation.

Debt restructuring was strictly off-limits. For the Eurozone, giving debt relief to a member state running a 16% annual fiscal deficit would be to condone fiscal excess; and doing so for a country which had lied about its fiscal statistics would add insult to injury. On the other hand, the ECB was apoplectic about anything that resembled a Eurozone member "not honouring its sovereign signature". It strongly believed that any debt relief would in effect be the first step to the dissolution of the Euro.

This posed a problem for the IMF. Its lending to Greece was exceptionally large and the Fund's statutes required it to be able to state that "there is a high probability" a country's debt would be sustainable in the end; that is, to make sure it would not be lending into a black hole. With a 2009 debt to GDP ratio of 130% and high deficits feeding that debt, this was a tricky proposition. So they changed the rules. The IMF board amended the statutes, allowing the Fund to lend when, "there is a high risk of international systemic spillovers".

The second problem for the IMF was that, as a Eurozone member, Greece could not devalue to correct its balance of payments problem. Barring exit from the euro, the only alternative was "internal devaluation"; eliminate an external deficit the hard way, through painful adjustments to wages and prices, and a deep recession.

This was understood. However, the depth of the necessary adjustment was not fathomed in May 2010, either by the Troika or by the Greek government. Nor did we know back then that the starting point (the 2009 deficit) would end up being even worse, or that the recession that year would end up being deeper, exceeding 4% (as opposed to 2% which was the assessment at the time); or for that matter how much the whole adjustment exercise would suffer from misguided European decisions and by the complete lack of political support for the programme within the country.

The cornerstone of the programme was fiscal consolidation, and an almost brutal deficit reduction up front; what was innocuously known as "front-loaded adjustment". Allowing for a more gradual deficit reduction would mean a higher debt burden (as cumulative deficits add to the debt), and even more money from the EU and the IMF, which was simply not there. Hence the need for €30 billion of measures, adding up to 13% of GDP during the 2010–14 period, in addition to the 5% of GDP in fiscal measures already adopted before the bailout. Of the total 18 percentage point reduction attempt, almost half (7.5 percentage points in old and new measures) was in 2010.

The magnitude of the task meant that expenditure cuts and revenue increases were both necessary. On the revenue side, everyone knew the problem was tax evasion. But when we argued that cracking down on tax evasion could increase revenues by 1-2% of GDP, we were rebuffed. Fighting tax evasion takes time, we were told (they were right); the IMF never counted tax evasion receipts up front – only as a "bonus" in the end. Hence we had no alternative to hiking VAT (the top rate going to 23%), excise and real estate taxes, and to instituting a crisis levy on profitable firms.

The emphasis of the adjustment, however, was on expenditure cuts (two-thirds compared to one-third coming from the revenue side). Government expenditures had doubled during the decade; so cutting back on the public sector wage bill – the bulk of overall spending – was inescapable. The first wage cuts had been instituted before the bailout. Now on the negotiating table was the full suppression of the 13th and 14th salary for public servants. We agreed to keep a cushion for the lower paid and postponed implementation until 2011.

A few days later, the Troika came back and insisted on

immediate implementation. "Circumstances have changed," was the explanation.

The situation was indeed getting worse by the day, despite the fact that we were negotiating in record time. Ambivalent statements – especially from Berlin – made the markets nervous; this raised the "credibility bar" for the programme and made the Troika ask for more. There was a lesson to be learned from this: time and delays are not on your side; a deal today is better than a deal tomorrow.

After wages came pensions. In the Greek system people would often retire with pensions exceeding their final salary, and early retirement schemes allowed some people to retire at 50. By 2009, the state was spending four times more on pensions than at the beginning of the decade. So we included measures to reduce them in both the private and public sectors (concentrating most on higher pensions), to eliminate early retirement and to bring the retirement age into line with increases in life expectancy.

Similarly, health costs had spiralled in recent years. There was a need for rigorous cost cutting to curtail hospital expenditure, reduce so-called "guaranteed" i.e. statutory (and exorbitant) profit margins for pharmacists, introduce generic drugs and control the system of drug prescriptions by doctors that had run amok.

The time to close a deal was almost up, and we did not have a good hand. The Troika was under pressure not to give ground lest the package appeared "too soft". Nevertheless we managed to soften the blow to the most vulnerable citizens. In the public sector, low-earners would get means-tested bonuses to offset some of the reduction in their salaries. Low-income retirees (two-thirds of the total) were protected from cuts.

The Troika wanted to extend the elimination of the public sector 13th and 14th salary to the private sector. We argued this would set a bad precedent by replacing collective bargaining amongst social partners by government-imposed reductions. We won the day. But our largest prize was to extend the time to bring the deficit below 3% of GDP from three years to five – the longest period given to a country.

While we did our best to soften the edges, a programme of such aggressive fiscal consolidation can never be fair; it does not spare anyone. Also, the government had limited its margin of manoeuvre – and I believe its ability to sell the project to Greek society – by excluding outright public sector redundancies.

I was happier when we were negotiating structural reforms. With a system based on patronage and protecting vested interests, I believed Greece was in a way the last Soviet economy in Europe. So when it came to opening up closed professions, breaking down barriers to new business, liberalizing critical sectors such as electricity and transport and, in general, rolling back the state, I was delighted I had an ally in the Troika.

We went through the final draft of the agreement line by line. The various sections were sent to relevant ministers for comments. I was the chief negotiator and it would be my signature on the final agreement. But I could not shoulder all responsibility; this had to be a collective effort. However, most comments that we received concentrated on trying to avoid or delay reforms and difficult measures. Few of these made it to the final text at the conclusion of the negotiation.

On April 30th, the prime minister convened the cabinet to discuss progress in the negotiations, get a consensus over the outcome, and plan how to handle it. There was a lot of reticence around the table. Some ministers expressed surprise there would have to be more measures in 2010, such as the near-abolition of the 13th and 14th salary. Others focused on the political manoeuvring. And there was the inevitable "how did we get here?" comment.

Towards the end of the meeting, one of the ministers summarized it all too well: "This is the end of an era," he said. Only to add despondently, "…and ours too".

The negotiations concluded on May 1st after a marathon all-day and all-night session. Fearing May Day demonstrations, we had moved to a government building out of the centre. While I was going over final details with the Troika, next door senior staff from Papandreou's office and some ministers were examining the texts with an eye on the legal and political consequences. I had the authority to negotiate and sign, but I was still seen as a technocrat finance minister whose instincts were considered too "non-political" and liberal and therefore not fully to be trusted.

As we concluded the "staff level agreement" and all the texts were agreed, it occurred to me this was the first time ever that the Greek state had a fully-fledged business plan. It was a policy blueprint for the next three years, complete with timetables, specific and fully costed measures and with a monitoring mechanism to ensure commitments were translated into actions. If not, there was the ultimate sanction: the withdrawal of financial support, leading to bankruptcy.

It was unfortunate that we had to get to this point to develop such a business plan. Parts of it were harsh, unfair and would prove politically impossible to implement. But I believed then and continue to believe today that despite the popular demonization of the *Mnimonio*, the vast majority of what was in those documents should have been done ages ago by successive Greek governments themselves – Troika or not.

The next morning – a Sunday – the cabinet approved the package. Not many had read the whole set of documents, but everyone had full information on what they contained and knew what they were agreeing to. Papandreou opened by saying, "no Greek family should live through the consequences of the country's bankruptcy". He then addressed criticism that the government had no "red line" (line in the sand) with respect to the Troika's demands: "avoiding bankruptcy is our national red line." And, in a statement that would prove all too prophetic – even optimistic – he added, "friends tell me that with these decisions I will only do one term as prime minister. I do not care. I want to do what is right for the country."

After cabinet approval, I went across Syntagma Square to the finance ministry for the announcements. I was the designated bearer of bad news. The press room was packed with media from around the world. I soberly went over the agreement – the negotiation, the measures, what we had managed to avoid, how it would help Greece avoid bankruptcy and help the country emerge stronger in the end.

"How do you feel being the most hated man in Greece?"

The question came from a British journalist and felt like a punch in the stomach. For a short moment, I just stared at him. I had never thought of it that way. I felt passionately about my country and had given everything to get the best possible deal in extremely difficult circumstances. I also believed we would be able to explain that we were doing the right thing and convince the people to back us.

My answer must have sounded defensive. It was the answer of someone in shock. After all, it was not many months since I had the highest popularity ratings of any government minister. I said, "this is not the moment to think of the political cost or of our personal careers. I am not in this job in order to lie to people or talk to them about a future which simply does not exist, if we do not take these measures. So we will do whatever it takes."

The Eurogroup was scheduled to meet that afternoon in Brussels to approve the programme and give the loan the green light. The Troika mission had a draft agreement and it had been formally approved by the Greek cabinet, so it was time for the finance ministers of the lending countries to give their blessing and pledge the money.

Olli Rehn presented the main elements of the programme: a huge fiscal effort to reduce the deficit by 10 points and bring it below 3% of GDP within 5 years, by the end of 2014. The economy would contract severely, but would recover in 2012. There were radical reforms in the public sector, the labour market and the business environment to make the economy more competitive.

He outlined how much money would be needed: a whopping €150 billion until mid-2013. There would be a €110 billion loan

(€80 billion from the Eurozone and €30 billion from the IMF), paid in quarterly instalments, to cover financing needs for the first two years and part of the third, when Greece would partly regain market access. The loans would have a maturity of 3 years and carry a variable interest rate, which came to around 5%, including the service fee (it was lower for the IMF loans).

It was clear the lending terms were punitive and the repayment period too short, but that was what lending countries would accept at that point. Rehn acknowledged this by saying, "we should consider lengthening the maturity to 5-7 years", and "review the need for the service fee at a later point". He urged countries to ask their commercial banks to "voluntarily maintain positions" in their Greek bond holdings by rolling them over when they matured and not selling in the secondary market. Thomas Wieser, the Euro Working Group chairman, pointed to a problem that was obvious to any analyst: "there is a maturity bunching for repayments after 2013; we cannot change the parameters now; but it is a real issue and we will have to come back to it later."

Everyone was waiting for Wolfgang Schäuble to speak. He confirmed that Germany would play its part: "we are prepared to give assistance quickly". The cabinet would meet next morning to approve and, by May 7th, the Bundestag would vote on it. There was a palpable sense of relief all around. "It was not easy but we will do it," he continued. But there could be no changes now and no discussion on debt restructuring. And while the substance of the agreement had been achieved, "the final decision will be by the heads of government of the Eurozone".

Christine Lagarde followed. France was ready to move immediately, would participate in a bridge financing exercise if the need arose – as long as at least three other countries did – and would ask its commercial banks to maintain their positions in Greek bonds. There was a nod to me: "I wouldn't like to be in George's shoes, but we are impressed; we have confidence in you."

The final word came from Jean-Claude Trichet: "we will have further problems beyond Greece; be lucid and alert." A much-needed reality check.

We were not out of the woods just yet.

Chapter 12

IT'S SYSTEMIC

The Eurogroup decision was received in Greece with trepidation rather than relief. "The great sacrifice" was how newspapers put it, publishing detailed tables with how much public servants would lose in the wage cuts, and the consequences of the tax hikes for everyone's pocket. The unions immediately announced strikes that would shut down ministries, tax offices, schools, hospitals and public services.

Abroad there were positive accounts of the agreement in the major news outlets. But these were quickly supplanted by concern that the fire "had not been doused". Spreads in peripheral countries dropped on the Monday after the agreement, but were rising again by Tuesday. Spanish PM Zapatero had to make a statement, dismissing as "complete madness" a rumour that Spain would ask the Eurozone for €280 billion in aid.

Most analysts argued that there would still be a Greek default and that the rescue package would not avoid contagion to other vulnerable countries. Their concerns: the aid package was insufficient to meet Greece's borrowing needs; the government would prove unable to implement what it had promised because of social protests; and a debt restructuring would still take place.

While policy makers across Europe were swimming against this tide of adverse commentary, the cabinet in Berlin approved Germany's contribution (€22 billion in total), and the ECB suspended minimum credit ratings for its collateral rules "until further notice". This allowed the ECB to continue accepting all titles issued or guaranteed by Greece as collateral, thereby continuing to fund the country's banks which all held substantial Greek debt. In one fell swoop the decision cancelled the impact of any further downgrades.

Meanwhile, we were working around the clock to prepare the parliamentary bill that would formulate the agreement as binding law – a "prior action" before the first loan tranche could be disbursed. We had decided to invoke parliament's so-called "extraordinary procedure". The bill was to be tabled on Tuesday and discussed in Committee on Wednesday, with a vote in full session on Thursday. A very short space of time for such an important bill – but necessary if we were to be in time for Friday's meeting of Eurozone leaders, convened for the final blessing of the Greek bailout.

We knew this was going to be the mother of all political battles. At stake were €110 billion, the survival of the government and – most importantly – the future of the country.

Before the parliamentary discussion the next day, I spent the afternoon with the PASOK parliamentary group, going over the bill, explaining patiently and fielding questions. I was exhausted – and they were not convinced. They would vote "yes" because of what was at stake, but wondered whether we could change this or that, make the wage cuts less steep or find less painful alternatives. No, we couldn't. This was the bill that was consistent with the agreement, and no changes were possible. It was a take-it-or-leave-it proposition.

The next day, while we were debating the bill in committee, a well-attended demonstration was in progress outside parliament. It started mildly, then got increasingly aggressive, with cries of "Thieves", "Traitors" and "Burn! Let the whorehouse burn!", directed at the parliament and all those inside. I was astounded. This went beyond protesting against what were indeed harsh measures – it was wholesale rejection, a collapse of the political and social consensus formed since the end of the dictatorship in 1974. It was not long ago that people had died so that democracy could be restored in the country and this "whorehouse" parliament actually function.

On the fringe of the demonstration groups of extremists in hoods and masks had assembled, intent on turning the protest into a violent clash with the police. To stop them, parliament was cordoned off by large armoured police buses parked one behind the other, creating an impenetrable wall. Riot police had taken positions around the building. Soon, tear gas filled the air, and the cat and mouse game began, the police firing tear gas and the extremist groups responding with Molotov cocktails.

And then time stopped.

Parliament is a very large building and, once inside, you cannot hear what is going on outside. But as the discussion on the bill was advancing, word filtered in: three people were dead.

Makeshift petrol bombs had been thrown into the offices of a bank whose employees had chosen to continue working despite the strike. The place had been set ablaze and, as smoke engulfed the building, panicked employees scrambled to get out. Three of them did not make it – a man and two young women, one pregnant. They were discovered too late, suffocated by the fumes.

We were all absolutely devastated. And, for a while, in the face of this tragic event and with violent clashes continuing in the streets, there was a sense that the situation was now out of control, that we were close to a wholesale revolt, and a storming of parliament. But the murder of the bank employees produced the opposite effect than what the perpetrators had intended: sanity prevailed, as it made people realize how close to the brink we had come.

The parliamentary discussion continued, but we all knew that the day's events – instantly prime time news all over the world – had changed the country forever. We had entered a dangerous period, in which old maxims were rejected, comfortable truths no longer held, established politics and politicians of all shades would be called into question, and disillusionment and distrust would easily transform into blind fury, leading to the most atrocious acts.

I went home that night completely shattered. The exhaustion brought about by months of endless work and lack of sleep combined with the awful realization that what lay ahead was a long, dark road. Jacoline, the strong presence in my life, gave me a long hug. The boys were still up, had seen the news and wanted to talk about it. Throughout this dreadful period, we had talked a lot about the situation, the difficulties and what had to be done. But how could one explain that day's events?

The horrific deaths cast a shadow over the discussion in plenary the next day. Every political party expressed their horror at what had happened. Some tried to make political capital out of it, but their hearts were not in it; most understood that the situation needed to be stabilized. In a dramatic statement Karolos Papoulias, the President of the Republic, summed it up well: "Our country has reached the edge of the abyss. It is the responsibility of all of us to ensure we do not take the next step."

As far as the parliamentary bill was concerned, it became clear that New Democracy and its new leader, Antonis Samaras, would vote against. This brought to the fore an important issue of substance and procedure. An article in the constitution stipulated that an enhanced three-fifths majority was required in cases where a bill ceded national sovereignty in certain policy areas, as had been the case with our EU accession. In a legal sense, the bill did not fit this description; but there was a debate on whether the government should ask for the 180 votes anyway to force cross-party support and send a message of broader political unity.

We discussed this in a meeting at the PM's office with senior ministers and the speaker. By asking for a three-fifths majority, we would put pressure on New Democracy. But what if we did not get the 180 votes? This would mean dissolving parliament and calling elections. Could we risk the country sliding into bankruptcy and anarchy during an election campaign? Would it not be an act of cowardice not to use our solid 160-seat majority to ensure passage of the bill? With so much at stake, as finance minister, I could not advocate a high-risk strategy.

In the end, we opted for a simple absolute majority. As an

aide to the PM put it, "I'd actually like 250 votes for a bill like this. But do we have them? No". Much later, when everyone started discussing "what if" scenarios and looking for scapegoats, some claimed that, if we had insisted on an enhanced majority, we would not have allowed New Democracy to play the populist card. Perhaps. But at that moment nobody was willing to risk consigning the country to chaos. Taking it upon ourselves was the responsible thing to do.

The discussion in the plenary produced a clash between Papandreou and Samaras. The prime minister put the dilemma starkly: "either we vote and implement the agreement, or we condemn Greece to bankruptcy. [...] I, we in PASOK, will not allow that. [...] We want to be able to live with our consciences." He asked Samaras how he could vote against the measures when parliaments throughout Europe were voting to help Greece. Samaras replied disingenuously: "they vote for assistance; we are asked to vote for specific measures." He added, "you are looking for accomplices and we will not be your accomplices!"

Unfortunately, on that day the conservative opposition did not rise to the historic occasion. They refused to accept their responsibility for the situation the country found itself in, or to lend support to the only possible way out. Starting on that day and for the following two years, Greece became the only one of the bailout countries without cross-party support for the adjustment effort – and the country paid dearly for this populism.

The bill passed with 172 votes out of 300. PASOK MPs voted in favour apart from three, who were summarily expelled. New Democracy voted against, with the sole exception of Dora Bakoyanni, daughter of conservative ex-prime minister Konstantinos Mitsotakis. She had been a contender for the party leadership a few months earlier, but lost out to Samaras. She was immediately expelled from the ND parliamentary group. There was also a surprise "yes" vote from the far right LAOS party, led by flamboyant George Karatzaferis, who decided to do the right thing.

The majority vote secured the assistance package and avoided the prospect of immediate bankruptcy, but it did little to calm markets. Greek 10-year bond yields reached 12% the next day. Spreads in Portugal, Ireland and Spain reached levels similar to those which prevented Greece from accessing markets in April. And interbank lending between European banks almost ground to a halt, pointing unmistakably to an acute systemic crisis in the making.

The sense of things rapidly spiralling out of control was captured in that week's Economist, which had the riots in Athens as its cover, and the cheeky title "Coming to a city near you?" The Friday Eurozone summit, originally called to give its final blessing to the Greek rescue package, would have to do much more than that.

The mood in the meeting was sombre. The assembled leaders had finally realized that the integrity of the entire Eurozone was in jeopardy. Overwhelming action was needed to avert catastrophe, over and above what was done for Greece.

The final communiqué reflected this. It announced "a European stabilization mechanism to preserve financial stability in Europe". The decision had been taken to create a bigger, more powerful bazooka (in the spirit of what the US had done after the 2008 crisis) to convince the markets that governments meant business and that no Eurozone country would be allowed to fail. The buck passed to finance ministers to hammer out the details; and they would have to do it by the weekend, before the markets opened on Monday to a meltdown.

The first step to revisiting the institutional architecture of the Eurozone since its inception had been taken.

I had accompanied Papandreou to the Brussels meeting on Friday afternoon, in case I was needed. We flew back after the meeting, I spent Saturday in the office, and then flew back to Brussels on Sunday 9th May for what turned out to be a marathon 14-hour meeting of the 27 EU finance ministers.

The gathering did not get off to an auspicious start. On

arrival we learned that Wolfgang Schäuble had been taken to hospital. At this critical juncture we could not start before the biggest Eurozone country had a minister at the table. So we waited for some hours until Thomas de Maizière, the German interior minister, had flown in to stand in for his cabinet colleague.

Commissioner Rehn spoke first. He was no longer the imperturbable Finn. "We have a systemic crisis – these are exceptional circumstances...We have been behind the curve, now we need to get ahead of it...We need more consolidation in 2010 – Portugal and Spain need to announce new measures – *today*. We need a financial backstop – *today*."

It was the ECB's turn to speak. On Friday, Jean-Claude Trichet had participated in the Brussels Eurozone summit and lobbied hard for leaders "to live up to their responsibilities" by creating that credible financial backstop. However, he knew this would not be enough, so he had organized an "activist" response: buying bonds of peripheral countries in the secondary market to stabilize the situation. But the ECB was not about to announce this yet. It would intervene in the market only after Ecofin reached and announced its own decisions.

Trichet was at that moment in Switzerland, presiding over a meeting of the ECB Governing Council in Basel (as part of the Bank of International Settlement meetings of central bankers from around the world) in parallel to Ecofin. Meanwhile, at the Ecofin in Brussels, Lucas Papademos, the ECB vice president, was stubbornly refusing to admit to what exactly they were planning. The ECB was not going to let finance ministers off the hook.

When a number of ministers asked Papademos point blank, but rather naively, to confirm that the ECB would be purchasing government bonds as of tomorrow morning, the response was firm: "the ECB is independent; it is inappropriate for you to make specific suggestions as to what it should do."

Frustration and anxiety were evident around the room. This was the full Ecofin, not just Eurozone members. Non-adherents to the euro also had their say. Alistair Darling, the UK finance minister, saw parallels to the 2008 crisis, but warned that the UK "could not be seen as explicitly supporting the euro". Jan Rostowski of Poland, in his unmistakable British accent, wanted the ECB to state explicitly what its plans were. And Anders Borg, the Swedish finance minister, known for his tough fiscal stance and trademark ponytail, stressed that we all needed to find "a larger number".

The pressure was on Spain and Portugal to immediately announce more austerity. Fernando dos Santos, the embattled Portuguese finance minister, pledged more in 2010. Elena Salgado, his Spanish counterpart, thought the urgent issue was to agree on a new stabilisation mechanism. Finland was worried that the package under discussion could be declared unconstitutional in Helsinki. Dutch minister Jan Kees de Jager indicated that any discussion on a "European Monetary Fund" was not helpful back home. And Austrian Josef Pröll reminded everyone of the obvious: "this is our last chance."

As for me, I was in a completely new situation. Greece was no longer the issue. The €80 billion from the Eurozone for us had been decided, and the remaining €30 billion from the IMF was being approved at that very moment in the Fund's board meeting in Washington DC. For the first time I was no longer the one being asked to explain, pledge more measures or negotiate. As one of my colleagues said, "You are off the hook, George. It's the rest of us that have to worry now." I smiled wearily. Not quite.

Germany and France had come to the meeting determined for a decision by night's end – notwithstanding the unfortunate absence of the German finance minister. As Christine Lagarde put it, "we need to stay here until we have a package" – only to add, recognizing that the price to pay for more money was the additional austerity about to be decided, "growth was just picking up, but so be it".

Soon enough, the package took shape: immediate and substantial additional austerity measures (the dreaded "frontloading" again); a nod of approval to ECB activism in the bond markets; a financial backstop; and a broader governance package to be determined later. But, given that the ECB would be taking its own decisions, everyone knew that what the world was expecting from this particular meeting was a number.

A big number.

And €60 billion certainly wasn't it. That was the number mentioned by Olli Rehn in his initial intervention; it related to funds from the Community bucket – and had to be supplemented and leveraged with money from member countries and from the IMF. Everyone knew that this wasn't anywhere near enough; Greece alone had needed €80 billion. As the evening progressed, the magic number kept going up – but more in the corridor discussions during breaks than in the meeting itself.

Reaching a decision was difficult on two counts: one political and one practical. The political difficulty was that while everyone understood the need to announce a big enough package to convince the markets, the sheer magnitude was daunting. The practical issue was to find the right legal vehicle. It could not be straight bilateral loans as in the case of Greece – the amounts involved were too high; nor could it be a European Community instrument. It had to be a stand-alone fund, backed with guarantees from countries.

The Legal Service was called in to give advice and explain how this would be compatible with the EU Treaty. It would be, but at a stretch. Many countries were getting nervous. And we got word from Washington that, while the IMF board meeting to decide on Greece was going well, they were worried on that side of the ocean that things were not doing the same in Brussels.

It was almost one a.m. and there was no agreement. There were panicky voices that the Sydney stock market was about to open, potentially starting a domino effect from east to west as day broke and stock markets around the world followed suit, with the news that Europe had not solved its problem. Christine Lagarde took the floor. "With due respect to our friends in

Australia, we can survive the Sydney opening. It's Tokyo we should be worrying about. We need an agreement by the time it opens."

And we got one.

After many breaks for bilateral negotiations between the main players and a number of delegations needing to check the different formalizations of the proposed mechanism with their capitals, finally there was a breakthrough – attributed by many to an idea originating from the Dutch delegation. The European Financial Stability Facility (EFSF) was born.

It would be based on a joint guarantee by Eurozone governments for a special purpose vehicle (SPV) to raise €440bn of market funds. To this would be added €60 billion of an existing mechanism administered by the Commission; it had so far been used for countries such as Hungary, Latvia, and Romania. This €500 billion total would then be supplemented by another €250 billion by the IMF, making a grand total of €750 billion, a sizeable 8% of Euro area GDP. We had our number.

"The nuclear option". "Shock and awe". "*Whatever it takes* crisis management". "Europe has thankfully replaced the water pistols with bazookas". The decision had impressed analysts. The markets were in agreement. The gamble had paid off. Most commentators were of the view that for the first time Europe's leaders were one step ahead of markets, rather than trailing behind them. Not only because countries had agreed to stand up for each other to a previously unthinkable extent, but because in doing so they had agreed to give up some of their fiscal sovereignty.

There was also caution. In the Financial Times Wolfgang Münchau pointed out that "by throwing money at the problem, mostly in the form of backstop guarantees, the EU has merely bought itself time". Others added that, by pooling more sovereignty than ever previously planned, the EU was at the mercy of its most indebted members.

Nevertheless, the markets were celebrating. Greek spreads

collapsed from close to 1,100 to just over 500 basis points. Portuguese, Spanish, Italian spreads followed suit. The Athens stock market rallied by 10%, as did markets around the world.

The euphoria had as much to do with the EFSF as it did with the ECB decision, announced simultaneously, to activate "exceptional measures" – mainly secondary market sovereign debt purchases. A week later, the ECB would disclose that it had bought €16.5 billion in government bonds in the first week since taking the unprecedented step of intervening in markets.

This new "activist" ECB was not to everyone's taste. The decision was backed by a large majority in the board, but it was not unanimous. In addition to Germany's Axel Weber, the Dutch central banker had also objected, as had Jürgen Stark of the executive board. But the criticism was blunted by the conditions attached to the decision (the creation of the financial backstop by Ecofin) and the fact that the intervention was "sterilized" by operations to re-absorb the liquidity injected by buying bonds, and therefore did not represent monetary easing – which would not have gone down well with the "hawks" on the ECB board.

And even critics conceded that, without the ECB intervention, the Ecofin decisions, brave as they were, would not have had anything like the impact they did.

On the day of the decisions, Chancellor Merkel's party suffered its worst post-war defeat in North Rhine-Westphalia, Germany's most populous state. The result cost Merkel control of the upper house of parliament. This was the regional election that had played a prominent role in delaying the German government's response to addressing the crisis. I couldn't help but remember that we had warned them it was no use waiting; given the timetable of Greek bonds maturing in May, it would all end up blowing up just before their election, as it did.

On May 10th, Papandreou and other party leaders met with Greek president Karolos Papoulias in an attempt to fashion some sort of consensus that the country would accept so that we could move forward. I was asked to give an account of the situation and then leave the room for the leaders to continue the discussion.

No agreement emerged on the difficult decisions that had to be made. The leaders of the two parties of the left – SYRIZA and the Communist Party – did not even show up. Among those that did, there was some agreement on the obvious – measures to root out corruption, the need for political reform and transparency – but none on economic issues. Samaras announced that his party would vote against the bill on pension reform, due in parliament in the next few days.

The next day, Greece officially requested disbursement of the first tranche of the bilateral loans. The German government decided to contribute guarantees to the aid package of up to €150 billion. Angela Merkel had delivered, despite her election defeat. And over the following two days, Eurozone countries in the danger zone unveiled initiatives to rein in their deficit. There were to be public-wage cuts and a pension freeze in Spain, and salary cuts of top officials and higher taxes in Portugal.

On Tuesday May 18, Greece received the first tranche of Eurozone aid, €14.5 billion in total. To this was added €5.5 billion from IMF, making a total of €20 billion. On the phone, the head of our debt management agency was happy: despite the complicated procedure, everything had worked as planned. The money had arrived in time for him to be able to pay the €8.9 billion bond which matured on Wednesday May 19th. And the rest could be used to continue paying salaries and pensions, and keeping the government going.

We had done it. Disaster had been averted; we would not be the first Eurozone country unable to repay its debts or honour its obligations to citizens, and go bankrupt. We would live to see another day and fight other battles.

But the real Odyssey had just begun.

Chapter 13

A VERY BUSY SUMMER

Greece doesn't have a spring season like the rest of Europe. Sometime in May suddenly, without warning, temperatures shoot up. From one day to the next, it is summer – the unmistakable, simmering hot Greek summer. Beautiful and breezy on the islands, hot and heavy in the cities. Glorious for holidays by the sea, tough for those who work in town. Life suddenly slows down. It's as if someone, somewhere, presses gently on a giant brake.

Not so in the finance ministry. The summer of 2010 was the first under the bailout. We had signed the agreement in May, the first implementation review was in August (with an interim one in June to keep us on our toes), and we had a mountain of work. Bills to pass, hundreds of small and large "actions" to complete, and a host of ministries (including my own) to convince that they had to adjust in record speed to a brand new environment – or else.

We were off to a good start: the monthly bulletins on budget execution showed that over the first six months of the year the deficit had a year-on-year reduction of over 40%. This helped counter criticism that the government had not taken any measures before the May bailout. However, sustaining that pace would not be easy.

Meanwhile, my Brussels trips were becoming increasingly frequent. I flew over on May 25th for the fifth time that month, this time to attend the first meeting of the Van Rompuy Group. The European Council had set up a task force to prepare the new EU "fiscal institutional architecture": strengthening budgetary discipline, better policy coordination, improved crisis management and economic governance.

At that first meeting not everyone was on the same page. Calls for removing voting rights from errant countries were quickly shot down by ministers, who realized that was a rapid way to lose democratic legitimacy at home. Automatically triggered sanctions were hotly debated, as well as proposals for a clear insolvency process for states. The ECB made clear its red lines early on: no Eurobonds, no default of a Euro country; and it reminded everyone that "when you activate a support mechanism, a country loses *de jure* or *de facto* its fiscal autonomy". The decisions taken in May marked a policy break in all Eurozone countries, not just Greece. It was clear that we had ventured where countries had not dared go before, but also that the decisions required some finessing for our internal audiences.

Germany's announcement in late May that it would ban "naked" short-selling – investors selling securities before they had actually borrowed them – was in the same vein. It was not just a reaction to the part such practices had played in exacerbating the crisis. It was also aimed to show to the Bundestag, which had agreed to bail a fellow EU country out, and to an electorate suspicious it would end up footing the bill, that the financial sector would also face up to its responsibilities.

My daily schedule when I was not travelling started early in the morning, extended well into the night, and was punctuated with continuous meetings. Many were internal: ensuring expenditures were kept in check, pushing for changes in tax administration, monitoring and helping restructure public companies, or designing a large-scale privatization programme.

Most, however, were with other ministries: with Transport to relaunch concession agreements frozen for lack of international finance, and to cajole public transport companies to reduce costs; with Health to rein in runaway costs and social expenditures; with Public Administration to figure out – finally! – how many employees were on the public payroll (close to 900,000 it turned out) and to design a new wage grid system.

That summer, we all felt that things were moving; the cogs

were slowly turning again and the machine was starting to work, sanity was being restored to a system run wild, responsibility was again the order of the day, and long-overdue changes were beginning to materialize.

These were not restricted to Troika-related fiscal reforms aimed at cutting the deficit; they extended to areas such as improving transparency and accountability, a stab at overhauling the calcified education system and reforming the public sector. At the same time we were worried we lacked the critical mass of people to bring about change; "capacity-building" was a rallying cry by the prime minister in many meetings.

But most of all we worried that the voice of change would be drowned out in an increasingly hostile and suffocating political environment, one with all the wrong political reflexes: rejection of anything new, empty slogans and confrontation, and complete inability to generate cross-party consensus that could support change. Worst of all, there was total denial about the harsh realities the country was facing.

Perhaps the clearest sign of the cynicism and denial in the Greek political system was the attempt by New Democracy to sketch out its "alternative" to the bailout agreement. In the first of what became known as the "Zappeion presentations", Antonis Samaras attempted simply to rewrite history.

He accused PASOK of having inflated the 2009 deficit since it took over in October, reiterated his position that the bailout agreement was the "wrong medicine" and presented a programme that, within two years, would bring the deficit down to zero and reduce debt by €50 billion. All this would be achieved without any pain; as he put it: "Without additional austerity measures. Without unbearable recession. Without higher unemployment." Well, which would you rather be? Poor, ugly and in bad health? Or rich, healthy and good looking?

During that summer, I also received a very interesting invitation.

The annual Bilderberg meeting is unlike anything else of its kind. Over the years, an aura of mystery and intrigue has arisen around its proceedings. To conspiracy theorists everywhere, it's nothing short of a congregation of unaccountable politicians and the business people who rule the world that meet in secret to take dire decisions for the future of mankind.

Obviously I would fit right in.

That year's meeting was to be held early June, in Spain. And, given that Greece was currently the centre of world interest, the Greek finance minister was a reasonably logical choice as a guest.

Soon after I had accepted the invitation, an elegant blue folder arrived, with practical instructions and the names of the other participants. In an attempt to convince the world that the whole event was not as sinister as some thought, the organizers had even put the names of the people attending on their website. The package also contained luggage tags with a mysterious, bold blue "B" on them, lest we forget that this was – after all – Bilderberg.

The list of about 150 participants was indeed impressive, an eclectic group drawn from politics, academia, business and civil society. It included regulars such as Henry Kissinger, past and present US government heavy hitters, such as Larry Summers; European politicians and commissioners from Brussels; the chairs and CEOs of major companies on both sides of the Atlantic; high-profile academics and presidents of think tanks and institutes; a few journalists (operating under strict confidentiality rules); and the obligatory superstars such as Bill Gates.

I flew out to Barcelona on a Friday unaccompanied – no spouses or support staff were allowed at these meetings. I was met by a black limo and driven the short distance to the conference venue down the coast, a hotel on the hills overlooking the beautiful seaside town of Sitges. The agenda for the next few days was only available on arrival, so I quickly changed ("casual dress at the conference sessions and *tenue de ville* at dinner") before rushing to the various sessions.

I hate to disappoint conspiracy theorists; no earth-shattering decisions were taken in the sessions. But in an agenda ranging widely from current events, security issues and the growing influence of cyber technology, to the crisis of the euro all the way to the promises of medical science, new energy sources and the role of social networking, the debates were fascinating and lively.

When discussing Europe, it was clear participants from both sides of the Atlantic did not think the crisis was behind us. US participants in particular voiced frustration at the glacial pace of European decision-making. I couldn't disagree. We always thought and argued with our European partners from the very beginning of our government's tenure that this was not solely a Greek crisis, it was a European crisis. And it was increasingly understood and acted upon in those terms, though it had taken a lot of time and effort to address it as such.

At some point during the discussion, I asked Larry Summers about his view on debt sustainability in Greece and other highly indebted Eurozone countries. Did he think there would eventually be a need for some debt management exercise? I got a very diplomatic answer. Afterwards, he came up to me and expressed his surprise that I had raised this issue publicly. Debt restructuring, in whatever form, was still considered taboo, even in the confidential Bilderberg environment.

Then there was dinner, with a speech by the Spanish PM José Zapatero. More importantly, we had been warned the meal was prepared by the team of El Bulli, the famous Spanish restaurant, at the time considered the best in the world.

What I had not been prepared for, however, were my table companions.

I arrived first, was shown to my table and located the nameplate with my name. Then I looked to my left. The nameplate read "Queen Sofia of Spain". And to my right, "Queen Beatrix of the Netherlands". I was to be seated between two queens.

I soon realized the seating was not accidental. Queen Sofia, sister of Greece's last king, Constantine, very much enjoyed the opportunity to talk about Greece; and the organizers had discovered that my Dutch mother-in-law knew Queen Beatrix well – as a young woman she had taught her three sons. So I spent two delightful hours with two fascinating women, alternating between speaking Greek to Queen Sofia and being told by Queen Beatrix that she had attended every single Bilderberg meeting since 1954, when her father sent her to the inaugural meeting of the group at the Bilderberg Hotel in the Netherlands to "sit in a corner and listen".

At the end of the dinner, I turned to Queen Beatrix. "May I ask you for a favour?" She looked at me quizzically. I took out my mobile phone. "Do you mind speaking to my wife?" She thought this was a splendid idea. So I dialled the home number in Athens, and Jacoline picked up. "Can I pass you to someone to say hello?" Before she could answer, I gave the phone to Beatrix. "*U spreekt met uw koningin*" – "you are speaking to your Queen". "Your Majesty, what a pleasant surprise," was my wife's deadpan reply.

I was back in Athens for only a day before I had to jump on a plane to Luxembourg for Eurogroup and Ecofin meetings.

This was the first meeting since the "bazooka" solution was adopted – the €750 billion envelope agreed to in May. The mood was hopeful. Jean-Claude Trichet reported on the ECB buying bonds of peripheral countries: the total so far was over €30 billion, spread across the last month. "We are paying a price for lost time", he added. As far as Greece was concerned, he reminded everyone that "the maturities profile will need to be extended" – the ECB had done the maths and thought Greece could never pay back the official loans it had received under the current loan terms.

More generally it was a time for crossing the t's and dotting the i's, and performing the practical steps required to implement the Europe-wide bailout mechanism. But most ministers were also in a reflective mood after the recent tumultuous weeks.

Christine Lagarde reminded everyone that "EU time is different from market time", while in a candid statement Wolfgang Schäuble admitted that "maybe we have been late in the Greek case". But for Greece there was only praise, with Commissioner Rehn reporting that "the Greek programme is being implemented fully".

Back in Athens we were frantically preparing for the first visit of the Troika, while trying to clean up the mess from the past, such as the €6 billion of arrears for medical supplies so as to avoid the threatened disruption to the normal operation of hospitals. We settled on a combination of cash upfront and government bonds.

Every day was made up of difficult meetings. The public sector union was apoplectic about wage cuts and suspicious about our efforts to record the actual number employed in the public sector (supposedly "a prelude to dismissals"). They were against the implementation of a new wage grid and worried they would never receive their pensions.

Meetings with the Transport Ministry made painfully obvious the near-bankrupt state of our railways and bus companies, as well as difficulties with privatizing airports and trains. In meetings of the Systemic Stability Council created for the banks, the Bank of Greece governor painted a bleak picture of deposits (still bleeding, the pace not slowed) and available bank collateral (dwindling fast), while stressing the need to move fast to consolidate the banking sector.

Just before the arrival of the Troika, the prime minister asked me to accompany him to Vienna for a lightning visit, which involved leaving Athens after lunchtime and returning the same evening. He had been invited to speak at the annual Institute of International Finance (IIF) meeting on June 11th.

Papandreou gave a candid and persuasive speech, prompting Deutsche Bank chief and IIF chairman Joe Ackermann to say he was confident that Greece could repay its debt because the nation was committed to reforms, reversing his view that a restructuring might be necessary. The Greek PM captivated his audience and got a standing ovation with a single sentence: "I do not care if this is my only term as prime minister. I did what I had to do to save my country from disaster." I have often wondered if he knew at that point how close to the mark he was.

But our progress with the programme was still not good enough for the credit rating agencies. On June 15th, Moody's downgraded Greek risk by four notches to junk. This meant that some investors were no longer allowed to buy Greek debt under the terms of their investment mandate. We were furious, and this time we were not alone. Olli Rehn called the downgrade "surprising and unfortunate", while Jean-Claude Juncker blasted the decision as "irrational". But the markets clearly continued to believe the risk of debt restructuring was very much present.

The view was not an isolated one. The more successful we were in reaching deficit reduction targets or implementing reforms, the louder popular protests were at home and the more dubious foreign observers became of our ability to carry on. In June, the foreign press was filled with stories of striking seamen blockading the main port of Piraeus, seriously disrupting the summer tourist season. A terrorist bomb attack, when a booby-trapped device disguised as a gift exploded in the hands of one of the public order minister's closest aides and killed him, gave the impression of a government increasingly losing control.

The Troika arrived in mid-June for a short visit to take stock of the situation since signing the agreement and to plan for the August full review. Taking stock was not too hard: after spending some days in the General Accounting Office, the boys in black rendered their verdict. We were on the right track, but still had not managed to fully control expenditures outside central government, in local authorities, social security funds and hospitals.

A large part of our discussions focused on strategy and tactics for the next steps of the programme – the big picture. The Troika insisted there should be clearer communication from all parties that debt reduction was not an option, and that the financial and economic risks of debt restructuring in any form were too high. We agreed to go on a joint "road-show" in autumn to convince the sceptics. We also tried to identify "low-hanging fruit" – quick-win reforms which would increase the credibility of the programme in Greece and abroad. But there was also practical talk, such as when to lengthen the maturities of the support programme loans, which everyone understood were too short.

While everyone thought our first steps were positive, there was still concern around the table. The international economic and financial environment was deteriorating and this would hurt us. The Troika fretted that there was still no full "ownership" of the programme by the government, with some ministers implementing its provisions reluctantly, while we urgently needed national consensus and support by all political forces. On a practical level they were concerned that a "minimalist" approach ("do only as much as is strictly necessary") was settling in.

This overall positive Troika assessment was not shared by our fellow PASOK MPs. They were not happy, and were vocal about it every time I discussed the bills to be tabled to parliament with them. They had voted for the bailout, but were intent on challenging every single bill that would come before them. As one of our MPs put it, "we have been colonized". He later defected to the far-left SYRIZA party. Their frustration was palpable, and there was no shortage of questions about whether we had "negotiated strongly enough".

Our parliamentary group would grumble and complain, but at least it eventually voted for the bills we presented to Parliament that summer: pension reform, the "fiscal responsibility" bill and the bill establishing the Hellenic Financial Stability Fund (HFSF). Not so the other political parties. The outright rejection that is so much a characteristic of Greek politics was very much in evidence.

Most of their criticism was directed at pension reform. As one SYRIZA MP put it, "this is a crime of historic proportions". After all, "pensions are not a fiscal issue". Well, perhaps, but someone has to foot the bill. Even New Democracy, despite having attempted its own pension reform a few years earlier (which, I have to admit, we had opposed at the time) weighed in, asking that we show more "social sensitivity" to women, who would now have to retire at the same age as men.

The bill establishing the HFSF as an entity where we would "park" €10 billion from the programme to be used for recapitalizing Greek banks was similarly rejected by the opposition, and also came under fire from our own MPs. Politically, helping the banks was tantamount to helping the bankers. When we were in opposition we had bitterly disagreed with the extension of guarantees to Greek banks when the European crisis started. So the rejection of the bill now did not come as much of a surprise, though the crisis should have made everyone wiser.

Of all bills to go through parliament that summer, the one about "fiscal responsibility" gained the broadest – though still not unanimous – approval. It involved establishing expenditure and commitment controls, rules and procedures for disbursement and monitoring, binding cash ceilings and closing loopholes for expenditure overruns. As one MP said, "we should have done this thirty years ago". Better late than never.

The July Eurogroup was the last before the summer recess. The Troika team had reported that macro developments seemed to be "broadly in line with the scenario underlying the programme". We were on our way to achieving the biggest deficit reduction by a Eurozone country in a year, and our reform progress was acknowledged even by sceptics such as the Financial Times ("Greece Wins Plaudits for its Reforms", was the title of an article at the time).

We were on track. However, Jean-Claude Trichet warned, "the main challenge is perseverance". The general view was summarized by Jean-Claude Juncker in the press conference afterwards: "The Greek programme is impressive and has outpaced our expectations."

The Symi symposium is an annual get-together that George Papandreou inaugurated in 1998. It is not quite a Davos-by-the-sea; it has however brought together progressive politicians and thinkers to exchange ideas in pleasant surroundings. The 2010 event was held in the island of Poros, close to Athens, and as the point man in the unfolding events, I was also invited. I was looking forward to some feedback on what we were doing from a group of highly talented people – among them Joe Stiglitz, the Nobel-prize winning economist, Segolène Royal, the French presidential candidate, Kemal Dervis, ex-finance minister of Turkey, Richard Parker from Harvard.

I was not disappointed. Stiglitz worried that in a closed economy such as Greece our policies would impact immediately on demand, while the positive supply-side effects would take time to materialize. In such a centre-left gathering, it was not surprising that concerns about equitable sharing of the pain were high on everyone's mind. The "IMF recipe" was not exactly their cup of tea ("it's like a boa constrictor" quipped one participant) but they understood the bind we were in ("a superb job against the odds" was how another put it). The round of applause at the end of the discussion warmed my heart; and then I left to go back to Athens and face the real world.

The Troika showed up in Athens for the first full review on July 27th. It turned out they did not believe in August vacations, so we had to accommodate that. By the time the "principals" showed up in Athens, their technical teams – young, eager, extremely professional and not easily fooled – had already been to the various ministries to figure out what was really going on, and it was impressive to see how quickly they had understood Greek finances.

Having gone through the bailout negotiation as well as the June interim review, at the finance ministry we pretty much knew the ropes and what to expect. Not so in the other ministries. In a political environment where the minister is the absolute ruler of his domain, the Papandreou government ministers were about to discover what the "man-to-man" Troika surveillance system meant. They were not going to like it.

In successive meetings, most held in my office, the main ministers involved in the bailout agreement (Transport, Health, Social Security, Economy, Defence) engaged in long meetings with the Troika on the "actions" under their purview. These were not easy meetings in substance or in format. To many ministers, the meetings tested the limits of the right of a democratically-elected government to run its own affairs.

Each side gingerly felt the other out. The Troika wanted to encourage ministers to move ahead with projects, as well as take them to task for delays. The ministers, on the other hand, had difficulty adapting to this kind of monitoring. Some were open and forthcoming; others formal and distant. Some chose to speak English so as to get the work done faster; others stuck to Greek because that felt more comfortable, but also to retain a sense of control.

There were difficulties all around. The transport minister wanted more time for the restructuring of the loss-making railways. The health minister had to explain why hospital arrears were again on the rise. The defence minister wanted to make sure the Troika understood the particularities of his sector; and the Troika wanted to make sure he understood the high cost of defence expenditures in the budget. The economy minister was worried about lack of liquidity in the real economy; the Troika was reluctant for the state to extend any further guarantees to struggling firms, and countered with criticism about delays in market liberalization.

All in all, however, it was not too difficult to conclude the first official review. As the statement by the EC, ECB, and IMF on the first review mission to Greece said: "Our overall assessment is that the programme has made a strong start. The end-June quantitative performance criteria have all been met, led by a vigorous implementation of the fiscal programme, and important reforms are ahead of schedule. However, important challenges and risks remain."

And so the Troika left – for the time being.

It was finally time for a short vacation. I joined my family on my favourite Greek island, Serifos – where you can be alone on a beach even in the middle of summer.

Chapter 14

THESSALONIKI

What a difference a year makes.

In September 2009, we were preparing for what we believed – correctly, as it turned out – would be Papandreou's last appearance as opposition leader at the annual Thessaloniki International Fair. The Karamanlis government was collapsing and we were looking forward to winning the elections.

A year later, in his first appearance as prime minister in the same venue, it was not quite the triumphant return we had hoped for. We were under siege, and battered, a few months after making a Faustian bargain – signing an agreement which had saved the country from bankruptcy, but for which we were increasingly vilified.

During the summer, we had won plaudits abroad for our robust implementation of the agreement in its first months, even silencing some of the most vocal critics. The general mood in Europe seemed to be better, with an increasing number of analysts now proclaiming that the Eurozone crisis might have turned a corner. But the lingering fear of Greek debt restructuring remained.

At home we had succeeded in passing the landmark pension reform without too much trouble, and faced down striking truckers who had blocked the main road between Athens and Thessaloniki; at the same time the disruption caused to tourism by picketing seamen turned out to be less than expected. But we were facing an increasingly hostile political environment, economic disruption and social unrest.

Before the Thessaloniki speech, Papandreou reshuffled his government – less than a year after winning the election. It was a facelift, which also involved some political compromises, following the maxim that it is better to keep your critics close by. Reuters succinctly summarized the message that was sent: "Greek PM reshuffles cabinet, stays fiscal course."

I was not affected by the reshuffle. At that point it would have been tantamount to challenging the bailout. In fact, on the very day the reshuffle was announced, I was in Brussels for the September Eurogroup meeting.

It was a good meeting, with praise all round for Greece. But the Eurogroup was absolutely furious with Slovakia. The new government which had taken over following national elections had reversed the decision of the previous government and would not participate in the Greek bailout. The actual amount involved was relatively small (about €800 million), but there was an issue of principle. Slovakia was breaching the Eurozone's united front on Greece.

Ivan Mikloš, the new finance minister, had come up to me before the meeting. He was apologetic; and I was polite. I was not going to be his main problem on that day. Mikloš was in his second stint as finance minister, and expected to be welcomed back to the club. Instead, he listened to an irate Jean-Claude Juncker blast the Slovak government as "irresponsible". Jean-Claude Trichet was "appalled", and added, "if I had known, I would have been against the entry of Slovakia [into the Eurogroup]". I was pleased by this solidarity, the result of good work done in recent months.

Back home a wave of September polls just before we headed to Thessaloniki lifted our spirits. They showed PASOK still clearly ahead, and by a healthy margin. People were hurting financially, but they continued to give us the benefit of the doubt.

In his speech at the opening of the fair on September 11th Papandreou was unapologetic. He reminded the audience of what was achieved in one year and gave a solid performance, intended to show friend and foe alike that we were still in charge and we meant business. We would continue the hard work of reducing the deficit and implementing reforms, and we promised the Greek people that there was light at the end of the tunnel. The message seemed to go down well in the room, but not outside, where the police were struggling to keep demonstrators under control. The scenes outside gained as much airtime as the message inside, prompting the Wall Street Journal to report, "social unrest brings bankruptcy closer".

But what really made the news was "the shoe incident". As Papandreou got out of his car to walk to the conference hall for his speech, a man took off a shoe and threw it at him, shouting, "traitors, down with the junta". He was a doctor, not exactly hard-pressed and more interested in protesting against what he considered Papandreou's "sell-out of Macedonia", that is the overtures made to our neighbouring country in order to find a mutually acceptable name that would end the dispute over the use of the Macedonia name. We also learned the incident had been rehearsed: the man had told a BBC crew that he would throw his shoe at the PM and they filmed him practicing the previous night. They then set up cameras to record the moment for the world to see.

In his Thessaloniki speech a few days later, opposition leader Antonis Samaras was in full denial mode. He delivered a mix of populism laced with painless solutions: "they should have borrowed enough for the year in January, when money was on offer" (from China? Russia? Mars?), "the Memorandum increases the debt" (yes, because we still have a yearly deficit), and "with our own plan, the deficit will be zero by 2011" (of course).

After Thessaloniki, I went on a "road show" around European capitals to convince the sceptics that we were delivering the goods. I was accompanied by the Troika principals. If investors did not believe me, maybe they would at least take the word of the representatives of creditors.

At a lunch in the City in London, on the day the Hellenic Republic paid almost 5% to borrow €1 billion for 6 months, the assembled investors pointed to the huge hump in our debt obligations, with large maturities occurring in 2014 and

2015. It was obvious Greece would not be able to repay around €130 billion in those years. Poul Thomsen of the IMF readily admitted this: "we can also do the maths; rest assured, we plan to do something about it." And he added, when asked what would happen in three years if Greece fully met EU/IMF demands, but failed to convince markets: "We would not walk away from Greece."

Similar meetings were held the next day in Paris and Frankfurt. I insisted that, given the programme and the progress achieved, Greek risk is "massively overpriced". "Is Greece's charm offensive working?" asked the Wall Street Journal, echoing my tour and Papandreou's similar message delivered in New York. The consensus was that, for now, as the paper put it, "The government hasn't flinched, and despite public-sector wage and pension cuts, as well as tax hikes, it still commands support".

Back in Athens we struggled to push forward reforms. We passed legislation to open up road freight to competition. It was a business where no new licences had been issued in decades, and existing licences were changing hands at hundreds of thousands of Euros each. In parliament the infrastructure minister declared, "past governments have shirked from taking this initiative. We are daring to do it". Outside parliament riot police fired teargas at some 200 truck drivers after they tried to storm the building.

At the same time, we were desperately trying to find ways to mitigate the pain that austerity was increasingly causing in an economy going deeper into recession. It was not an easy task. Against a background of our banks continuing to haemorrhage deposits, with the interbank market effectively shut to them, I met with the CEOs of Greece's biggest lenders. We agreed on a so-called "liquidity pact" to maintain at least some economic activity; but the banks were hard-pressed and could not really deliver the liquidity needed by the economy.

In the midst of all this, late in the evening of September 29th, after yet another day of meetings and anxiety, an envelope containing a CD-ROM with information on Greeks with accounts in a Swiss bank arrived at my office from France. Its contents would change the course of my life. But more on that later.

On October 2nd, a Chinese delegation arrived in Athens. Premier Wen Jiabao said that following the bailout China was prepared to buy Greek bonds – a vote of confidence that drove spreads lower. He also announced the creation of a fund to help Greek ship-owners build vessels in Chinese shipyards. Jiabao made much of the large investment the Chinese had already made in the port of Piraeus, and outlined plans to double the bilateral volume of trade. He did not omit to ask for our help in convincing the Europian Union to lift the embargo on Chinese gun imports.

Over dinner at the roof-top of the new Acropolis Museum, with a majestic view over the Parthenon lit up against the Athens sky, Jiabao waxed lyrical about the ties between Greece and China, talked of our "strategic partnership", declared that "true friends prove themselves in difficult times", and dipped his bread into some excellent Greek olive oil (increasingly exported to China, together with wine and marble). There was substance to the visit; but – with Portugal next on his itinerary – it was also a part of a carefully choreographed Chinese public relations exercise.

A few days later, I was on a plane again – this time to New York and Washington, for the twice-yearly IMF meetings. In one busy day in New York, I was hosted for breakfast at the NY Federal Reserve, went around to the Wall Street Journal, CNBC and CNN for interviews, and then met with funds and investors. Greece was still a hot item, and we were doing the right things (Moody's had just stated "we are impressed by the reforms by the Greek government"). Everyone wanted to ask whether we could continue despite the protests, and if we thought we could get the job done without debt restructuring (answers: yes, and yes).

My three days in Washington were very different from those at the April IMF meetings, shortly before we signed the agreement. No negotiations this time around, but still a lot of questions about the future, which were discussed in bilateral meetings with DSK, Tim Geithner, and the Russian and Chinese finance ministers. I also gave a well received speech at the Institute of International Finance, where a room full of hard-nosed bankers seemed to suspend disbelief and give the Greek government and its finance minister some credit.

In a nod of approval for the work done, I was invited to participate in a BBC World debate alongside Dominique Strauss-Kahn, Nobel Prize-winning economist Joe Stiglitz and the governor of the Bank of China. "Any second thoughts?" I was asked, about our decision to seek help from the EU and the IMF. My answer "no, we had no choice" was echoed by the rest of the panel. It seemed to capture a general feeling that the Greek government had done the right thing and was actually not doing too badly under impossible circumstances.

Compared with the packed press conference of a few months before, the one I gave at the IMF this time around was poorly attended. I noted, as I started, that this was a positive sign. Most of the journalists were Greek; what they wanted was my reaction to a comment made by Jean-Claude Juncker the day before. He had said that the EU had known all along about Greece's problems, but that "France and Germany were making large sums from their exports", so he could not say publicly what he knew. Would I care to comment? No, I would not.

That was not all. It seemed that a certain Greek prime minister had also told Juncker he was governing a "corrupt country". Who was that prime minister? I was getting increasingly irritated by this line of questioning, so I ventured that it might have been the previous PM, Kostas Karamanlis. After all, wasn't it during his term that Greece slipped badly in the Transparency International corruption rankings?

That landed me in a huge storm back home. It transpired Juncker was actually referring to the current PM, George Papandreou, who had talked to him about the need to tackle corruption (but had never actually said, "the country is corrupt"). The opposition asked for my head on a platter for having slandered Karamanlis. For days, this issue was the main item on the evening news. I was stunned. Rather than facing up to the problem, people were upset that someone had dared speak its name.

By the end of October, dark clouds were again gathering over Europe.

Ireland had revealed a crippling deficit and acknowledged that massive debts by Anglo Irish Bank could bring down the country. It was an incredible turn of events for a country that had been a paragon of virtue. Irish banks had accumulated a huge portfolio of non-performing loans; when the property bubble burst, they lost €100 billion. The economy collapsed and, despite harsh austerity, the budget swung from a surplus in 2007 to a deficit of 32% of GDP in 2010. It was being pressed to ask for a bailout, but was resisting – for now.

Further to the south, Spain was hit with a credit downgrade and tough new cutbacks were proposed in Portugal. A general strike in Spain and mass street protests across European cities against spending cuts and tax hikes stirred new fears. It seemed once more that the crisis was not contained; it kept mutating.

And yet… in the midst of the gathering doom and gloom in most of Europe, Greece seemed to be doing all right, comparatively. In the preceding quarter, Greek bonds were the top performers in Europe, making gains for the first time since the debt crisis began. Investors seemed to think record high yields compensated for the possibility of a default.

At a time when spreads in the rest of the periphery were widening, spreads on 10-year Greek bonds had tightened by 300 basis points; a number of international banks were recommending them, and Norway's $450 billion sovereign-wealth fund, the world's second biggest, had purchased Greek securities. Bloomberg noted that in "insuring against Greece defaulting within a year is [now] cheaper than buying cover for longer" – a sign of declining risk.

In short, the programme was actually working. The deficit numbers were going in the right direction. Reforms were happening. Confidence was slowly returning. All of this, however, came with a very high economic and social cost: a deepening recession and increasing social unrest, both of which had replaced concerns on government inaction as the main preoccupation of the foreign media.

True, predictions of impending default were never far off. They were only kept in check by rumours that creditors were considering options for extending Greek loans if refinancing risks lingered. But, overall, there was a grudging acceptance that we were actually beating the odds and – improbably – exceeding expectations.

And then we hit a roadblock.

Chapter 15

DEAUVILLE

The picturesque French town of Deauville is an unlikely setting for momentous political decisions. It is a sophisticated seaside resort in Normandy, best known for its long wooden promenade and its film festival. In October 2010, it was the venue for a Franco-German summit, and it was in Deauville where the Eurozone crisis lived one of its worst moments.

Whatever the intention at the time, the decisions taken in Deauville transformed a crisis which could have been contained into a fully blown-out systemic disaster. They opened the gates of hell for the Eurozone, and prompted the entry of Ireland and then Portugal into support mechanisms akin to that created for Greece.

On October 18th, while Eurozone finance ministers were meeting in Brussels, Nicolas Sarkozy and Angela Merkel – both clad in raincoats – went strolling on the famous Deauville promenade. In the culmination of months of behind-the-scenes negotiations, they sealed a deal that took even their closest aides by surprise.

Germany backed down on automatic sanctions for countries breaching fiscal rules and accepted "qualified majority" decision-making, which gave greater discretion to governments, something France badly wanted. In exchange France accepted a proposal for a limited EU treaty change that would, as of 2013, turn the temporary bail-out fund into a permanent mechanism. Crucially, that decision involved the possibility of a country defaulting on its debts. In such a case, private investors would participate in the eventual bailout, taking losses through a "haircut".

It was a bad decision because the message it sent to the

markets was terrifyingly simple: come 2013, they would very likely suffer losses on their bond holdings. So why should a rational bond holder continue to hold – let alone buy – peripheral country debt?

There was, no doubt, a need to create a permanent bailout mechanism. And it is difficult to fault the chancellor's political logic in making banks pay alongside taxpayers. She was, as always, responding deftly to the climate at home, as well as to rising pressure from the impending Irish bailout. But the execution failed spectacularly to take market reaction into account. Papandreou did in fact tell her at the time that while her intention was to punish the banks, in effect she would end up punishing countries.

European banks immediately took the announcement to imply the prospect of losing money on the Greek bonds they had decided – in a gentleman's agreement with governments – to retain a few months earlier, during the May bailout. And the logic easily extended to other countries in trouble.

The tsunami set in motion was not immediately recognised. When news filtered to the finance ministers meeting in Brussels, reactions centred more on the fact that Germany had backtracked from automatic sanctions. Only Jean-Claude Trichet, an ardent opponent of any private debt haircut, immediately understood the enormity of what had been decided. "You will destroy the euro," was his furious response to the French and German delegations.

The markets understood too. The first impact was on Greek bonds, whose spreads immediately leapt by 150 basis points. The clarification given, that any such "private sector involvement" would apply only to new debt issued from 2013, when the new European Stability Mechanism (ESM) would come into force, was not believed by anyone – and rightly so.

Promising future losses is not the smartest way to keep investors. The pre-announcement in 2010 that, come 2013, bond holders could end up making losses, drove up borrowing costs immediately, reversing the positive assessment markets held of the Greek programme up to then. The momentum was lost, never to be regained.

But the *coup de grâce* for the Greek programme was yet to come, in a month's time, with the final revision of Greek statistics by Eurostat. The European Council held on October 28th ratified the "Deauville decision". In doing so they also opened the door to Ireland – a mere three weeks later – and then Portugal to join Greece in the "bailout club".

In that meeting Papandreou issued an impassioned plea against Merkel's plans to strip errant member states of their voting rights. He was joined by the Irish prime minister, Brian Cowen, who said he would never be able to win a referendum on a new treaty if it involved denying Ireland its voting rights. Merkel backed down, but not before Papandreou told her that if she went ahead with her notion of "second-class" EU membership, she might as well take back Berlin's loans to Athens.

On November 8th, I flew to London to speak at my UK alma mater, the London School of Economics. As protests against our policies had now gone international, the LSE was understandably worried the event might be disrupted. Apart however from some energetic Q&A at the end of a well-received speech to a packed auditorium, there were no incidents. In an evening full of memories, my host, Professor Kevin Featherstone, introduced me by noting how ironic it was – given the state of the country – that the LSE had produced a number of Greek finance ministers.

Back in Athens we held our breath until the results of regional and municipal elections, held on November 14th, were in. On the night, we were not disappointed: the candidates we backed won the two largest cities, Athens and Thessaloniki, as well as eight out of the 13 regions, including Attica, home to almost 40% of the country's population. We rejoiced, as did many analysts and the international markets.

It was a tremendous result, which seemed to suggest we were still in the game. But we also missed an opportunity: the chance to use the occasion of local elections to call snap national elections and secure a fresh government mandate.

In view of our increasing problems, a number of ministers had recommended that move to Papandreou. Their argument was politically solid: due to unforeseen circumstances, we were implementing largely different policies from those we had been elected on, and the people needed to be given a chance to have their say. Plus, we could actually win at that point. Fearing disruption to the economy, I was one of those that disagreed.

In retrospect, we missed an opportunity. A fresh mandate would have allowed us to soldier on longer than we eventually managed. Papandreou decided not to take a risk with the country and its fragile economy. He felt it would have sent the wrong signal. And we still believed that recovery was on the way and that the programme would show results in 2011. We paid a political price for forgoing that chance, and gave breathing space to the opposition, on both right and left; but nobody can accuse us of having put the party's interest above that of the country.

On the day of the election itself, as always in Greece a Sunday, I was in my office with the Troika. What worried us all was not the election results; it was rather the repercussions of the Eurostat announcement the next day of the revised deficit and debt figures for 2006-2009. The final figure for the fateful 2009 deficit was actually calculated at 15.4% of GDP, not 13.6% as previously thought. And the 2008 deficit figure was 9.4% of GDP – proving that, under the previous government, the economy had started to go off the rails even earlier.

The revision meant that, despite our best efforts, the plan to reduce the deficit in 2010 by 5.5 percentage points (from 13.6 to 8.1% of GDP) was no longer good enough. Our starting point was now higher so, if we did not move the goalposts, we would need an additional reduction, bringing the total deficit reduction to a mind-boggling 7.3 percentage points in one year

– never done before anywhere.

Could we not just adjust the 2010 target accordingly? The Troika objected to this on two grounds. First, the markets were still nervous; increasingly so because of Ireland. There would be negative reaction to the deficit revision and it would be even worse if we did not stick to the original plan. The second reason was political: any additional effort should be made when we still had – some – political capital left.

The announcement had predictable results. Spreads jumped 100 points, reaching 900. We were now stratospheric, in orbit. Markets had the "not again" feeling of yet another revision in Greek accounts, and responded to the fear that the Greek government now had to achieve additional deficit-reduction in increasingly difficult social and political circumstances. This reaction overshadowed an important milestone: this final revision lifted all remaining doubts and asterisks on Greek fiscal data, finally declaring them clean and on a par with all other EU countries.

Getting a clean bill of health from Eurostat had been a long and arduous process. Even before the 2009 election, I had insisted on including the pledge to grant independence to the statistics service in our party manifesto. Then, following the discovery of the manipulation of the figures, as minister I pushed through a bill granting it independence, hired an ex-IMF official to head the new Hellenic Statistics Authority (ELSTAT) and cooperated with Eurostat to clean up the accounts.

The new statistics chief, Andreas Georgiou, was hired in August 2010 and proved to be the right man for the job, helping to make Greek statistics credible. I was less lucky with some of the other people appointed to the ELSTAT board. One of these started hacking into Georgiou's email account, a breach confirmed by the Greek Police electronic crime squad. The official in question was sued and had to resign. Another challenged Eurostat's role in our national accounts and accused Georgiou of "inflating" the 2009 deficit data "to bring in the IMF".

The accusation was totally absurd. First of all, Georgiou had actually taken up his post in August 2010, *after* the bailout agreement was signed. So how on earth could he have inflated the figures "to bring in the IMF"? Secondly, and more importantly, Eurostat validated the 2009 data after many months of work in Athens in 2010. And Georgiou was as straight as they come. Late one night, I called him to ask about the quarterly GDP growth figure that was to be announced the next morning. He answered that he could not tell me, unless the press release included a footnote that the finance minister was told the figure the previous night. I hung up, secure in the knowledge that at least no-one could tell ELSTAT to massage the numbers anymore.

And yet the ridiculous allegations that we had manipulated the data resonated with the public. It was just so convenient: if we had shown the figures to be much worse than they really were, that would have made the 2009 deficit more manageable. Hence, no need for a bailout and all the measures accompanying it. We could have gone on with our lives, were it not for the people who brought in the IMF to sell out the country.

Both the opposition on the right (primarily Mr Samaras) and that on the left lapped it up. Soon the justice system was involved. Prosecutors brought criminal charges against Georgiou for actions having caused billions of damage to Greece. We were suddenly in a parallel universe; rather than bringing to task those who had lied about the true size of the deficit, we were accused for having told the truth!

Eurostat's deficit-revision announcement came one day before the November Eurogroup, and other finance ministers were not amused by this latest episode concerning Greek statistics. They could see that it would spook the markets and that it was the last thing we needed, with Ireland on the brink of a bailout.

The Eurogroup tried to put a lid on the affair with a "terms of reference" paper – that is, a script for everyone to follow. First, it was acknowledged that we had so far done a good job with deficit reduction. Then they noted that there had been a substantial revision of the 2009 data; and finally they welcomed our commitment to include additional measures in the 2011 budget. That of course made it clear I had to redraft our budget for the next year, and not for the better.

But, this time round, Greece was no longer alone. There were now three countries in the line of fire: the usual Greek suspect had been joined by Ireland and Portugal. While I had to explain how the data revision would not undermine our efforts, the other two ministers had to answer criticism that they were not doing enough to avert their own bailouts. They trotted out the measures they were taking, with the Spanish and Italian ministers watching, wondering when their turn would come.

That particular day, the spotlight was on Ireland. Brian Lenihan was defending his efforts to rein in the country's huge deficit, the result of the state taking on the debts of the Irish banks. Their decision some years earlier to guarantee all deposits had come back to haunt them, and it was clear to observers that the recent Deauville decision had not helped things one bit.

At that point the details of Ireland's ongoing tug of war with the ECB were not publicly known. The ECB letter threatening to cut off liquidity to the Irish banking system if the government made banks bear some of the adjustment pain came to light only much later.

At the beginning of the Greek saga in the last months of 2009, Lenihan had been particularly critical of Greece, comparing the chronic lack of effort in Greece to rein in the deficit with the pain already incurred by Irish citizens over many years. Back then, I felt that while he was right when referring to previous Greek governments, he was not giving enough credit to our efforts; but, today, there was no feeling of satisfaction on my part for his troubles, only sadness. Here was a good finance minister doing his best against the odds, in what was clearly a losing fight.

True enough, over the next few days, yields on Irish bonds

went over the 8% mark. By the weekend, it was not a question of if but when. A hastily convened Eurogroup teleconference on Sunday evening, November 21ˢᵗ, confirmed that the Irish government was ready to throw in the towel. The next day they formally asked for EU/IMF assistance and intensified negotiations with the Troika team already in place to reach an agreement.

Throughout the week, the markets were unrelenting. By Sunday 28ᵗʰ, it was time for the official decision, again in a teleconference.

In his opening remarks, Olli Rehn called this "a more grave situation than in the spring". It was necessary to agree the Irish programme on that day. The Irish government had approved it and so it was up to the Ecofin ministers to sign off on an €85 billion facility, €17.5 billion of which would be provided by Ireland from its own reserves. Of the total, €50 billion would go to plug the hole in the deficit and the remainder to recapitalize the banks. Unlike in the Greek case, the UK, Denmark and Sweden would also participate.

This, however, would not be all. We were under a "blatant systemic attack", said Rehn, and "a systemic crisis calls for systemic reform". So we needed "to resort to the nuclear option", in other words, to agree on a permanent assistance mechanism in line with IMF standards.

He went on to outline the main elements of such a mechanism. There would be case-by-case participation of private creditors, with EFSF loans having preferred status. For solvent countries, creditors would be encouraged to retain exposure; however, if a country were insolvent, it would have to negotiate a debt restructuring plan with its private sector creditors. But, more as a wish than real expectation, "private sector involvement would not be effective before mid-2013."

I was not happy with this. We were all in favour of agreeing to the Irish bailout, but the rest of the proposal was half-baked and potentially downright dangerous. It was the practical manifestation of the Deauville decision, and I had already seen its results on our spreads. Who and how would determine "solvent" and "insolvent"? I asked for clarification and Jean-Claude Trichet immediately agreed with me. But with Deauville already blessed by the leaders, it was a done deal.

I also had a Greek issue to resolve. Having learned from past mistakes, the EU finance ministers had decided that the bonds in the Irish programme would have longer maturities – 7.5 years as opposed to only 4 in our case. We could not agree to this without a pledge that our loans would be treated accordingly. We had discussed this extensively with Papandreou, and I was under instructions to block the Irish bailout without such a decision.

It was an obvious stand to take in terms of equal treatment, but also a necessity; it would help us avoid the €130 billion repayment "hump" that analysts had identified for 2014 and 2015 and would give us till 2024 to repay the last tranche. We got it as a pledge at the end of the Eurogroup statement: "the Eurogroup will rapidly examine the necessity to align the maturities of the financing for Greece to that of Ireland."

So, after all was said and done, another piggy had gone to the bank.

And more were to come.

Chapter 16

SELLING THE FAMILY SILVER

The annual Financial Times rankings of EU finance ministers is a closely watched affair, not just by those named. It is based on three criteria: political, from a poll of leading analysts; economic, based on a country's latest economic data; and credibility in the markets, based on the yield on 10-year bonds.

On the last two criteria any Greek finance minister would be languishing near the bottom. However, to my surprise and delight, the 2010 edition of the rankings published at the end of the year ranked me first on the basis of the political criterion and eighth overall, with Wolfgang Schäuble first overall.

The Financial Times thought I had shown "panache" in handling the crisis. Of the analysts they polled, one called me "remarkably effective at navigating treacherous EU politics, securing domestic acceptance of unprecedented austerity, and rebuilding some measure of investor confidence – almost impossible tasks." Another added that I had undertaken "more budget and structural reforms than any EU country ever". A third: "My vote for finance minister of the year goes to Greece's Papaconstantinou... Greece's miserable performance leaves him in only eighth place overall but, if his economy begins to recover in 2011, he could emerge as next year's star."

That last part was not to be. Nevertheless, it was humbling stuff, giving me some measure of satisfaction for what had been achieved that year. But the fact that such international recognition got barely a notice in the Greek press should have been a warning: the hourglass containing my political capital was emptying fast.

Before November was out, the second Troika review was concluded. It was smooth sailing in the assessment of what we had achieved. The joint EU/ECB/IMF press statement noted the programme was "broadly on track". They praised the 2010 deficit reduction, which was larger than targeted, but pointedly noted that, due to the 2009 data revisions, extra effort would be needed to meet the 2011 target.

In early December, Dominique Strauss-Kahn attended the Eurogroup meeting in Brussels. He urged "ring-fencing Portugal and Spain" and also offered help: "if you increase the money available, we will follow; even change the ratio, go 50-50." Meanwhile, Trichet launched into an attack on speculators who have endless resources ("they have four trillion!") and work on the basis of "a mixture of greed and fear". He reminded everyone that the ECB was refinancing Irish banks at 100% of GDP, Greek banks at 58%, and Portuguese ones at 32% of GDP.

Following the meeting, I hitched a ride from DSK to Athens on a small jet chartered by the IMF. The visit was a chance for him to offer encouraging words and to call for perseverance. In a *tour de force* speech to the Economic and Financial Affairs Committee of the Greek parliament ("I am your doctor", he told MPs), a confident DSK defended the programme, praised the efforts by the government and the Greek people, and promised light at the end of the tunnel with growth returning as early as next year.

In a one-two sequence of support visits, DSK was followed by Olli Rehn, with whom we went over the programme's next steps. On the plus side of the ledger, there were rapid fiscal retrenchment and competitiveness adjustment. On the minus side, consolidation was still not enough to hit the targets set, due to the deficit revision and worse than expected fall in GDP. But we could look forward to the extension of official loan maturities – it would help the return to the market. And we should expect an economic turn-around in the spring or summer.

Rehn's parting words: improve coordination within the government and get society behind the reforms. Easier said than done.

With the visitors gone, we were immersed again in the harsh reality of numbers and measures: an emergency bill in parliament for the additional 2011 fiscal measures, and then the 2011 budget itself which incorporated the measures. Both passed, but not without plenty of grumbling. Compared with last year, I received a markedly cooler response from PASOK MPs.

Numbers aside, I was particularly proud of this, our second budget. Not only had we left "Greek statistics" behind, but we were breaking new ground in terms of process and transparency. The 2011 budget was the first with expenditure caps, borrowing limits, procedures for controlling commitments and obligations for the regular reporting of execution. Mundane stuff in most countries, revolutionary in Greece.

In the midst of continuing market volatility and the ECB stepping up its secondary market purchases of Greek, Portuguese and Irish bonds, George Papandreou attended the European summit on December 16th. He had been busy travelling to make our case abroad. Part of the narrative he was pushing on these travels was that peripheral countries would never cease to be targeted by speculators as long as there was no risk-sharing mechanism, some kind of debt mutualisation, amongst EU countries.

Enter Eurobonds. At the concept's core was the idea of a supra-European entity issuing bonds, which would tie the borrowing costs of major European economies to those of peripheral members – with economic policy "conditionality" attached. Germany was strongly opposed, fearing such bonds would raise its borrowing costs, but also create moral hazard problems. Despite German rejection, the idea gained traction. In an article in the Financial Times, Jean-Claude Juncker and Giulio Tremonti called for such joint European sovereign bonds to be issued by a European debt agency to assert the "irreversibility of the euro". But Merkel, aided and abetted by Sarkozy, killed the idea at the December summit. It did not even make the agenda.

On December 18st, we got the sad news of the death of Tommaso Padoa-Schioppa, Italian economist, policy maker, and one of the founding figures of the euro. About six months earlier, he had approached us and offered his services. No charge, he just wanted to help. I had met him a number of times since and had spoken at length with him on the phone. Few people in Europe possessed his wisdom and experience.

In one of our last meetings, the Italian had sensed my frustration as internal politics got in the way of implementing the programme. As I had walked him to the elevator, he turned towards me and said, "George, don't forget: in your position, you have much more power than you think. Don't hesitate to use it". I should have taken those words more to heart.

As 2010 drew to a close, I reflected on an incredible year. A year in which Greece's long-standing problems had caught up with her and demanded unprecedented and painful solutions. A year in which we realized how lucky we were to be members of a European family which would – reluctantly and in extremis – come to our rescue when the markets decided we were no longer worth the risk. A year in which we signed the biggest loan ever; and agreed to conditions which would involve tremendous economic and social costs – and would soon cost us our jobs.

The January 2011 Eurogroup meeting took stock of the situation in Greece and I presented the progress so far. Greece in 2010 had achieved the biggest public deficit reduction ever by a Eurozone country: more than five percentage points of GDP. Adjusted for the economic cycle, the fiscal correction was equivalent to cutting the deficit from 10% of GDP in 2009 to 1.5% in 2010.

I rattled off our reforms: in a single year, we had created an independent statistical authority; overhauled the tax system; passed sweeping changes in pensions to make the system fairer and more viable; reformed local government; liberalized professions; simplified procedures to establish a business. The sheer magnitude of the changes showed what was achieved –

but, even more, what was still needed.

But I also raised red flags: the worse than expected recession and associated social hardship, the bleeding in Greek banks from continuing deposit outflows, and the rating agencies treating our bonds as junk. The planned 2012 return to the markets was becoming an increasingly untenable prospect; and the same applied to our political fortunes.

As had been promised, the Eurogroup revisited the issue of the dates that official loans would mature. Jean-Claude Trichet proposed extending all official loans to Greece, those from the EU countries and from the IMF, including the repayment for tranches already disbursed. Wolfgang Schäuble wondered aloud whether even this would be enough to convince the markets that Greek debt was sustainable – the first oblique reference to the words that dare not speak their name: debt restructuring. The elephant in the room was beginning to be acknowledged, but it was still too early for decisions on that.

At the end of January, I accompanied the prime minister to the 2011 Davos meeting – a very different affair from that of the previous year. This time, Greece – while still of global interest – was no longer the bomb about to explode. Plus, we had a story to tell: we were actually delivering.

We took this message, complete with numbers and graphs to back it up (we called it "From Davos to Davos") to one-on-one interviews with major news outlets, a well-attended media roundtable, the heads of large international banks, and a number of other events. People were receptive, but sceptical about whether we could persevere, and whether it was feasible without debt restructuring – a point I argued over coffee with Zanny Beddoes from The Economist. She was not convinced.

Davos is all about networking, mostly done outside the official meetings. Walking down the corridor of the conference centre, I bumped into Axel Weber, the hawkish German central bank president. We started talking, got to the debt issue and I was astounded to hear him propose extending all Greek debt to 50 or 70 years. I told him this was an excellent idea, very much in line with our own thinking – maybe he should work on it with the ECB governor and the German government? He soon left the German central bank in a row over the succession of Trichet, but debt restructuring – the "R" word – was finally quietly making its way into polite society.

The trip was not without its perks. On the way over, on entering Swiss airspace, our government plane was escorted by two Swiss fighter jets, flying alongside each wing – a nod to the PM on board. And, on the way back from Davos to Zurich to join our plane, we were treated to a magnificent helicopter ride – again, courtesy of the Swiss Air Force. Strapped in uncomfortable seats facing the side doors, wearing massive headsets to drown out the noise, we were more than rewarded by the skills of the military pilots. Banking their massive machines hard into deep valleys, flying close to inaccessible mountain peaks painted an intense purple by the evening sun, they turned the ride into an unforgettable Alpine tour.

Back home it was time for the Troika visit – again. This was the third review and a routine had set in. To coordinate ministries on Troika-related action, we had set up an inter-ministerial group to monitor progress and prepare a regularly updated "state-of play" table, with actions and deliverables. This enabled us to use a "red alert" system before the Troika appeared on our doorstep.

Once the Troika rolled into town, I would initially see the principals in my office to go over the visit schedule. The Troika people would then fan out across ministries to collect data and discuss policies. Based on their findings, meetings with ministers were scheduled, which I would only attend if there were serious problems. This process would typically last 2-3 weeks, and at the end we would go over the documents line-by-line, negotiating policies and numbers or drafting expressions until we shook hands over a "staff-level agreement".

This time round, Poul Thomsen was fretting about the need

for a "game changer". Spreads were up in peripheral Eurozone countries and market analysts were increasingly vocal about the need for some sort of debt restructuring – for them a precondition for Greece to access the markets again.

So in our first meeting, on a Sunday afternoon, he felt we needed to address that concern in the review. Debt restructuring – even in the milder form of reprofiling obligations – continued to be off-limits. We needed to resort to other solutions. How about a big push in the privatization agenda to show that proceeds from sales could reduce significantly the debt over the next few years?

Privatization had, for a long time, been a dirty word for the Greek centre-left. The supposed reason was ideological: we stood for public services, and these were endangered when private investors took over state-owned companies. But the real reason was patronage – and it applied to both the left and the right. Successive governments had used publicly owned companies for political appointments. They had siphoned money from their advertising budgets to fund electoral campaigns, or to support local teams and cultural organizations. Over-manning was rife, productivity dismal, and public service poor; deficits and debt had gone through the roof.

Cold reality had nevertheless forced the hand of previous governments. Revenues from privatizations from 1997 to 2009 were €18 billion, equivalent to 10% of GDP; of those, the majority (€11 billion) had been under PASOK governments until 2004. Most entailed stock market listings and gradual share sales, without the state ceding overall control. They aimed at raising money and injecting some private sector discipline into public behemoths, as in the case of OTE, the telecommunications provider. But they stopped short of the kind of transfer of power that would change corporate governance.

It was time for a bolder approach. The logic behind a large-scale privatization programme was compelling. Private investors would radically change the stifling corporate culture, inject much needed capital into critical sectors and send a clear message attracting foreign capital. As a bonus, eliminating – or reducing, where there was a public service obligation – the deficit of state companies would lower the fiscal deficit, while revenues from mass privatizations would reduce the national debt. In this respect the programme signed in May 2010 was not very ambitious. It aimed to raise "at least 1 billion euro a year during the period 2011-2013". At that point, urgent fiscal and structural reforms dominated. The restructuring of public sector enterprises to prepare them for divestment took precedence over immediate asset disposals.

In June 2010, I had made a first stab at bringing the privatization agenda to the forefront. My careful presentation of options to a cabinet meeting had been met with hostility; I had few, if any, allies. Most felt the issue was more trouble than it was worth; didn't we have enough problems already? As in other areas I was reduced to invoking obligations under the agreement with our creditors to advance the issue.

In a classic pre-commitment strategy, I had corralled three other ministers into a joint press conference, to announce that the government was considering options for asset divestment in areas as diverse as gaming (a state monopoly), the rail network (for passenger traffic and freight), ports (Piraeus, as well as other ports around Greece), airports (Athens airport and regional facilities), roads, water, energy, and telecoms. I presented the options: outright sales to strategic investors, initial public offerings, public-private partnerships and concession agreements, and the listing of holding companies (SPVs) with a basket of corporate and real estate assets.

Over the following months, we prepared the ground by hiring advisors to explore options, and kick started the as yet untouched project of selling public real estate – a potential goldmine, fraught with legal, planning, bureaucratic and political problems. Our effort resonated internationally, with the Wall Street Journal claiming "Greece's Massive Privatization

Thrust Will Change Its Economic Landscape". By December, I was ready with an action plan, which I presented to the cabinet. The plan talked about accelerating asset valuation and disposal (as in the former Athens airport at Ellinikon, the largest urban development project in Europe), and included specifics for individual projects. Reservations were muted; I had avoided including politically explosive assets (for example, in energy), while leaving final decisions on the shares that would be sold to be decided after the financial advisors hired in each case had made their proposals to the government. The plan was approved. In the second Troika review, we revised the privatization proceeds target from €3 to €7 billion over three years. Now, in the third review, we were about to take this to a whole new level.

"Shall we set a target for €50 billion?"

The proposal came from the IMF, but had obviously been discussed with the European Commission and the ECB before landing on the negotiating table. €50 billion? How could we achieve that? Market capitalisation of the state share in publicly listed companies was no more than €10 billion. Even if all were sold, where would we find the rest? The Troika countered with reports estimating the total value of state property in excess of 300 billion, most of it land and real estate. So it was feasible, at least in theory. It would also send a powerful message to the markets about debt sustainability, as it would entail cutting the debt to GDP ratio by more than 20% of GDP over the next five years.

I took the issue to the prime minister. I did not hide my reservations: I did not think the plan would be feasible, but I could see the logic behind it – and, if it were implemented, at least in part, there would be less pressure on us for additional fiscal tightening. Plus, opposition leader Antonis Samaras had announced in his "Zappeion" speech back in July that, if ND came to power, they would launch a vast privatization and real estate programme intended within two years to bring revenues of – yes, you guessed it – €50 billion.

So at least we seemed to be safe from the main opposition accusing us of selling out the country. That could only come from the left – and of course, from our own ranks. In fact, that was an understatement of what was about to happen.

The Troika review finished on the morning of February 11th. Most of the staffers started leaving town, with the principals staying behind for an afternoon press conference. Then I got a frantic call from my press officer. During the Q&A session at the Troika press conference, the Commission representative had dropped a bombshell while answering a general question about privatizations: the review incorporated a €50 billion privatization drive. Journalists were speechless. In fact, one of them had asked: "Did you say *fifty?* Or *fifteen?*"

By the time of the evening news broadcasts, the situation was out of control. The largest TV channel led with the story that the Troika had "revealed" a massive sell-off of state property. The commentators slaughtered us. Who was running the country – the Greek government or the Troika? It transpired that, a day earlier, there had been a demonstration outside the TV network against their "pro-bailout bias"; they were rattled so they needed to prove the opposite.

At around 9pm, the dedicated government landline rang. It was the prime minister and he was clearly not happy.

I had never heard him as angry as this before. Over the last hour he had been on the receiving end of a number of calls from his staff and ministers, all expressing their horror over the "50 billion plan", and, most importantly, about the fact that this had been announced without any prior discussion in cabinet.

I conceded this looked bad, but stood by the substance of the plan, which we had in any case previously discussed. I then offered my resignation. If he believed my handling was at fault or if he wanted to backtrack on our commitments, I could not remain in my post.

I spent the next few hours talking to the Troika in Athens and the institutions in Brussels and Washington, giving everyone a piece of my mind. They had breached a rule they kept lecturing us about: programme ownership. By pre-announcing a major policy decision rather than letting us discuss it first in cabinet and handle its communication, they had played into the hands of those who claimed the Troika issued orders and the Greek government executed them.

The statement issued by the government spokesman lashed out at the Troika's "unacceptable behaviour", reaffirming that all such decisions were taken by the government alone and making clear that, while we stood by our privatization and real estate development programme, that did not mean "a clearance sale of public land".

There was no backtracking on commitments and hence no resignation. The Troika tried to make amends in a statement issued the next day: "our role is to advise and support the government while considering options during the decision-making process. It is regrettable if a different impression was perceived at any time."

The "50 billion" incident came and went, but it left scars. In agreeing to go ahead with the plan, we had underestimated the opposition to some of our policies within the party, in powerful constituencies and in the media. In failing to avert such a misstep at the Troika press conference, we gave the impression we were no longer in control of the agenda. As a result there was now a clear lack of trust in much of the media and the political system in the way I was doing my job; and the first serious crack in the most important relationship a finance minister can have: that with his prime minister.

I was a wounded man and the hunting season for me had begun in earnest.

Chapter 17

THE R WORD

"R" for restructuring. In other words, a reduction in the nominal value of someone's debt – the so-called "haircut" on Greek national debt. Or more mildly, "R" for reprofiling: extending the maturity of a loan held by a private investor, and moving it to the distant future to avoid a big repayment hump that is impossible to make. Until spring of 2011, both words were banned from Eurogroup meetings.

It is not that the question of Greek public debt sustainability was new. It had been raised by Greece before the May 2010 bailout (the investment firm Lazard had been hired by the government at the time to explore alternatives in this respect) and explicitly put aside. Countries had barely agreed to put money on the table and Greece had not yet proved that it would mend its fiscal ways, so at that point nobody was willing to entertain the idea of debt forgiveness.

There were some voices in the IMF arguing in that direction, with its Latin American experience in mind; but these were overruled by the IMF leadership when it became obvious it was a deal-breaker with the ECB and EU countries. Still, the IMF hinted at some sort of debt reprofiling in its May 2010 report: "there may be scope for bolstering this [market access] by seeking coordinated voluntary rollover understandings among creditor groups."

While officials were unwilling to discuss the issue, bankers and analysts were not so shy. In May 2010, the Financial Times argued that "Europe and the IMF have bought no more than another six months to a year before a restructuring". The same went for the Wall Street Journal, which was saying, "The arithmetic adds up to a Greek restructuring".

Our position was delicate. Unilateral debt restructuring – simply deciding not to pay back our debt – would be catastrophic. It would at a stroke make Greece a pariah, shutting it out of all international markets, and would make it impossible to finance our large primary fiscal deficit. Only coordinated, "voluntary" debt restructuring could work, with lending banks as well as governments on board. That was not on the cards; we understood that any statement or hint we were considering debt restructuring would seriously backfire, making our already difficult access to markets impossible.

Economists love discussing debt restructuring as a liquidity versus solvency issue. If the state is simply illiquid, i.e. short of money now but can service its debts later, there is no need to restructure the debt. All that is necessary is some money to tidy it over. If it has a solvency issue, i.e. debt cannot be serviced in the medium-term, then it needs debt relief. Analysts have criticized the 2010 bailout as having mistaken a solvency problem for a liquidity one, by throwing money at it rather than taking the hard decision of debt relief early on.

It is always easier to make such calls after the fact. Debt sustainability is a slippery concept. Is a debt to GDP ratio of 200% sustainable? Clearly not, except if your name is Japan. Is 60% of GDP sustainable? Yes, it is. How about 120 or 130% of GDP, the Greek level in 2009? Well, it depends.

It's not just a matter of the headline number. It depends on many things. Maturities – is your debt to be repaid immediately or does it stretch into the distant future? Interest – how much of your GDP goes to interest payments? And, crucially, growth prospects – debt is sustainable if the economy can grow so that it can be serviced.

Equally important is something beyond numbers: perception. At the end of the day, debt sustainability is in the eye of the beholder. If the markets believe debt is sustainable, they continue lending and it will *de facto* be sustainable – a virtuous circle. If they decide it is not, they stop lending and it becomes unsustainable. And markets are not rational: they were happy to lend to us at almost the same rate as Germany for many years; but, in 2010, they decided it was game over for the country.

What we knew in 2010 was that, even if all €300 billion of outstanding debt were somehow forgiven, if nothing else changed the Greek state would still be spending €24 billion more than it received as revenues every year. So the EU/IMF money was necessary to reduce that deficit gradually (with austerity) rather than immediately (with even more austerity). The liquidity versus solvency debate was interesting, but we had to ensure we could actually pay wages and pensions the following month.

This does not mean we remained idle. We started off by convincing our European partners that the maturities of the official EU/IMF loans needed to be pushed back in time and repaid at lower interest rates. Their original lending profiles with punitive rates and short maturities were a child of political necessity; they were subsequently improved.

As far as privately held debt was concerned, we worked on options behind the scenes with advisors and debt restructuring experts. When major international banks approached us with ideas for reprofiling, i.e. chopping off "debt peaks" and moving them to the distant future, we sent them to discuss these with Brussels, Frankfurt, Berlin and Paris. If they got some traction there, we would be on board. We then talked to the IMF, the only part of the Troika open to discussing this issue. Two IMF debt experts worked intensively with our debt management agency to examine the structure and profile of the debt, and come up with options.

By early 2011, sentiment on debt restructuring was shifting, even in the Eurogroup. In February, following a cautiously positive report by Olli Rehn on the programme ("it is broadly on track, challenges remain, there is no guarantee of success"), Wolfgang Schäuble surprised everyone. After asking, "what does it mean, 'broadly on track?' Is it or isn't it?", he broached the subject no-one else would, stating bluntly, "we need to open the issue of restructuring". In this he was joined by Dutch Finance

Minister Jan Kees de Jager.

Jean-Claude Trichet would have none of it. He warned of repercussions if the discussion leaked, and threatened he would leave if it continued. He believed the Eurozone would be destroyed if a country's "signature" was put in question.

In the Eurozone leaders' meeting in March, PM Papandreou tried to force decisions. He proposed the extension of official loan repayment dates, the lowering of interest rates, a debt buyback and some debt liability management. He spent many frustrating hours trying to convince Dutch PM Mark Rutte of the need to reduce the rate paid by Greece on official loans. In the end, the rate was reduced by 1% (Rutte wanted only 0.5%) and the maturity of official loans was increased to 7.5 years. This would help us go over the repayment hump in 2014 and 2015, but we knew it would not be enough to convince the markets.

On April 6th, at the beginning of the fourth programme review, I called the Troika principals into my office. I presented a document entitled "Greek Capital Markets Recovery Plan", prepared after consulting with major international banks, advisors including Lazard and experts such as US economist Adam Lerrick and debt restructuring lawyer Lee Buccheit. In addition to extended maturities and lower rates for EU/IMF loans, we had prepared detailed proposals for a debt buy-back by the EFSF, and reprofiling – not restructuring with a "haircut" – of privately held debt. The Greek government was now formally requesting the Troika to examine debt reprofiling as part of the programme review.

The next morning, a letter arrived, addressed to the prime minister and signed by Jean-Claude Trichet. It started by informing Papandreou that pursuing a strategy of debt rescheduling "would put Greece's refinancing in euro at major risk".

How so? He was explicit. First, the ECB had decided to continue accepting Greek government bonds as collateral despite their low rating because of the programme, and "no debt rescheduling is compatible with the programme". So the ECB would no longer do that. Second, even voluntary debt rescheduling would lead to further downgrades and make other Greek bonds ineligible as collateral. Third, a rescheduling could trigger huge losses for Greek banks; without recapitalization funds, banks "might have to be suspended from monetary policy operations".

Translation: cease and desist, or we will pull the plug on your banking system.

The April 2011 Trichet letter shows that claims – still made today – that Greece could somehow have obtained debt relief with the first bailout in 2010 are totally unrealistic. One year later, with significant fiscal consolidation behind us, with goodwill at least partially returned and with debt restructuring being openly discussed in the Eurogroup, the ECB was still threatening to use the nuclear option.

Nevertheless, this letter was also a kind of last stand by the ECB and Trichet. Under the influence of the shifting German position and IMF support, the debate was evolving fast. In the summer of 2011, the central bank would agree to debt reprofiling with bondholders accepting net present value losses. Finally, in October 2011, it would accept a nominal haircut on the Greek debt; but not before Trichet had retired as ECB president.

Meanwhile, we were facing mounting opposition to our reforms. A landmark bill to open hundreds of hitherto closed professions passed, despite objections from the many vested interests that were threatened by provisions to simplify entry into particular professions, as well as to remove pricing and other restrictions. We had opted for a "Columbus egg" approach: rather than dismantling regulations one by one, which would have been incredibly complicated, the bill mandated professions "open" by default, except where specific provisions were enacted.

I learned two important lessons from that bill. First, you have to pick your battles. One of the provisions removed the prohibition for Athens law firms to open offices elsewhere in the country (meant to "protect" local lawyers). A cross-party group of MPs insisted I let matters be. I pointed out the absurdity: by virtue of EU legislation, a London law firm could open an office in any Greek city while an Athens firm could not. "Let them go to court", I was told. Facing a revolt, I yielded, dumbfounded.

The second lesson was that, at least in Greece, passing a law does not guarantee it is actually implemented. For real change to happen you have to persevere for years with painstaking changes in secondary legislation and in accepted practices – you are up against vested interests that will fight you all the way.

Opposition in parliament was matched by a surge in the "Can't Pay, Won't Pay" movement on the streets. From motorways tolls to property taxes to issuing receipts, there was a citizen's revolt, openly aided and abetted by opposition parties, in particular SYRIZA. It was a movement that had turned into a political platform and it eventually propelled the radical left to power.

The news bulletins were a never-ending reel of the catastrophe brought by the bailout: increases in VAT, reduced pensions, cuts in wages. In your face, with no perspective and no critical analysis; just pandering to the general mood. Not for a moment was the counter-factual examined: was there any alternative to these tough measures? Would people be better off or massively worse off? But the power of experience is immense; what you do not experience has no comparable weight.

As the point man of austerity, I had increasingly become the lightning rod for all criticism of the government. Numerous newspaper articles were targeting me personally, attempting to create the image of an arrogant and out of touch finance minister. I could not recognise myself in these descriptions; but the truth is of course that politicians in positions of responsibility tend to become cut-off and isolated from people. And when you are the finance minister of a country in acute crisis, this isolation takes extreme characteristics.

I ended up drastically restricting my movements – I would

pretty much circulate only between the ministry, parliament, carefully chosen and screened events, and my house. My presence in airplanes when travelling abroad for meetings would often trigger reactions such as those of an irate gentleman who started shouting at me "we don't wanted to be saved like this any more!" In another, a lady heading a small business told me that what I was doing was criminal. I told her she would not want to be in my shoes and only have bad choices to choose from.

Around that time, a bullet hole was discovered in one of the large windows in my office, behind a conference table that was regularly used. We had no idea when or how it had got there. Forensics officers could not shed much light. I decided to leave it there and keep quiet; there was no need to over-dramatize what was already a difficult situation. Instead I would invoke it, half-seriously, during difficult negotiations with the Troika. One of my successors eventually had the windowpane changed.

We felt increasingly under siege at home and abroad. Internationally we were getting battered by the credit rating agencies. Following Moody's downgrading in March, I had sent a letter to the Eurogroup expressing my frustration: Greece was in a bailout programme, the programme was on track, and yet we were in an unwinnable fight to get back to the markets because of these downgrades. That did not stop Standard and Poor's and Fitch from following suit in the months to come.

The downgrades reflected the expectation that sooner or later, there would be some form of debt restructuring. There was plenty of speculation around that premise, and many market participants were making money on its back. As of the beginning of April, Greek spreads had hit the 1,000 mark (10% above German rates) and further rises seemed unstoppable.

The spreads fed on rumours, such as an email distributed by a London trader on April 20th, saying that "there seems to be increased noise over Greek debt restructuring as early as this Easter weekend". The email caused the Athens stock market to crash. It incensed me and we requested an Interpol investigation of potential market manipulation. At the ministry, we had a strong feeling of *déjà vu* – exactly the same thing had happened a year earlier. What was it about Easter weekends? It wasn't just Greek spreads; the whole periphery was on fire. Already all three main rating agencies had downgraded Portugal. Prime Minister José Sócrates then resigned after his austerity package was rejected by parliament and, on April 6th, Portugal threw in the towel and requested an EU bailout. The situation in Spain was not much better; markets expected it to be the next casualty, with Italy also facing increasing pressure.

With panic mounting, I got a call from Jean-Claude Juncker, summoning me to yet another secret meeting in Luxembourg on Friday May 5th. Now it was definitely *déjà vu* - all over again.

The Eurogroup president had also invited the finance ministers of France, Germany, Italy, Spain, as well as Commissioner Rehn and the ECB chief to his home turf. The topic was Greece, and I was told to show up with a plan.

I informed the prime minister, got my marching orders, told no-on except my wife where I was heading, booked a flight to Germany to avoid questions about why I was going to Luxembourg when there was no scheduled meeting, and caught a connecting flight. When I landed in Luxembourg and switched my phone back on I had hundreds of unanswered calls. The meeting had been leaked and the media all over Europe was buzzing with rumours of an impending Greek exit from the Eurozone.

I arrived at the small château where the meeting was being held to discover over twenty officials deep in discussion at tables that had been put up *al fresco* in the courtyard. I was greeted with some unease; there seemed to have been be a preliminary meeting, to which the Greek finance minister had not been invited. As I arrived, Jean-Claude Trichet was leaving. To anyone asking why, his response was that he would not participate in any meeting about debt restructuring. It was extraordinary.

We were ushered into a small dining room – ministers and

senior commission staff only. It was to be a working dinner. Juncker wasted no time: Greece could not access the markets in 2012; it needed a new programme. Olli Rehn followed, insisting the programme was not a failure, pointing to the deficit reduction that had been achieved, but warning us to step up implementation or there would be no more money. He lamented that the Greek opposition was not helping and added that it was time to consider voluntary debt reprofiling.

I was asked to present our case. I reminded them that the programme had been designed to allow Greece time to regain market access and make the debt load sustainable. But, despite significant effort and notable successes, the market attitude was negative.

Despite the huge fiscal consolidation achieved, markets focused on the 2010 deficit target that had been missed. Despite the landmark reforms which had been completed, all the talk was about "reform fatigue". Despite our government having a strong majority and still leading in the polls after a year of austerity, the discussion was all about social unrest and political difficulties.

After an early decline in the spreads of up to 300 basis points, the markets were now assuming there would be debt restructuring and our 10-year bond spread had exceeded 1200. There was a risk that the uncertainty would create a double-dip recession and a bank crisis. It was also eroding any remaining public support for the programme and the government.

I outlined a proposed policy response, which would also recognize the market reality. It involved continued fiscal consolidation – we would aim to reach a primary surplus in 2012 and would announce measures totalling €26 billion (over 11% of GDP) for the period to 2015, including €4 billion of additional effort in 2011. We committed to raise €15 billion from privatizations by 2013 and a total of €50 billion by 2015, thereby reducing debt by 20% of GDP.

But this needed to be complemented by a voluntary offer to lengthen or exchange bonds maturing up to 2020, with no haircuts. It would give Greece more time to pay its existing debt, and allow time for fiscal consolidation and structural reforms to bear fruit. Finally, we wanted a commitment for additional financing, but only if necessary. We did not want a new programme.

Christine Lagarde took the floor when I finished. "George, you are a very good advocate; but 'no new programme' is too high a bar. We need a significant drive to deliver the existing programme, and also a new programme. Additional money would not change the situation but would buy time."

Giulio Tremonti's tone was different. He was visibly rattled by the way the markets were treating Italy: "It is necessary to convince the market and me. I cannot go to parliament and ask for more money. We need a plan or no money." To his demand "pledge your patrimony as collateral in a trust!", I responded acidly, "do you mean the Acropolis, Giulio?"

Wolfgang Schäuble focused on debt restructuring: "Is there something between Vienna-plus [the voluntary rollover of maturing bonds] and reprofiling on a voluntary basis? Trichet says it is dangerous; but without debt restructuring it will not be possible. Germany agrees voluntary reprofiling has got to be part of a solution. The markets say yes; the IMF too; why do the Commission and the ECB say no?"

Olli Rehn tried to find middle ground. He defended the programme and our record ("seven percentage points of deficit reduction is not peanuts") while raising the bar ("the key is a substantial primary surplus in 2014"). There was a case for voluntary reprofiling, but the ECB needed to be part of the discussion ("they are not against a Vienna-type initiative, with rollover of exposure").

The discussion now zeroed in on debt restructuring. Lagarde mused, "reprofiling is necessary, but if we push our banks, we make it compulsory and it becomes a credit event. If Trichet says no, I cannot recommend this to Sarkozy". She turned to Schäuble: "can you give more money without reprofiling?" His reply left no doubt: "no, the programme needs to be sustainable." Juncker tried to pull things together: "Is asking Greece to leave the Eurozone an option? No. Is restructuring an option? No. Reprofiling? The ECB says no; I am not against reprofiling but if ECB says no, it's a no go." At this Schäuble exploded: "what is the ECB proposing? Programme, programme, programme... that is not enough!" And Tremonti chimed in: "the absence of the ECB from this meeting is tragic."

It was obvious that the meeting was getting nowhere. I had been partially successful in deflecting the worse – and totally unfair – criticism, while shifting the emphasis from the collateral required for a new loan, which was simply not acceptable to us, to the issue of reprofiling, where the frustration lay with the ECB's position.

Juncker knew the entire world was waiting to hear word from the meeting. "Our communication is: no Greek exit; no restructuring; we leave open reprofiling and ask for a stronger adjustment programme with more ambitious timing for primary surplus, with bipartisan support. Greece needs to regain credibility – this is not personal; George has been the most responsible of all Greek finance ministers. If the Greeks say no, a Grexit cannot be excluded, though I personally exclude it."

And with that the meeting was over.

From the discussion it was clear to me that we were repeating some of the mistakes made a year earlier, blaming implementation problems in Greece for the overall European systemic problem. But at least some of the decisions taken, such as the move towards some form of debt relief, were in the right direction. Would that be enough? I doubted it.

The Eurozone was once more on the brink.

Chapter 18

THE RESHUFFLE

"Do we really need to discuss this now?"

From the very first presentation of the main elements of the Medium Term Fiscal Strategy (MTFS) to the cabinet meeting in February 2011, a couple of months before the bill would go before parliament, I had been in trouble.

Charting a multi-year fiscal path to bring the deficit below 3% of GDP by 2014 was a key part of the May 2010 agreement. There was an obvious need for that, bailout or not; but it did involve up front decisions about expenditure cuts and tax hikes at a time when we were reeling from all the measures already taken. Hence the attempt by the PM's office to bury the discussion on the MTFS as item no. 7 in the list of 10 items on the cabinet agenda, tucked between more innocuous bills. They were hoping it would pass unnoticed. It didn't.

The same denial was evident in March when I sent letters to the opposition parties, inviting them for a discussion on the forthcoming MTFS. I believed it would help them understand that there were no easy options; plus, they might have some good ideas. New Democracy, SYRIZA and the communist party all refused to send representatives. Three small parties showed up. Their representatives listened politely, offered no alternatives and left. One was frank enough to say to me, "I would not want to be in your shoes".

The MTFS framework was approved by cabinet in mid-April, to be elaborated and pass into law in May. Papandreou committed his government to curtailing expenditures from 53% of GDP (the record level in 2009) to 44% (the EU average), and to boost revenues from 38% of GDP (at their lowest level in 2009) to 43%, the level when Greece adopted the euro. Nobody could dispute the logic of the arithmetic; the difficulty arose when it was incorporated into specific measures.

After the secret Luxembourg meeting on May 5th, I requested an informal cabinet meeting to brief ministers on what had transpired. I was very candid in describing the atmosphere, the requests for more measures, and the demands that we post collateral for the new loan which had by now become inescapable. I could see that a number of my colleagues no longer had confidence in my handling of the situation.

Evangelos Venizelos, the defence minister and long-time Papandreou rival, was the main critical voice. His statement during the discussion that "we need to regain the political direction of the country" was really aimed at the prime minister. But he finished with a scathing reference to "the arrogance of the finance ministry, which keeps announcing the need for new measures without presenting a national plan".

On the way out, I caught up with him and complained. I had bent over backwards to accommodate colleagues in what was an impossible situation. He looked at me and said, "you have to understand; my time is running out". Initially I was taken aback, but then I understood. This was about so much more than deciding on what was best for the country. The crisis was quickly erasing political careers that had been painstakingly built over decades.

With the government losing traction internally, the opposition was upping the populist ante. A year after his first speech, ND leader Antonis Samaras returned to the scene of the crime with Zappeion II. His speech had everything from conspiracy theory (we planned to bring in the IMF from the start) to promises of tougher negotiations, "like Ireland and Portugal did, unlike Greece" (a year earlier he was saying Ireland would never seek a bailout).

And yet, populist rhetoric still was not convincing the Greek public. One year after signing the agreement, and countless harsh austerity measures later, PASOK was still ahead in the polls. Despite opposition in the streets, despite the fact that only a few days ago, during the traditional May 1st demonstration, Athens had seemed like a city in chaos. We were in trouble, we were politically wounded, but we were not dead – yet.

As May unfolded, the markets got jittery and so did politicians across the EU. In late April, Eurostat had announced the final 2010 fiscal deficit for Greece: 10.5% of GDP. We missed the target by two percentage points, mostly due to the upward revision of the initial starting point of the 2009 deficit. Still, the five percentage point deficit reduction (half a point less than the 5.5 percentage point original target reduction) was the largest ever achieved in Greece and the Eurozone in a single year. It had taken hard work from us and painful sacrifices from the Greek people.

A Eurogroup teleconference was called for May 11th. We were one year after the bailout, and Olli Rehn talked of a situation more serious than then, with political fatigue in the north and reform fatigue in the south. He told everyone Greece was unlikely to return to markets in 2012. Jean-Claude Trichet once more excluded any debt restructuring ("it would be an abominable catastrophe"). He would only countenance voluntary debt rollovers. I was asked to present yet more proposals at the upcoming Eurogroup.

The days between the teleconference and the Eurogroup meeting were taken up by intensive and often testy negotiations with the Troika. Their instructions were to push us as much as they could. My staff was angered by both the demands and the tone. In one meeting the normally mild Matthias Mors from the Commission rejected our latest proposal with an abrupt, "there is nothing more to discuss". I replied "no, there isn't", packed up and walked out, thus suspending negotiations. They resumed a day later, after tempers had cooled and explanations were offered.

In their June 16th meeting, finance ministers approved the €78bn assistance package for Portugal (spanning three years, with €26bn from the IMF). The agreement was supported in

Lisbon also by opposition parties – a precursor of what would happen also with Greece's second bailout. But the substantive work on Portugal had already been done; the announcement was just the ceremonial part. The real work on that day was once again devoted to Greece. As I had been asked to show up with proposals, I was given the floor first.

I started with a bold statement: the programme was not a failure. A lot had been achieved since May 2010. Deficit reduction, reforms, a stable financial system: check on all three. But there was no return to the markets; on that we had failed. Why?

Admittedly our own shortcomings had played a role: lack of implementation capacity, wavering political will and a lack of broad political support. But more important were external factors outside our control: the latest – and final – upwards revision of the 2009 fiscal deficit figure, the lingering debt restructuring issue and the Deauville decision were much to blame. Last, but not least, were design problems in the programme – both in its conditionality as well as in the repayment schedules, with short maturities and a repayment hump that scared off investors.

To move forward I suggested we needed to restore confidence that we were delivering, deal with the financing gap and address debt sustainability. For our part, we would stick to the 2011 fiscal target, taking €6-7 billion of additional measures. And we would pass a robust MTFS; I reminded everyone that in the end we would be achieving a massive 13% of GDP deficit correction in the 2009-2014 period, with 6 points already done.

The discussion that followed had to resolve a problem particular to the Troika: because of its charter, to disburse its part of the next loan tranche the IMF needed either a new 3-year programme, assurances that the financing gap would be filled or some kind of debt management exercise. EU countries were not ready to give those assurances and Germany would not commit to a new programme without the IMF on board. We had an impasse.

Olli Rehn tried to break it by arguing for a primary surplus of 5.5% by 2014 that would subsequently be maintained ("Belgium has done it for 10 years"), complemented by €15 billion privatization revenues in 2011-12 and cross-party support for the programme. This would allow the Eurozone to commit to more money. He was not getting very far in convincing the others.

Jean-Claude Trichet wanted us to dismiss public servants, eliminate all tax exemptions, means-test social benefits, close state-owned organizations and cut wages in state-owned enterprises. The ECB wanted a tough new programme, signed by both government and opposition. He admonished the finance ministers: "if you say further financing is impossible, we have debt restructuring; but what happens to Portugal, Ireland, others?"

The risk of contagion to other non-programme countries, notably Spain and Italy, was on everyone's mind. The Spanish finance minister complained that contagion risk to Spain feeds from debt restructuring rumours, and asked everyone to agree to buy time with new money and stop talking about restructuring. To this, Germany responded: "if we buy time, what exactly are we buying it for?"

The IMF had its red lines: to disburse, they needed stronger measures – financing assurances for €60 billion or a new 3-year programme, and a sustainable debt profile. They turned to the ECB and asked if it would consider a debt-management operation. Trichet was adamant: no reprofiling; no exchange of bonds. "We can accept only Vienna-type rollovers." Schäuble interjected, "this is not just an IMF and ECB issue; it is an issue for EU member states."

Olli Rehn pleaded, "the air is thick with 'red lines' – make them pink!" Juncker tried to summarise: "Greece takes new measures, strengthens privatizations, passes the MTFS; meanwhile we prepare a new 3-year programme and some kind of debt management exercise." Germany interjected: "no announcement today of a new programme; we will announce only that Greece will take additional measures." Then France: "the new programme will go over the political cycle, so we will need opposition support. They will have to sign."

But the last word belonged to Klaus Regling, the CEO of the EFSF. He would be disbursing the new loan. "Just keep in mind, we will need more than 100 billion."

A reality check.

Two days after the Eurogroup, my mobile rang. It was Poul Thomsen. He was dumbstruck. "Are you following the news?" No, it was 1 a.m. and I was actually trying to get some sleep. Dominique Strauss-Kahn, the IMF's powerful managing director and potential candidate for the French presidency, had been arrested in New York and charged following allegations of a sexual assault. For the next few hours I followed developments (DSK taken out of plane, DSK in handcuffs, DSK in court). I was stunned but also sad, drawn in by the human interest of this story but also trying to figure out what it all meant for the Greek programme, for Greece and for Europe in general.

About a month earlier, as I was leaving DSK's IMF office in Washington DC after a bilateral meeting during the annual IMF spring meetings, I had asked him whether he would be running in the forthcoming French presidential election. He had smiled, mentioned the need "to discuss things with the family", and artfully dodged the question. Had he run, by all accounts, he would have been a shoe-in. Now he was in handcuffs, doing the infamous New York perp walk for the entire world to see.

The next days the rumour was he had been on his way to meet Merkel and argue for immediate Greek debt restructuring. Whether this rumour was true or not, DSK's arrest (after much legal juggling, the charges were dropped some months later) and his resignation as the Fund's managing director threw a spanner in the works of the delicate balance in the Troika. IMF staff remained professional and went through the motions, but leadership was absent at a critical juncture. That had to wait till the end of June, when Christine Lagarde was named the first female managing director of the IMF.

A week after the Eurogroup, I was back in Brussels for the last meeting of the EU task force meeting chaired by Herman van Rompuy before its conclusions and proposals would be tabled at the European Council. Greece had been the canary in the coal mine in the broader systemic crisis hitting the EU. I felt the lessons learned in our case had a broader relevance and needed to be shared.

I suggested there were four. The first: things catch up with you. In our case, lax fiscal policy, broken institutions, governments not willing to confront problems. There comes the moment when you just have to deal with them. It is never easy, and there is never enough time. The second: even if you do things right, you are not out of the woods. You need to convince the markets, but markets are not rational. The third: time is expensive: the more you delay, the more you pay. That was also a lesson for the EU as a whole, as we had seen in 2010. And the fourth lesson: ad hoc solutions are only second best and don't work for long. The gaps in the EU's institutional architecture needed to be addressed.

In that vein, I offered my thoughts on three elements of any reform effort. On fiscal consolidation and improved coordination, we needed more community instruments, more practicality and less morality, and to pay attention not only to levels but also to quality of expenditures. And yes, we needed Eurobonds. On the hugely important issue of financial regulation, I pointed out the obvious: we were being heavily outplayed by markets. We needed to better understand their concerns; but we could not simply be reactive and led. We needed to regain some measure of sovereignty over speculative behaviour. For that, collective decisions were required, and we were shying away from taking them.

And finally, investment and growth. It just couldn't all be blood, sweats and tears. While in cases such as Greece there was no option but to consolidate, this was not the case for a number of other countries wich had fiscal room. And we needed to improve the supply-side response in our economies; competitiveness was above all about investments and positioning in international markets. At the end of the day, Europe was a political project which needed to make economic sense, but also remain convincing to citizens.

On that last part, all over Europe, incumbent governments were losing the battle, proving the old Juncker line that "we all know what to do, we just don't know how to do it and then win elections". On May 22nd, Spain's ruling socialists suffered their worst local election defeat in 30 years, a prelude to losing power later in the year. On June 5th, the Portuguese socialists were routed in national elections. Bailouts were deadly for signatory governments. And we were on the ropes, now overtaken in the polls.

May and June were months from hell. There were successive cabinet meetings to finalize the additional fiscal measures for 2011 and the MTFS; sessions with our MPs and discussions in parliament; and demonstrations, as the opposition successfully channelled popular discontent with our policies into often violent protests.

I presented the additional 2011 fiscal measures and the draft MTFS to a cabinet meeting on May 23rd. Everyone was immensely frustrated by our predicament – as one put it "we are cleaning up a 40-year mess". There was self-doubt ("do we have the legitimacy to continue on this path?"), self-criticism ("why have we not achieved our targets?) and side-swipes at me ("why do the measures come pre-decided?").

There was anger at the Troika ("their demands have no bounds"); but also self-awareness and political courage ("we should stop blaming the MoU", "enough with the rear-guard action"). There was lucidity ("as long as the EU has not addressed the systemic problem, they will keep squeezing us") and legitimate concern ("are they trying to push us out of the Eurozone?"). There was even poetry ("the darkest moment is just before dawn").

The next day, we announced details of the additional €6 billion in 2011 budget cuts and a plan to speed up asset sales.

The Greek political system abhors consultation and compromise; it is entirely geared towards confrontation. But to extract broader political support behind our effort, Papandreou asked President Papoulias to convene again a meeting of leaders of political parties. I was also invited; for a second time after the meeting in May 2010, the PM wanted the others to hear about the economic situation directly from me.

The meeting was a complete failure. The opposition did not give even an inch towards a broader "national understanding". Papandreou expressed his disappointment publicly, but said he was open to broadening his government by including politicians from other parties. Samaras entered the meeting saying, "we will not be blackmailed" into agreeing with wrong policies, and then offered cooperation only if we rejected the MoU. SYRIZA leader Alexis Tsipras asked for the government's resignation and fresh elections.

Negotiations with the Troika concluded on June 2nd. The "staff-level agreement" covered the additional fiscal measures and the detail of the MTFS. It was approved in a Eurogroup teleconference a few days later and the corresponding parliamentary bill was then submitted to parliament for debate on June 9th. All that remained was for it to be voted through. But, Houston, we had a problem.

Its magnitude became apparent to me when I presented the bill to PASOK MPs – a process which always preceded the debates in parliamentary committees and in plenary. There was always criticism, but I had never before faced this. Many of our own MPs were speaking as if we had created the problem in the first place; as if we had achieved nothing since we took over ("the sacrifices were in vain" was a commonly used phrase).

The same people who had opposed any difficult measures were now saying we should have taken measures earlier, and that we did not "use our biggest weapon and default"; they warned that the MTFS would be the last straw that would ignite a social revolt. Many called for elections – a way out of their predicament of having to vote for these measures. Not everyone took that line; some simply expressed their anxiety, while supporting the bill – but their voices were drowned out.

I was asked to replace permanent measures with a one-off "solidarity tax". I could not do that. I was asked for reassurances that there would be no further austerity – I could not do that either (I had paid dearly for saying "there will not be any new measures" a year earlier). I was told that parliament should not be blackmailed into voting under threat of bankruptcy – I agreed, but the threat was real. I was repeatedly told that Greek society could not take any more austerity.

How to respond to that last criticism? It was true, of course. Greeks were finding it increasingly impossible to make ends meet, with taxes going up, salaries down, and public services struggling with reduced funding. The unemployment rate was shocking and was still rising, especially amongst the young. The economy was in deep recession, not about to create new jobs any time soon. A lost generation was forming before our eyes, young educated people who felt they had no hope and no future.

But at the same time I was struck by two things. The first was that everyone was describing the problem; nobody had a coherent alternative to what we were trying to do. Nobody had a realistic way of keeping the country funded while avoiding austerity; and everybody chose to forget that part of the austerity and all the reforms were necessary anyway, bailout or not.

The second was that those protesting most vehemently were usually not the weakest. In the main it was not the unskilled builders, the struggling private sector employees earning the minimum wage, the farm labourers or the poorest of pensioners who were on the streets. It was not the unemployed graduates or the struggling small businessmen and women.

The most vocal were the high-earning civil servants whose salaries we had cut, the pensioners of state-owned enterprises who had retired at 50 on high pensions, the upper and middle class property owners who had never paid property tax and were now furious, the pharmacists whose guaranteed profit margins had been reduced by law, and the doctors and lawyers who routinely declared only a fraction of their earnings.

After 12 gruelling hours of fielding questions from PASOK MPs, it was clear that I had lost our parliamentary group. Outside the meeting some were openly calling for me to be replaced. They were aiming at me so as not to attack the prime minister directly. I could not go on.

I was not the only one thinking that. Rumours started circulating of an impending cabinet reshuffle that would see me replaced as finance minister. I tried to ignore them and get on with my job, as meetings in both Brussels and Athens multiplied. Time became dense. We were coming to some sort of resolution.

In yet another Eurogroup teleconference on June 8th, the Commission tried to convince increasingly doubtful ministers that debt sustainability could be achieved by very high primary surpluses and a revamped privatization programme. Bond rollovers and debt-exchange options were openly discussed for the first time, and fine distinctions between a "rating event" and a "credit event" were elaborated.

Jan Kees de Jager declared that the Dutch parliament would not approve a new loan without private creditors taking a hit via debt reprofiling. Trichet responded tersely that he sympathized, but had problems with his own governing council. He admonished everyone: "we saved European banks; we need to do the same for Greece." De Jager retorted, "we never agreed to bail out countries under *any* circumstances. Greece has derailed. When will it access markets again?" Trichet shot back, "Before Deauville, Greece was on its way back to private markets".

Finland's Jyrki Katainen reminded everyone that he could not move without collateral. Portugal, Ireland and Spain fretted about contagion risks. Christine Lagarde was concerned about the lack of cross-party support for the programme, and revealed that the French PM François Fillon, had tried to convince

Samaras to adopt a bipartisan approach to no avail.

The decision was taken to work on both bond rollovers and exchanges, to explore options on collateral, and to look into what would constitute a credit event and a trigger for credit default swaps. It was clear: there were no risk-free solutions. We would revisit the matter in a week.

The informal Eurogroup and Ecofin meetings convened on June 14th, one day after Standard and Poor's cut Greece's sovereign credit rating to CCC, the lowest rating for any country it reviewed in the world, with spreads on 10-year Greek government bonds having broken the 1,300 basis point barrier. As an informal meeting, it could take no decisions. But we were clearly running out of time and decisions would have to be taken at the formal Eurogroup scheduled for June 20th.

I was also running out of time. This was to be my last appearance at the Eurogroup and the Ecofin as Greece's finance minister.

The stage was set for a final showdown on debt restructuring. Vittorio Grilli, new Chair of the Euro Working Group, laid out the alternatives that had been developed: no private sector involvement (PSI, the acronym used for the various forms of debt restructuring); a "soft Vienna approach" – asking banks to maintain exposure to Greek bonds by rolling them over at maturity, based on moral suasion; "Vienna-plus" – the coordinated rollover of maturing debt with positive incentives; and the upfront exchange of existing debt with new bonds, using positive and negative incentives. He outlined the trade-off in each case: size and participation of bondholders versus the impact on Greece and the potential contagion in other countries.

Trichet did not like the direction things were heading. "We strongly advise against any PSI which has an element of coercion. There should be no compulsion, no credit event, no rating event. You will take your decisions; and I will take mine. But you should reflect on the risk of a deposit run. When the US let Lehman go I said it was an enormous mistake. Let's not repeat it."

Wolfgang Schäuble entered the discussion: "We all understand there is a need for a new programme; but, without some kind of PSI, there is no solution." Lagarde concurred: "without PSI it is politically impossible."

Not everyone was in agreement. The Portuguese minister, battling his own bailout, thought PSI was a big mistake. Jean-Luc Frieden of Luxembourg believed it risked further destabilizing the Eurozone. Northern countries worried a new loan would not pass their parliaments. This prompted Tremonti to interject, "we also have parliaments! When your neighbour has a fire, you offer a fire extinguisher".

Everyone was waiting for Germany. Schäuble said he was ready to disburse the next loan tranche, if there was a modest but robust PSI. "We need to respect the Greek effort," he added, "but who knows if it is feasible politically?" Then he added, in a precursor of things to come: "maybe in September we will be discussing a different question…"

Germany was already thinking beyond simple reprofiling, but was waiting for Trichet's term to finish before revisiting the issue. For the moment, all Trichet was willing to give was, "we can have an organized – not wild – voluntary PSI. Greece should organize it, with our help". He added, "any new programme needs to be negotiated also with the opposition. It is a disgrace there is no political consensus."

In recent months, Syntagma Square in the centre of Athens had became a tented village, with people spending the night in protest. The *indignados* movement from Spanish squares was transplanted to Athens, with a twist. At the top half of the square you had the extreme right and the neo-Nazis; at the bottom half the left and the anti-globalization movement.

In addition to this now longstanding situation, a general strike was called for June 15th. The square filled with protesters intent in encircling the parliament building in a bid to prevent the MTFS bill passing. Police in full riot gear used water cannons and tear gas to maintain access to parliament.

In the debating chamber a number of our MPs openly disagreed with the MTFS bill that was currently going through committees; a couple resigned their seats. George Papandreou understood that he could not let that go on. To break the impasse he called the leader of the opposition, Antonis Samaras, and asked him to join forces - if necessary with Papandreou stepping down as prime minister.

It was a bold and courageous move, at the limit of his constitutional mandate – after all, he still commanded an absolute parliamentary majority. Smelling blood and mistaking the offer for unconditional surrender, New Democracy leaked it to the press, and in doing so effectively killed the idea. Papandreou addressed the nation, announcing he would be reshuffling his government and asking for a fresh confidence vote.

The call finally came. A very apologetic prime minister wanted to inform me of his decision to relieve me of my duties as finance minister. "George, I hope you understand". I interrupted him. "You don't need to explain your decision. I can no longer convince our own MPs." I knew that to continue with a policy you sometimes needed to change the person leading it. That was the only way for the PM to continue – finance ministers are the proverbial sacrificial lambs in politics.

The new cabinet was announced the next day. I was replaced by Evangelos Venizelos, who was also appointed deputy prime minister. I was tipped to take over foreign affairs; instead, I was appointed to the energy, environment and climate change portfolio, replacing Tina Birbili. Along with others, she paid the price for the need for Papandreou to sacrifice some of his longtime close collaborators. They had been unfairly called "his gardeners" by former PASOK ministers who had been left out of Papandreou cabinets. It was a sweeping reshuffle meant to embrace "the whole of PASOK" and signal party unity. But all it would do was buy us a few more months.

I was finance minister no more.

Chapter 19

HELIOS

The first Eurogroup of the new finance minister did not go well. Venizelos flew to Luxembourg the day after he was sworn in as finance minister and the customary speeches were given at the change of guard. I ended mine by wishing my successor what Olli Rehn had said to me from the same podium a year ago: "*kalo kouragio.*" Good luck. He was not amused. I left, reassured I was leaving behind my entire senior staff team, that would fill him in on all pending issues.

The reality check came when he landed in Luxembourg. In the Eurogroup meeting Venizelos spoke a language devoid of numbers, laced with politics and legalese, guaranteed to irritate finance ministers suspicious of the sudden reshuffle. His calls to renegotiate the agreement and delay the MTFS vote in the Greek parliament angered them. The Financial Times summed it up, quoting an unnamed Eurozone diplomat: "He managed to say everything he shouldn't have said." So the Eurogroup engaged in classic "hazing", impressing on the newcomer that rules were rules. There would be no changes.

Or rather there would be some – but not in the direction the Greek government would have wanted. The new minister had reopened negotiations on a completed agreement, hoping for a better deal. By the time the final agreement got the Eurogroup's blessing and its measures were approved by the Greek parliament at the end of June, over two days marred by violent protests, there was more austerity. The lack of trust led to the demand for more sure-fire fiscal measures.

However, the June Eurogroup also marked an important milestone. It officially opened the way for debt restructuring – as the statement at the end of the meeting put it: "private sector involvement in the form of informal and voluntary roll-overs of existing Greek debt at maturity." That was meant to lead to a substantial reduction in the programme funding required.

At its July 21st meeting, the European summit approved more money for Greece – initially €109bn, raised to a massive €130bn in October. They also agreed on private sector debt rescheduling, a debt buy-back, further lowering of loan rates, and even longer maturities (15 to 30 years). Also, to stave off contagion, leaders made the EFSF/ESM more flexible, allowing it to act on a precautionary basis, to intervene in secondary markets and to lend money to governments so that they can recapitalize banks.

These decisions had been forced upon European governments by events. They were driven by the market perception that the crisis would not end without some sort of debt relief. Also, the decision in late June for Mario Draghi to succeed Jean-Claude Trichet as president of the ECB undoubtedly removed a major obstacle.

I had met Mario Draghi earlier that year in the context of the IMF spring meetings. He was at the time still the Italian central banker but his name was increasingly discussed as the most likely successor to Trichet – hence I wanted to have a bilateral meeting. He was careful and measured in our discussion, as one would expect from a central banker; but it was obvious to me that he would be more flexible on the debt restructuring issue.

The July summit decisions did not prove to be the silver bullet Europe needed. A few days after the summit, Moody's and Standard and Poor's joined Fitch in again downgrading Greece. In early August, Spain's 10-year bond reached a record 6.5%. Alarmed, the ECB voted to resume its bond-buying programme, picking up Portuguese and Irish debt, and then Italian and Spanish debt as well. In Italy, spreads soared higher than the Spanish ones.

Over the summer, one after another, a number of Eurozone governments announced more austerity, against a deteriorating backdrop which included the stripping from the US of its triple-A status by Standard and Poor's, and fears that France might lose its triple-A credit rating.

The July summit's decision was to be short-lived.

Meanwhile, in the Greek cabinet, seated in my new seat symbolically further away from the prime minister, I watched my successor run roughshod over procedure. Gone were the detailed explanatory notes and Powerpoint presentations that my colleagues had been used to. Venizelos explained orally what everyone was called to agree on. No one complained. I sat there feeling uncomfortable by the way he was trying to effectively replace the prime minister. But I made a point of vocally supporting my successor in those meetings; after all, I was the one person in the room who knew first-hand what he was going through. Now there were two of us.

In any case, I had enough work of my own. I threw myself enthusiastically into my new portfolio, determined to make a difference. Over the next year, with a small and dedicated team, I tried to address the overregulation and stifling bureaucracy dominating land use, environment and energy policies.

In the field of environment policy, we moved to revamp waste management systems that were stuck in old-fashioned thinking and were out of touch with modern practices. With Greece as the only EU country still lacking a national land cadastre, we advanced the completion of land and urban planning, and tried to deal with the more than one million illegal dwellings by implementing a system of regularization – in the process also producing significant revenues for the state (once a finance minister, always a finance minister...).

In energy, we brought in long overdue legislation to liberalize the electricity and gas markets, and pushed to break up the state monopoly; oversaw a large increase in Greece's renewable energy capacity; pursued participation in international gas routes; and brought forward the exploration of Greece's hydrocarbon potential to which so many attached (often unrealistic) expectations.

I faced constant opposition from bureaucracy and entrenched interests. Simplifying environmental permits horrified those who made fortunes from the protracted and costly process – but did our environmental protection record really justify having ten times the required environmental permits per capita than France? The decision to allow diesel cars in Athens and Thessaloniki drew howls of protests but was quickly embraced by consumers – should Athens be the only European capital to ban modern technology diesel engines? (This was before the VW diesel scandal).

Signing off on the permit for a large foreign gold mining investment in Chalkidiki, in the north of Greece, gave activists another reason to dislike me, even though the project had passed the most stringent environmental tests. Creating a level playing field in energy upset major players, who favoured the status quo to the detriment of consumers. My decision to merge environmental research centres to create a critical mass created more enemies – those who had been feeding off the state, unchecked for decades. Even deciding to move the ministry from its rented 30 locations around the city into one building met significant resistance though, of course, the aim was to save money.

Some of the most explosive policy areas in my new portfolio were directly related to the MoU. Opening up the energy sector and privatizing the Public Power Corporation were flatly rejected by the latter's powerful trade union. I visited my former constituency, in the northern Greek prefecture of Kozani, where most lignite-based energy was produced. As I made my way into a building for a meeting, I ran into a wall of insults. I was a double traitor, for wanting to sell off the company and for doing so as an ex-MP for the area.

I was desperate to shake up the calcified system. I wanted to show that the transformation of the country was not just about austerity, but mainly about changing the economy. What we needed were bold initiatives, concrete projects that could bring in large scale investment and unlock the country's growth potential for the benefit of all.

Enter Helios, the power of the sun.

Greece enjoys 300 days of sunshine a year. It has 50% higher solar radiation than Germany and other central European countries. We import oil and gas, but do not export energy from our major national resource and comparative advantage, the sun. Project Helios was conceived in order to export solar energy to other countries on a large scale.

Could it be done? There were a number of obstacles. Land was one: the 20,000 hectares needed for the installation of the planned 10GW capacity seemed large, but represented only about 0.1% of Greece's land surface. We managed to locate them, using public and municipal land in part. Electricity grid infrastructure was another: the existing network could carry up to 3GW of energy to northern Europe, so the remainder had to be phased in gradually, in line with EU plans for a more integrated European energy system. Transit through other countries was a third consideration; it required international agreements, but could be done.

This left us with one important issue: clients. I targeted Germany; the government there had recently announced a move away from nuclear power and set ambitious targets for renewables. Helios could be a cost-effective way of reaching renewable energy targets in 2020 and beyond, if German consumers were allowed to consume solar energy produced more cost-effectively in Greece and imported into Germany.

It was a perfect win-win situation. Europe could back a concrete growth project at a time of austerity, and Project Helios could act as a catalyst for integrating a fragmented European energy market. For Greece, the project would be a signal of confidence and of European solidarity based on economic common sense. It would bring foreign investment, and the revenues over its life cycle could also contribute meaningfully to the reduction of public debt.

In mid-September, I set off to sell the project to my German counterparts. Both the energy and environment ministers liked it. We set up a working group to work out the specifications and requirements of a pilot project, and crucially, to get the financing and make the numbers add up.

But the highlight of the trip to Berlin was a meeting with Wolfgang Schäuble. We arranged to meet partly to discuss Helios, and partly as a courtesy on his part to an old colleague with whom he always had a mutually respectful relationship. We met for lunch at Paris-Moskau, a restaurant close to the Brandenburg Gate. A small traditional building with a sloping roof, more at ease in a Bavarian village than in Berlin; standing at the time alone in the middle of a huge urban reconstruction project, it provided a setting straight out of a Cold War movie. The discussion was pleasant and easy. Schäuble had always talked about projects to generate growth in Greece; he had even mused about solar exports in the past. So he would support Helios, and nudge his colleagues to overcome obstacles relating to subsidies for solar producers in Germany. But he also wanted to know how the government was coping with protests and with the opposition that was refusing to help. And then this: "George, the [July] debt agreement will not work. We will need a real haircut of the debt. Maybe 50% or so." I was speechless.

As soon as we had said our goodbyes, I was on the phone to the prime minister to recount what I had been told. He listened attentively and did not seem surprised. I was just confirming to him the feeling he and the finance minister had been getting in recent weeks. Greek debt sustainability had worsened over the summer, and most analysts were arguing that the July decision had to be revisited sooner rather than later ("think bigger and bolder", as The Economist had put it).

Many large European banks had reduced their exposure on Greek bonds; these were now held in the secondary market by a multitude of investors. A simple debt rescheduling by leaning on a few big holders would therefore not work. So the German government was now pushing for a large nominal haircut. But this would have to wait for the departure of Jean-Claude Trichet from the ECB in October.

In the end Helios did manage to play a small part in the Greek debt sustainability saga. At the time of the October summit, at which the haircut on Greek debt was agreed, I was in Baku for discussions with Azerbaijan's President Ilham Aliyev about the gas route from the Caspian oil and gas fields, through Turkey and Greece to Europe. As I switched my phone back on after leaving the opulent presidential palace, I got a call from Venizelos, who was negotiating in Brussels.

He wanted to know if we could pledge the proceeds from Helios towards the calculations aimed at making Greek debt look sustainable – the Dutch and the Finns were insisting on an additional gesture from Greece based on revenues from our public assets, and Papandreou had convinced them to use proceeds from project Helios in this regard. Yes, we could, and that would have the added bonus of ensuring the project would go ahead. Indeed, the Euro summit conclusions on October 26th included the slightly cryptic line, "Greece commits future cash flows from project Helios […] to further reduce indebtedness by up to 15 billion euros".

But even that did not save Helios. Despite extensive technical and financial work, and a solid collaboration with both Germany and the European Commission to get a pilot project going, it died a quiet death after I left the ministry in mid-2012. The project was unmistakably linked with me, and was therefore politically toxic for my successors. They felt prospective oil and gas exploration ("Norway in the Aegean") was more popular and easier to sell to the public than a complicated plan to export solar power. Until, that is, oil prices tanked, taking with them the investment interest for Greek hydrocarbon reserves.

Meanwhile, in late August Venizelos orchestrated a show of defiance to creditors by walking out of the negotiations. The Troika promptly suspended Greece's programme review. A week later, the cabinet capitulated and hurriedly approved €7 billion of new emergency measures to plug a gap in the 2011 budget. They included an unpopular real estate levy to be collected via electricity bills.

In early October, the draft budget for 2012 was approved with a targeted deficit of 8.5%. A week after that, the Troika finally concluded its review, opening the way for the release of a loan tranche worth €8 billion to be paid in mid-October. The remaining financing gap would have to be bridged by a debt restructuring exercise.

What transpired between the show of defiance in early September and the final agreement on October 2nd was intense pressure from European capitals on Greece to live up to its commitments, which culminated in a teleconference between Papandreou, Merkel and Sarkozy. Then, yet another difficult Eurogroup.

It convened on September 16th in Poland's picturesque city of Wroclaw. When the discussion came to Greece, ministers told their Greek colleague that they wanted additional fiscal measures or there would be no tranche disbursement. But what really made for Venizelos' U-turn happened outside the meeting itself.

In the dark and deserted basement bar of the Hotel Monopol, with the presidency reception in full swing in the main hall above, Schäuble and Venizelos had a 90-minute tête-à-tête with only their deputies present. In that meeting, Schäuble proposed a "friendly" Greek euro exit, assisted financially and accompanied by measures such as controls on capital movements to help the currency change.

Was this a true proposal or – more likely – a gambit to make it clear to the Greek government that Germany was ready for all eventualities if Greece continued to refuse to play ball and take additional austerity measures? It was difficult to tell at that point. In either case, the Greek finance minister was shocked, realizing that the prospect of Greece finding itself on the way out of the Euro was no longer a theoretical possibility.

The Greek government had been put on notice.

Chapter 20

CANNES

By the time the Euro summit convened on October 23rd, it was clear it would be another make-or-break all-nighter.

In fact, it took two summits. At the first, Papandreou argued that the July decision had been overtaken by events and urged for a decision that would involve a large nominal reduction in Greece's debt. He was helped in this by the latest IMF debt sustainability analysis, which was arguing for a "deeper PSI". The mood in the room was leaning towards a nominal haircut, but more time was needed to draw up a solution. The meeting was suspended, to reconvene on October 26th.

As the second meeting approached, the rumour mill went into overdrive: the media reported that the Germans had been asking for a massive 60% haircut from private investors, who were refusing. No compromise meant Greece would default. In the meeting itself, the leaders explored alternatives: a voluntary debt buyback financed by the EFSF; or a cheaper and more coercive transaction involving the exchange of bonds and pressuring creditors into acceptance of the offer.

In a basement room of the Justus Lipsius building, as leaders were discussing in the fifth floor above, a Greek negotiating team assisted by the Eurozone, the IMF and international advisors (Daniel Cohen from Lazard, the US lawyer Lee Buccheit and economist Jeff Sachs among them) was facing off against Charles Dallara, managing director of the Institute of International Finance, and representatives of the banks which were major holders of Greek debt.

Their discussion had started even before the July summit decision and taken a dramatic turn in September as bankers were pressed to accept a "deeper PSI" and a hefty nominal haircut.

The negotiations intensified before the summit, continued throughout and it was now crunch time.

There were four issues on the table: how deep the haircut would be; what kind of compensation ("sweeteners", in banking lingo) the banks would get down the road; the level of the interest rates; and the dates the new loans would mature. Around 2 a.m., the bankers in the basement were refusing to accept more than a 45% haircut. Facing an impasse, the meeting of leaders above was suspended and the heavy guns were called in: Merkel and Sarkozy. They walked into the bankers' meeting and insisted on a 50% haircut. It was a take-it-or-leave-it proposition. The bankers took it.

Around 4 a.m., after more than 10 hours of talks both upstairs and downstairs, there was an agreement. The summit invited "Greece, private investors and all parties concerned to develop a voluntary bond exchange with a nominal discount of 50% on notional Greek debt held by private investors".

It was an absolute first – a nominal haircut for the debt of a Eurozone country, intended to bring Greece's debt to GDP ratio down to 120% by 2020. The Eurozone had bowed to the reality that Greece would be unable to pay back its debts as they stood, and had decided to force private bondholders to accept large losses. The leaders had opted for the coercive option, but were dressing it up.

And finally, lest we might imagine the rules had been changed and that other countries would follow, a quick rejoinder: "Greece requires an exceptional and unique solution. All other euro area Member States solemnly reaffirm their inflexible determination to honour fully their own individual sovereign signature."

In addition to the decision on Greek debt, there was also fresh money on the table. First, of the smoke-and-mirrors variety: in an attempt to stem contagion by building better firewalls, leaders agreed to "optimize" the resources of the EFSF by introducing leverage options, effectively boosting the EFSF's firepower to €1 trillion. And then, the real thing: a package of €130 billion for Greece, bringing the bailout total for the country to €240 billion, easily exceeding Greek GDP.

When Papandreou arrived for the post-summit press conference, he was exhausted, but satisfied. He had every reason to be so: over the last few months, the Greek government and its international advisors had negotiated hard for debt relief, whichever way entailed fewer risks. And, just before the summit, Papandreou had multiple meetings with José Manuel Barroso, Herman van Rompuy and the leaders of EU countries to reach a deal.

"It's the dawn of a new day", were his first words at the press conference.

That was not how things were perceived back home. Papandreou and the rest of the team flew back from Brussels and the successful deal to face social unrest and a political rebellion. Both opposition and the media refused to acknowledge the success and continued a Pavlovian, knee-jerk reaction of criticism.

Then things started getting out of hand. On October 28th, President Papoulias was in Thessaloniki, Greece's second city, to commemorate World War 2 resistance against the Axis. While he was attending the military parade, protesters broke through the barricades and interrupted the event, booing him off the stage. As he was whisked away by his security detail, visibly emotional, a war veteran himself, he faced the cameras: "It is an outrage to call me a traitor. I've fought for my country since I was 15 years old…"

Meanwhile, Athens was a city under siege. The city centre was cordoned off for the parade. Large armoured police vehicles flanked by riot police formed a "security corridor" to allow MPs and government officials access to parliament. It felt more like a Latin American country after a coup than the capital of an EU member. The prime minister's own car was pelted with bottles as he made his way to parliament for a cabinet meeting on the results of the summit.

These were not spontaneous protests. At the core of the

demonstrations was an orchestrated campaign by political activists, guided by parties of the extreme left and right, to force a change of government. SYRIZA, in particular, had refused to condemn the attack on the president and talked about "social civil war". The party's leader, Alexis Tsipras, said the government was behaving like a *junta* and warned that politicians would soon not be able to walk the streets. It was a scarcely veiled threat.

On October 31st, Papandreou convened PASOK's parliamentary group, in an attempt to regain the political initiative and rally the troops. He wanted to convince his increasingly worried – and, in some cases, openly hostile – MPs that, with the debt haircut and the additional money, the government could move forward and hope for a revival, both of the economy and of our political fortunes.

In the middle of his speech, he dropped a bombshell: he announced a referendum on the recent agreement. There were gasps in the audience, followed by applause. And then all hell broke loose.

I remember the first thing that went through my mind when I heard him: "I hope he's told Merkel." He had – in a way. At the chancellery meeting on 27th September the two of them had a private moment and he warned that he was thinking of calling a referendum. But he had not discussed the issue with President Sarkozy when he visited Paris.

The announcement came just days after the Brussels summit decision was supposed to put a lid on the Greek crisis and it stunned the political system and markets alike. The fear that a "no" majority in the referendum would push Greece into disorderly default and out of the euro led to stocks and bonds plunging around the world. The yield on 10-year bonds hit 25% and on two-year bonds an absurd 85%.

Not everyone thought this was a bad idea. According to Der Spiegel, "Papandreou is right to let the Greeks decide". Bloomberg agreed: "Greek citizens deserve a say on one of the most important matters in their lifetimes." And, while Financial

Times Deutschland though it was "madness. Pure madness", it also conceded that "if Papandreou manages to convince the people with his arguments, the euro rescue would stand on much safer feet than it has stood until now".

European leaders certainly thought it was a bad idea. The next day, Papandreou was summoned to the G20 meeting at Cannes that started on November 2nd to explain himself. The referendum was the main global news story and Nicolas Sarkozy was beside himself. The G20 meeting was supposed to be the springboard for his presidential re-election campaign. Instead, it was being hijacked by the Greeks.

As soon as he arrived in Cannes, accompanied by Venizelos, Papandreou was ushered into a meeting with Merkel and Sarkozy, who were joined by their finance ministers, as well as by José Manuel Barroso and Olli Rehn from the European Commission, Christine Lagarde of the IMF, and Eurogroup president Jean-Claude Juncker. According to the narratives of the meeting which surfaced later, people in the room were angry at not having been warned; they worried that by the time Greeks got to the polls – whatever the result – market turmoil would have destroyed the Eurozone.

The Greek prime minister was asked to explain his thinking. He made the case for Greek people to decide whether they accepted the Brussels deal or not. He explained why a referendum was the only solution. If the opposition had backed the agreement there would be no need for such a vote. It did not go down well.

What followed was a very awkward and aggressive discussion, led by the French president. It was peppered with words such as "betrayal" and "disappointment". Sarkozy had been told by his aides that France's Gaullist tradition favouring referenda would make him seem hypocritical if he asked Papandreou to drop his idea altogether. Instead he had agreed with the others to ask Papandreou to pose a clear question in the referendum: "yes" or "no" to the euro. Until that question was answered, there would be no money.

Chancellor Merkel was not exactly on the same wavelength. Possibly this had to do with the fact that she had been forewarned about the referendum. When Papandreou broached the subject with her about a month earlier, her reaction was that if a referendum became necessary, it would need to occur after a deal was reached. For her it was all a "win-win" scenario: if Greece voted to stay in the euro, it meant they accepted to play by its rules; if they voted "no", leaving the common currency would have been the country's own decision, not one imposed by its creditors. In any case, on that particular day she left the initiative to the French president, who was hosting the meeting.

At the end of the meeting, as the Financial Times later revealed, Barroso (who had also been forewarned of a possible referendum, as had Jean-Claude Juncker and Hermann van Rompuy) took Venizelos aside and told him in no uncertain terms, "we have to kill this referendum".

Despite the pummelling, when the meeting was over, Papandreou put in a brave face for the cameras as he was leaving, and insisted – rather vaguely – that the referendum would in fact take place.

The Greek delegation took the government plane back to Athens. As soon as they landed at 4 a.m., Venizelos released a statement opposing the referendum. Despite publicly backing the idea when it was announced (he had called it "a liberating initiative"), he would now be instrumental in killing it.

With the entire world against him and his own finance minister publicly dissociating himself, Papandreou was left with no choice. The next day he announced that the referendum would not take place. In any case, he did not believe he had the 151 necessary votes in parliament in order to have the proposal to hold the referendum approved so that it could actually take place.

The excuse for taking back the referendum was that Antonis Samaras had finally said he would support the agreement reached at the European Council – something creditors had long demanded. The level of frustration at the European People's Party, the umbrella organisation of EU conservatives, with the populist stance of Samaras had been running high for some time already. Barroso had also leaned on him heavily, as had others, Merkel chiefly amongst them. Samaras understood that backing the agreement was the only way to stop the referendum, which would have been catastrophic for him.

Was the referendum really such a bad idea? Papandreou's reasoning was simple: all the opposition parties (and half of PASOK) were pretending Greece could have its cake and eat it; that it was possible to stay in the euro but still reject the agreement and the sacrifices it entailed. This view had poisoned the debate in Greece and made it impossible to go on. So he was calling the opposition's bluff.

It would have worked. Papandreou would have won the referendum if he had been allowed to have it, no matter how the question was phrased. Both PASOK and ND would have backed a yes vote. People would have realized the country's European destiny was at stake, and voted accordingly. The result would have obliterated the pro- and anti-bailout division in society and in politics, and we would perhaps have avoided three more elections, as well as the third bailout accepted by a left-wing government four years later. It would have given Papandreou a massive mandate and a fresh start. And it was for precisely these reasons that everyone else in Greece opposed it.

Papandreou's mistake was not in the conception; it was in the execution. Leaving Eurozone leaders in the dark effectively killed the referendum idea.

Once Papandreou went back on the referendum, the door opened for a coalition government, and he would have to go. Prior to a motion of confidence scheduled for November 6th, a number of PASOK MPs made it clear they would only vote for the government on the understanding that the prime minister would immediately resign and give way to a national unity government. Indeed, as they arrived at parliament for the debate, a considerable number of PASOK MPs called for the prime minister to step down. Almost all of them belonged to the faction within PASOK that was close to Venizelos.

Papandreou spoke just before the roll call. He talked of the unjust criticism he had received in the last two years ("Was I the one who doubled the debt?", "Was I the one who left behind a 36 billion deficit?") and of the huge damage PASOK had sustained ("I have been picking up the pieces these last 24 months"). He talked of the tough choices he had been forced to make, and of the pain and anger Greek citizens felt. Of the alternative that we did not live through – and whose horrific nature we could therefore not fathom. Of the folly of "heroic and easy solutions" that would have sent Greece into the abyss. Of the need for the entire political system to accept responsibility.

He admitted that he had been taken aback by the opposition to the summit decisions. He defended the need for people to have their say in a referendum ("why is the opposition so afraid of it?"). He welcomed Samaras' willingness to support the agreement, and repeated that he was not clinging to his job ("the country is bigger than any of us"). All he wanted was to protect the effort of the last two years. He would work for a new government with broad support – with someone else at the helm.

It was a dignified, emotional and courageous speech. He won the vote, with 153 MPs supporting the government. But everyone understood it was a Pyrrhic victory.

The next days were a constant back and forth of party leaders to the Presidential palace. Samaras and Papandreou agreed that a new government would be formed. Its mission would be to lead the country to elections, after implementing the October summit decisions. Samaras insisted that the prime minister resign immediately; he wanted to parade his head and claim victory. Papandreou retorted that he would only do so after they had agreed on his replacement.

A quest got underway for the person to lead the coalition

government. Lucas Papademos, who had completed his ECB deputy governor term, quickly emerged as an obvious choice, both in Athens and in European capitals. He commanded the expertise and Europe's trust – both crucial in these critical moments. Papandreou proposed him. Samaras rejected him – "he is a banker" was the reason.

There followed a few tortuous days where names would be tossed into the arena, discussed, leaked to the press, then withdrawn. One was Nikiforos Diamantouros, recently retired as European ombudsman, another Greek who had international recognition, if not the economic background of Papademos. The names of the current and a previous Parliament speaker were also discussed. Neither had the international exposure required at this specific juncture.

When Papandreou convened his last cabinet meeting on Tuesday, four days after the vote of confidence, everyone was still in the dark. Discussions on a new prime minister were not getting anywhere. Venizelos informed everyone Eurogroup required five signatures on the programme: in addition to the finance minister and the Bank of Greece governor, the new prime minister and the leaders of PASOK and ND would have to put their names to the document. Towards the end of the meeting, Papandreou asked for our resignations.

It was the end of an era.

On Wednesday, after having explored other options, Papandreou phoned his ministers to say that he was going to formally propose Papademos. Everyone agreed apart from Venizelos; he seemed to think Papademos was beholden to the ECB. More likely, he harboured hopes that he would end up getting the nod himself. There were more calls, and an hour later the finance minister withdrew his objection. Papandreou informed Samaras and the president. This time, Samaras acquiesced. George Karatzaferis, the leader of the right-wing party LAOS, then joined Papandreou and Samaras in pledging to support Papademos and his new three-party government.

Lucas Papademos was sworn in as prime minister on November 11th. He would head an uneasy cohabitation of PASOK, New Democracy and LAOS in a "transition" government tasked with finalizing the debt restructuring exercise; and the country would take its first steps towards learning how to operate with coalition politics.

It would prove more difficult than anyone thought.

Chapter 21

THE HAIRCUT

Barely a week after Lucas Papademos was sworn in as prime minister in Athens, Mario Monti was nominated to head a caretaker technocratic government in Italy. A week after that, the centre-right People's Party in Spain defeated the socialists in national elections, bringing Mariano Rajoy to power. But this change of guard did not defuse the crisis. By the end of November, Spanish and Italian bonds had reached unprecedented levels. Italian short-term risk was up, with 2-year bonds now yielding more than 10-year bonds (for which investors were asking an unsustainable 7%). And the yield on 10-year Greek bonds had surpassed 30%.

The markets were reacting violently to the failure, yet again, to build an effective firewall. This was no longer about Greece. It was about Spain and Italy, whose debt pile simply made them too big to fail. In Cannes, Obama and Sarkozy had tried to convince Merkel to increase the money available. The US had come up with the idea of creating a big bazooka by increasing "Special Drawing Rights" (SDRs), a form of currency created in 1969 as the IMF's unit of account. It would now be used in a more flexible way to multiply the firing power of existing bailout funds. But Chancellor Merkel could not be swayed: the Bundesbank had vetoed the idea.

With nothing new to soothe the markets, the saga would not yet come to an end.

In Athens Prime Minister Papademos held his first cabinet meeting. He had kept on most PASOK ministers, including Venizelos in finance, and I still had my energy and environment portfolio; and he had added a few people from New Democracy and LAOS in ministerial posts away from the heat of Troika negotiations. This was by design; the leaders of ND and LAOS had opted for lukewarm support – they wanted to be both government and opposition.

Papademos was in a tricky position. He was a technocrat prime minister, whose job depended on the support of the three party leaders. His main job was to oversee the implementation of the Eurozone decision mandating a 50% haircut in privately held Greek bonds. But before that, the new government had to legislate the 2012 budget and negotiate the new bailout – not easy tasks.

The budget passed on December 6th with the support of all three parties backing the government, by 258 votes out of 300, a record. I was envious; my two budgets – with equal, if not less, austerity – had been bitterly opposed by New Democracy in blind opposition and denial of its responsibility for the mess and of what needed to happen to sort it out.

As a non-parliamentarian minister since 2009, I never got to vote on my own budgets. During the 2012 budget debate, I was a continent away, at the UN Summit on Climate Change in Durban, South Africa. I was also on a mission: to limit the impact the world embargo on Iran had on Greece's energy needs.

Before the crisis, Greek oil refining companies could buy crude oil on the international markets using open credit lines issued by international banks. Once the crisis hit, those credit lines closed. As importing oil then necessitated cash payment up front, Greek companies had to switch to the only supplier that still accepted Greek credit – Iran. In 2011, oil imports from Iran represented more than two-thirds of the total.

With the embargo in place, this avenue closed and we now faced an energy shortage. I raised alarms at the EU and with US officials. They were sympathetic, but nobody offered a solution. With no cash and time running out, I made the case to the Saudi oil minister of Greece buying from his country on credit, while Papademos spoke to the Saudi king on the phone. We did not get very far and, in the months that followed, we came very close to running out of oil reserves.

With the budget approved, negotiation with the Troika on the new programme started in January. This time, there were three coalition partners on the Greek side, with one – New Democracy – desperate to prove it could negotiate a better deal. The talks advanced with difficulty, especially in politically explosive areas such as labour market reforms, and almost fell apart over €325 million, the fiscal gap that required additional cuts, which Samaras was blocking. Agreement was finally reached on February 9th, but for some cabinet members it was too much. Two PASOK ministers and the four ministers from the LAOS party resigned.

The agreement passed in parliament with 199 votes, easily surpassing the 151 votes required, but with many of the "no" votes coming from the government majority. Over 40 MPs from ND and PASOK did not support the bill; they were promptly expelled from their respective parliamentary groups. It was a sizeable rebellion. Clearly, the coalition did not seem to have a bright and long future ahead.

Since coming to power in 2009, PASOK MPs had to explain to their constituents that spending cuts and tax hikes were necessary. In ND, a party with populist rather than reformist instincts, MPs now had to explain the about-face from the rhetoric of Samaras against the first bailout. Several could not take it, voted "no" and were summarily expelled.

Following the vote, Eurogroup gave final approval on February 21st. Unusually, the finance ministers' meeting was attended by the Greek prime minister, with Venizelos clearly unhappy at having a chaperone. The presence of Papademos was meant to reassure the Eurozone ministers of the Greek government's commitment to the programme.

During the meeting, the IMF noted that the debt trajectory had deteriorated since October and asked for an even deeper haircut; so, after negotiations with the bankers, the haircut was increased from the 50% agreed in October to 53.5%. In addition, the Eurogroup decided to lower interest rates on Greek loans retroactively, and agreed that any ECB and central bank profits from their holdings of Greek debt should be passed back to Greece.

The creditors had learned their lesson; the refusal of the opposition to back the first bailout had fanned the flames of populism and thwarted implementation. So they asked for letters from the prime minister and the leaders of both main political parties in support of the new agreement, "beyond the forthcoming general elections".

Following the €110 billion agreed in 2010, Greece now had its second mega-loan – this time €130 billion – and a new 3-year programme to finish the job started under the first one. From 2010, we had already received €73 billion; so we had about €167 billion to look forward to. But the Eurogroup made it clear that the money would be "subject to a successful PSI operation". No haircut, no money.

On February 23rd, the Greek parliament voted through legislation allowing the PSI to take place and, one day later, the Greek authorities launched a debt exchange offer for bonds with a total outstanding face value of approximately €206 billion.

Bonds held by the ECB and central banks were explicitly excluded from the offer; only private investors would take a hit. The Eurogroup also vetoed the intention of the Greek government to exclude small Greek private bondholders from the haircut. This would prove to be embarrassing for the government. Government bonds had traditionally been considered a safe, risk-free refuge for small investors, who were now also forced to exchange their bonds and suffer a haircut.

When exchanging existing bonds, bondholders would receive new bonds with a face value equal to 31.5% of the amount exchanged, as well as EFSF notes maturing within two years for 15% of the face value of debt exchanged. They would also receive a bonus from an upswing: an additional 1% in GDP-linked securities if growth exceeded specified targets.

Total: 47.5% of the original value. The new bonds would mature in 30 years, and pay an annual 2% coupon, rising in steps to 4.3% after 2021.

The success of "voluntary" participation in such an exercise lies in two elements: the credible threat that, if bondholders do not offer their bonds in exchange, they stand to lose even more; and large participation, which reduces the debt burden so that the risk of non payment down the road disappears or considerably diminishes.

To get bondholders to play ball, the Greek government used a carrot and a stick. The carrot was to set the new bonds in the framework of similar securities in other countries; they would be governed by English law and contain standard clauses. The switch from Greek to English law caused an outcry in parliament. But who in their right mind would exchange Greek-law bonds for new bonds under the same legal jurisdiction and run the risk of further restructuring down the road?

The stick was the law on collective action clauses (CACs). In the acronym soup of financial markets, CACs are provisions whereby bondholders' qualified majority decisions bind all bondholders. The old bonds under Greek law did not have such provisions, and this made it difficult to assemble the necessary critical mass for the exchange. Many investors would instead decide to hold on to their bonds, hoping that with everyone else exchanging, Greek debt would become less risky, and they would get paid in full. Hence parliament voted on February 23rd "retroactive CACs", i.e. to insert such provisions *ex post* in order to ensure there would be no holdouts.

Long before the exchange was executed, rating agencies had decided that the debt restructuring operation represented some sort of "default" by the country, albeit temporary. Once Greece retroactively inserted CACs, Standard & Poor's cut its credit rating to "selective default". Fitch followed by downgrading Greek bonds to "restricted default", and Moody's considered Greece to have defaulted.

Next, credit default Swaps were triggered. The International Swaps and Derivatives Association (ISDA) decided that Greece invoking CACs in order to force bondholders to accept the offer in effect constituted "a restructuring credit event". This meant insurance taken against such an event – which is what credit default swaps are – would have to be paid. Approximately €2 billion were paid to insurance buyers.

But would they come? Would enough bond holders participate in the exchange? Of all eligible bonds, 90% were under Greek law; once CACs were activated, all were compelled to exchange their bonds. But the Eurogroup set a 95% participation threshold for the exchange. It was an informal rule, not in any official document, but the understanding was that below that percentage all bets were off. To get to that number, a significant part of bonds issued under English law would also need to be offered for exchange.

This extremely high threshold raised concerns on the Greek side that the Eurogroup in effect wanted the exchange to fail. If it did, a plan B was under preparation, which included bank closures and provisions for the first ever default of a Eurozone country. The door to a Grexit would be wide open.

The exchange offer book at the Greek Public Debt Management Agency closed on March 9th. Officials were optimistic but, with so much at stake, everyone was nervous. As the offers started coming in, they were automatically tallied. When the magic 95% number showed on the screen, the Greek side immediately asked for a Euro Working Group teleconference and announced to the still dubious Eurozone finance ministry officials: "mission accomplished".

When all was said and done, over 96% of eligible bonds had participated in the exchange, with holdouts representing only €6 billion. This meant about €200 billion of debt would be slashed by more than half. Seen in net present value terms, i.e. taking into account the fact that a debt payable in, say, ten years is worth much less than the same debt payable next year, the gain was almost 80%.

So there it was: the Eurozone had its first haircut of privately-held debt. It was a show-stopper: the largest "voluntary" sovereign debt haircut in history, with over €205 billion debt involved, of which over €100 billion disappeared into thin air. In total it involved 130 bonds, with 5 governing laws, four currencies, more than 40 countries and 25 parties or institutions.

But this debt restructuring extravaganza still did not solve the problem.

It is true that the debt restructuring itself was uneventful. The EU and the IMF had come to the conclusion that even a large haircut now posed no systemic risk; few foreign banks' holdings of Greek government bonds were worth even 10% of their capital. In addition, by buying CDSs most banks had shifted their risk elsewhere – on to insurers, who were not as important to the financial system as a whole.

That was not the case with Greek banks. They were still heavily loaded with Greek government bonds, about €40 billion worth. Successive governments had arm-twisted them to buy large chunks of them. Between 2010 and 2012, the Greek banks had not sold bonds off as many European banks had done. So, come haircut time, they were effectively wiped out, and the new bailout had to include €40 billion earmarked for recapitalizing them. This money added to the debt; it meant the net haircut was not as large as the initial numbers suggested.

The markets took debt restructuring in their stride. It did not create the systemic tsunami that Jean-Claude Trichet's ECB had feared. The "selective default" credit rating was soon removed and there was no triggering of default clauses elsewhere in the system. Spreads on 10-year Greek bonds collapsed from a stratospheric 36% before the exchange to 18% after that. But they were still at dizzying heights.

Then there was the issue of how to deal with holdouts. To avoid long-term legal battles and despite some incendiary proposals in the Eurogroup to refuse payment, it was decided they would be paid in full when they matured. As Lee Buccheit had put it, "let's not bring Argentina to the heart of Europe".

At the same time, the PSI did little to calm fears in the rest of the Eurozone. The next few months were turbulent, with the focus on Italy and especially Spain. One after the other credit rating agencies downgraded Spanish bonds and, in June, the Eurogroup earmarked a €100 billion bailout package for Spanish banks, with the EU finally endorsing the concept of a banking union.

Also during this period, a more interventionist "new ECB" began to make its mark. It announced additional measures to support Eurozone banks, including increased collateral availability for banks by enlarging the pool of eligible assets, and would conduct two long-term refinancing operations (LTRO) to provide liquidity. The first took place just before end of 2011, with a take-up of €500 billion by 523 banks.

In Athens PM Papademos was diligently running his "special purpose" government, whose *raison d'être* was to take the decisions relating to the new programme and execute the PSI. Many came to believe that Greece could emulate Italy by making progress under a technocratic government with a wider mandate and no defined time limitation.

Not a chance. As soon as the debt exchange was complete and the programme was formally approved by the Eurogroup on March 14th, ND leader Antonis Samaras made it clear the government's days were numbered ("we expelled Papandreou; next we expel PASOK" was how he put it in a speech to party faithful), and the two major parties started jockeying for position in view of forthcoming elections.

George Papandreou resigned as president of PASOK in March – barely 30 months after he had led his party to victory, capturing 44% of the vote. History had accelerated since 2010 and was gobbling down prime ministers – he was the first of a series to follow. He was succeeded by Evangelos Venizelos, who finally got his 2007 wish to become the leader of PASOK. Venizelos resigned from the government and was replaced as finance minister by Philippos Sachinidis, who had previously served in the deputy minister post.

While many were urging him to soldier on, Papademos knew he could not do so without the support of the two largest parties. Samaras was in a hurry to become prime minister; it was time for the caretaker to throw in the towel. On 11th April Papademos asked the President to dissolve parliament and call elections; they were scheduled for May 6th.

For me it was time to run for a seat in parliament again. If I wanted to go on in politics, I needed to reclaim a parliamentary seat. Going back to the Kozani prefecture, which I had represented between 2007 and 2009, was not an option. Having left in 2007 to become an MEP, it was very difficult to come back. So I asked my party to run in the prefecture of Attica, in the vicinity of Athens.

Before the party lists were announced, I was summoned to the office of Venizelos. He asked me not to run. I was incredulous. I told him that if he believed I was a liability for the party, then all he had to do was exclude me from the lists. But it would have to be his decision – I would not withdraw. Withdrawing would be as if I believed that what we had done collectively and what I had done personally as finance minister were wrong.

Venizelos did not exclude me from the party lists. But I soon understood his attitude at that meeting when I saw the election campaign that PASOK ran. We were not defending our record; we were repudiating it. For the new PASOK leadership, the entire 2009-2011 Papandreou period was a mistake. People like me, who so clearly symbolized the first Papandreou government, needed to be removed from the picture.

More generally, in the election, PASOK candidates were facing an extremely hostile political environment, and were often openly prevented from campaigning. As I crisscrossed the vast Attica prefecture, which stretched from the affluent northern suburbs to the depressed western districts with their record unemployment, I found it increasingly difficult to reach people.

Our supporters were dispirited and terrorized by the thugs of neo-Nazi Golden Dawn on the right and SYRIZA fanatics on the left; and my security detail was increasingly unwilling to let me to go into areas they felt were not safe. After all, I was the man who had signed the first bailout – I had committed the original sin.

Election day in Greece coincided with Francois Hollande's election as president of France. In the streets of Paris, French socialists were jubilant; in Athens, there was nothing to celebrate. We had been crushed, and the old political system had imploded.

New Democracy was first, but its 19% of the popular vote was the lowest percentage it had ever achieved. Even when losing to PASOK in 2009, ND had still reached 35%. Some of its vote had gone to the Independent Greeks, a right-wing splinter party whose populist rhetoric helped them capture 10% on their first attempt. On the extreme right there was a very worrying result: the neo–Nazis of Golden Dawn, invisible in 2009 with 0.3% of the vote, had now reached an incredible 7%.

The real shocker was SYRIZA: from barely getting into parliament in 2009 with a little over 4%, this left-wing coalition had risen to second place, with 17% of the vote – ahead of PASOK. It had successfully managed to forge the anger on the street into votes. Next to it was its own splinter party, the Democratic Left (DIMAR), which gained a respectable 6%.

For PASOK the election was a disaster. Polling 13% meant it had lost more than 70% of its vote in under two years. We were punished for the people's suffering and for our tough decisions during the crisis. Fair enough. But our third place, below SYRIZA, was a direct result of not defending our record. We could have clinched second place if only we had defended what we had done in office. And if, after being so thoroughly vilified, PASOK had still managed to finish second, SYRIZA would not have emerged as the main alternative to New Democracy.

Our poor third place also cost me a parliamentary seat. In 2009, PASOK had elected six MPs in the Attica Prefecture.

This time around, we elected one. I came third on the list of PASOK candidates; had the party done reasonably well nationwide, I would have been elected. Nevertheless, given the public abuse and criticism I had suffered throughout the period, I was reasonably satisfied even with this ultimately unsuccessful personal result.

On election night, PASOK candidates were asked by the party leadership not to appear on the customary post mortem TV discussion panels; instead we were summoned to party HQ. Venizelos was trying to nip in the bud any challenge to his leadership after the disastrous result.

I arrived after 10 pm, with memories of election night in 2009 playing in my head. The street was almost deserted; a lone PASOK supporter forlornly waved a flag, desperate for reassurance that not all was lost. Inside there was an eerie silence; everyone was shell-shocked. I felt unwelcome; lots of sidelong glances at me and other prominent ministers from the Papandreou government. It was obvious who the new PASOK leadership was going to hold responsible for the result.

Even with the 50-seat bonus awarded to the first party under electoral law, New Democracy could not form a government alone. It needed allies – and not one, but two. PASOK and DIMAR were the obvious choices. In the ensuing talks, DIMAR refused to join a coalition. The president of the republic had no choice but to dissolve the newly elected parliament. He swore in a caretaker government under Council of State President Panagiotis Pikrammenos and called repeat elections for June 17th.

Antonis Samaras then managed a seemingly impossible political feat. From being down and out, the man under whose leadership New Democracy had sunk to its lowest ever vote, he deftly transformed the election result into an "us or them" dilemma. With SYRIZA second, he managed to portray the repeat elections as a simple choice: either ND would gain power or a SYRIZA win would lead to chaos, default and Grexit.

It worked because it reflected reality. Spreads of 10-year bonds before the June elections had reached 30%. The Athens stock market fell to a historic low, while uncertainty led to massive deposit withdrawals. Since the crisis started, liquidity had dropped by over €70 billion, one-third of the total. Between the two elections, more than €1 billion was removed daily, €13 billion in the last week alone.

The Pikrammenos caretaker government struggled to keep the country afloat. In his first – and only – European Council meeting, the urbane former judge was a reassuring presence. But in bilateral meetings with EU leaders, the urgency of the situation was impressed on him. Greece needed to respect its obligations and continue implementing the programme; "*pacta sunt servanda*" ("agreements must be honoured") was the expression he heard many times from Chancellor Merkel.

Meanwhile, the governor of the Bank of Greece was busy organizing for planeloads of emergency bank notes from abroad in order to keep the ATMs full and the banks open. And together with George Zanias, who had been appointed caretaker finance minister, they were busy preparing emergency decrees for closing the banks in case the election result led to a fully-fledged bank run.

Greeks went to the polls for the second time in two months with the whole world holding its breath, and the entire EU leadership willing Samaras to win. The preference was plain to see, often too much so. A few days before the election, Pikrammenos had to convince a well-meaning van Rompuy that an open letter to Greeks urging them to stay in the Eurozone could backfire.

This time, New Democracy jumped ten points to a shade under 30%. The in or out of the euro dilemma had worked. In the second election ND took votes from the smaller parties. It was still a worse percentage than the one with which they lost the 2009 elections, but it was good enough. SYRIZA had also picked up ten points since May, but did not succeed in producing the upset.

The storming of the Bastille would have to wait for another day.

PASOK and DIMAR were again the only possible coalition allies. This time, both agreed to support a government under Antonis Samaras. In a move at odds with the standard practice for the formation of coalition governments in Europe, they stopped short of participating in the cabinet and instead proposed non-party figures to take over certain cabinet portfolios.

On the 21st of June, Antonis Samaras was sworn in as prime minister, less than three years after New Democracy had been roundly defeated by Papandreou's PASOK. After having derailed the economy and brought Greece to the brink of disaster, they were again in power, albeit in a coalition.

The arsonists were back in charge of the fire station.

Chapter 22

NO-ONE IS SINLESS

In the summer of 2012, Europe turned a corner. And it only took one sentence.

"The ECB is ready to do whatever it takes to preserve the euro." Two sentences, actually. "And believe me, it will be enough."

These make-my-day comments at the end of July by Mario Draghi set off a huge global market rally and sent spreads tumbling. They convinced markets the ECB would use all the tools at its disposal to defend the integrity of the currency.

Was it really so simple? Would a statement like this made by the ECB one or two years earlier have stopped the crisis in its tracks and avoided all the trouble we went through? Not quite. After all, successive Eurogroups and summits had used the "whatever it takes" statement. It had not impressed the markets.

What made the difference this time was that the statement came at the end of a long period in which both Eurozone countries and the ECB had proved – step by step – that they had the political will as well as the tools to deal with the situation. Draghi's words came after the bailouts of Greece, Portugal, and Ireland, and agreements to lend money to Spain and Cyprus, as well as after the creation of the EFSF and the ESM.

They were uttered by a new more interventionist ECB chief, and were followed up by real firepower: the outright monetary transactions (OMT) programme. Under OMT, the ECB could buy government bonds from countries under duress, as long as they had requested help from the EFSF/ESM and were in a programme.

Crucially, Draghi's phrases also came after an important decision by European leaders on June 29th to break the vicious circle between banks and governments. They decided to move ahead with the unification of the European banking sector under a single supervisory body (the Single Supervisory Mechanism or SSM) and to give the new European Stability Mechanism the power to recapitalize banks directly.

Let us not forget that the European crisis did not begin in Greece in late 2009. The root of the problem was the exposure of European banks to toxic US banking products. As the 2008 US subprime mortgage crisis spread to Europe, the resulting banking crisis mutated into an economic and fiscal crisis. Economies went into recession, governments helped exposed banks and deficits increased. In turn this fed back into the banking sector as banks were weakened by exposure to government debt.

In this highly destabilised environment, in 2008 Ireland came close to being the spark that ignited the flames. Instead it was Greece a year later. Its large internal and external imbalances, coupled with the misreporting of fiscal data, proved to be the catalyst, souring market sentiment towards sovereign debt in general. Capital flight from south to the north exacerbated the crisis. Policymakers eventually realized they needed to address the banks' problems together with fiscal issues.

Meanwhile, in Athens the new prime minister decided it was better to have someone else bear the political cost and appointed as finance minister Yannis Stournaras, a technocrat from the centre-left rather than a politician from his party. Despite their ideological differences, Stournaras found a modus vivendi with Antonis Samaras, who by now had realized that the country's survival – and his own as prime minister – rested on implementing faithfully what he previously so vehemently denounced.

Throughout this period, a Greek prime minister's most important relationship has been with the German chancellor. Samaras knew this well, and was aware also that he had some fence mending to do: over the past two years he had made enemies at the European People's Party. Angela Merkel had been particularly vocal in her criticism.

So it was fitting that he chose to give his new credentials in Berlin. At the press conference after his first meeting as prime minister with the chancellor in late August, he was asked by a German journalist whether he bore some responsibility for the situation Greece was in after the last two years. His answer: "no-one is sinless."

It was an apology of sorts for the damage done. He had already prepared the ground by admitting a few months earlier in a Wall Street Journal article that the 2009 deficit bequeathed by New Democracy was indeed over 15%, and not lower, as he had tried to maintain since the true numbers were revealed. Now he was telling the world he had been wrong about opposing the bailout as well.

But all this came too late. The populist genie was out of the bottle and it could not be put back in. It would manifest itself in the birth of a new populist party of the right, in the explosion of the vote for neo-Nazi Golden Dawn, and was also to be seen in the eventual election victory of the far left SYRIZA two years later.

Following the Berlin visit and the U-turn by Samaras, relations with Germany improved quickly, culminating in a visit to Athens by Angela Merkel in October. It was a show of support in a city under draconian security, though that did not stop the chancellor seeing the "Stop the Fourth Reich" banners from her armoured limousine.

The improved relationship with Merkel was important for another reason: Greece seemed to have lost the confidence of the German finance minister. Wolfgang Schäuble's apparent change of stance towards Greece had already manifested itself in the basement bar of the Hotel Monopol in Wroclaw, in September 2011, when he suggested a "friendly exit" from the Eurozone to an astounded Venizelos.

To many analysts, Schäuble seemed to be flirting with the theory that allowing Greece to leave could serve as an example for the remaining euro members and create a stronger union. After all, history is full of currency unions that did not survive in their original shape. It is questionable whether he ever actually subscribed to this theory, but he certainly used the prevailing mood expertly as a negotiating tactic.

In a sense roles had been reversed. Back in 2010, it was Schäuble who persuaded a reluctant chancellor to accept the inevitable: a bailout for Greece. He convinced her to put aside her misgivings – which were partly on principle and partly with an eye on her electoral calendar – and agree to the first bailout, albeit on an *ultima ratio* basis and on punitive terms that would serve as a warning to others.

Fast forward a couple of years. Cautious politician that she is, Angela Merkel was now unwilling to countenance a Greek exit from the Eurozone. She would ask her advisors on the potential fallout from a Grexit and they would answer that they simply could not tell. Perhaps the markets had already priced a Grexit and contagion could be contained; but perhaps not, and then she would be the chancellor to preside over the disintegration of the euro. That was too high a risk for her to take.

In the end common sense politics prevailed. It is very different to argue that certain countries should never have been allowed into the Eurozone than to demand one should be kicked out. No-one could convincingly put a price tag on a Greek exit, let alone provide guarantees that more countries would not exit. The logic of "irreversibility" built-into the process of adopting the euro won the day.

The improved climate with creditors got a nod of approval at the October Eurozone summit. But soon there was trouble. In early November, the government brought to parliament the 2013-16 medium-term fiscal plan, which included new fiscal measures of €13.5 billion, of which over €9 billion for 2013. The bill squeezed through with just 153 votes, significantly less than the government's parliamentary majority.

Difficulties in Athens were soon compounded by problems

in Brussels. The Eurogroup was withholding payment of the latest loan tranche until the Greek government implemented all "prior actions" and until it itself resolved its differences with the IMF. The Fund insisted that the decision to postpone the 4.5% primary surplus target to 2016 had hurt debt sustainability, and that now more needed to be done about Greek debt.

After the 2013 Greek budget had passed in parliament, the Eurogroup held on November 27 eventually agreed to further reduce the interest rates of the official loans to Greece, defer interest payments by 10 years and extend debt maturities by 15 years. The Eurozone finance ministers also agreed to a debt buy-back programme to bring the debt to GDP ratio to 124% by 2020, while not excluding further debt relief by the official sector if all this did not prove enough to make debt sustainable. These decisions led to the disbursement in instalments of a large €49 billion loan tranche to Greece in December.

Once the buy-back programme was completed, we finally had a complete picture of how much the PSI and related operations had reduced the debt burden.

The February PSI had reduced the debt by €106 billion; with the debt buyback, it fell by another €21 billion, bringing the total reduction to €127 billion. But the net reduction was smaller; subtracting the €25 billion used to recapitalize Greek banks in 2012 – a direct consequence of the impact of the PSI on Greek banks – gave a net debt reduction of roughly €100 billion. Still a very large number, but not big enough to put to bed the discussion about Greek debt sustainability.

By the end of 2012, European leaders could look back and claim the worse was over. To cap it all, the year-end summit approved a blueprint prepared by Herman van Rompuy, with the title "Towards a genuine economic and monetary union". It included steps for stronger fiscal governance and for unifying the European banking system through common supervision, harmonised bank resolution and national deposit guarantee frameworks.

But there was still another roadblock ahead: Cyprus.

Compared to the other bailout cases, that of Cyprus could be considered insignificant – a mere one-tenth of Greece in terms of both population and size of economy. And yet, in a still unstable Europe, dealing with Cyprus was an important test-case for decision-making procedures and the new rules being put in place.

As a bailout case Cyprus was closer to Ireland than Greece. Its problem was a banking sector seven times larger than its GDP, and an economic model over-reliant on financial services and offshore accounts. The system came under strain as Cypriot banks became exposed to overleveraged local property companies, and came to breaking point with losses following the Greek debt restructuring, given the banks' large exposure to Greek sovereign debt.

Despite modest borrowing obligations, it became increasingly difficult to access markets. Successive credit rating downgrades and bond yields soaring to double digits led to an emergency loan from Russia in late 2011, and finally forced the government of communist President Dimitris Christofias to formally apply to the Eurogroup for financial assistance in June 2012.

But the Cypriot government delayed and procrastinated. Christofias preferred to let the Troika negotiations drag on and leave difficult decisions to his successor, conservative Nicos Anastasiadis, who was elected in February 2013. After a few weeks in office, the new president was called to deal with an ultimatum by the Eurozone and the ECB: the Cypriot government was asked to agree to a "bail in", that is, a deep haircut on bank deposits to top up the €10 billion bailout pledged by the EU and the IMF and fill an estimated €14 billion financing gap.

On March 16th, the Eurogroup, chaired by Jeroen Dijsselbloem, the Dutch finance minister, who had replaced Jean-Claude Juncker as president of the group, agreed to a Cypriot request that "insured depositors" with bank deposits below €100,000 also be included in the haircut, so as to reduce the losses to be imposed on higher deposits. The government believed it would thereby preserve the Cypriot financial model and Russian deposits in the island.

They were mistaken. But the Eurogroup should have known better and never have agreed to this; the decision breached an important tenet of trust in the European banking system, that of excluding insured deposits in any "bail in" scheme.

What followed was truly extraordinary. In a week rich in political drama, with people demonstrating on the streets of the capital Nicosia, the Cypriot parliament refused to approve the agreement reached by its president with the Eurogroup: no haircuts of bank deposits were acceptable. The Cypriot finance minister was packed off to Moscow to ask for another loan and came back empty-handed.

The Eurogroup reconvened a week later to deal with the situation – and to correct its mistake. The final decision on March 25th spared insured deposits, but was much more brutal. It involved closing Cyprus Popular Bank, the island's second largest bank, it imposed very heavy losses on uninsured depositors at the Bank of Cyprus, the largest bank, instituted capital controls, and led to a severe recession.

With this decision, the Eurozone entered uncharted territory. Rather than using the European Stability Mechanism to recapitalize banks, the Cypriot case tested a new "bail in" approach without thinking through the broader repercussions. In doing so, it showed how unstable decision-making in the Eurozone continued to be.

Markets seemed to shrug it off, but it had now become urgent to move from trial-and-error to a more systematic approach when dealing with failing banks. The framework was worked out by Ecofin in June. It was a decision which outlined burden-sharing amongst shareholders, bondholders and uninsured depositors in an eventual bank recapitalization; in effect, another step towards banking union in Europe.

For Greece, there was an important lesson from what

happened in Cyprus. The TINA adage – There Is No Alternative – was once more plainly evident for everyone to see. There was no money or shortcuts to be found in Russia, the Arab world, China or anywhere else. Solutions had to be worked out within the European framework and with the IMF, however imperfect that might be.

Above all, a government must always do everything possible to avoid the huge economic cost associated with capital controls and closing the banks. But many people's memories are short; some of the events in Cyprus in early 2013 would be repeated two years later in Greece by a freshly-elected government of the left.

In Athens, following the PSI, it was now urgent to recapitalize the banks. Greek banks had not participated in quasi Ponzi schemes with housing loans as had their counterparts in other countries. But they had two problems: many of their corporate loans were extended on the wrong kind of "know your client" basis (i.e. based on personal relationships rather than sound banking practices); and they were holding too much sovereign debt. They were hit once the economy soured after 2008; entered the danger zone once they started bleeding deposits in 2010; and were crippled by the PSI in 2012.

Deposit outflows were already monitored on a daily basis at the Finance Ministry since late 2009 – when we further extended the €28 billion government guarantees package started under the previous government in late 2008, as part of the Europe-wide response to the financial crisis. Meetings with bankers multiplied, and a Systemic Stability Council was formed to continuously assess the situation.

Once the May 2010 bailout was in place, €10 billion was earmarked for the banks and "parked" with the newly created Hellenic Financial Stability Fund. They were to be used – if needed – for recapitalizing the banks. They would soon be needed; and prove not to be enough. By end of 2010, Greek banks were funded exclusively by the ECB and government guarantees were increased by €25 billion.

The difficulties continued as foreign investors withdrew from Greece and Greek depositors also voted with their feet. Capital share increase efforts by banks did not stem the tide and restore confidence, and in mid-2011 government guarantees were increased further, now totalling €85 billion. The Troika kept pushing banks to gradually reduce reliance on the Eurosystem, but there could be no solution to the banking problem before the broader uncertainty lifted.

Once the PSI was completed in 2012, the losses for the six largest banks were so large that postponing decisions and half-measures would not work any more. Banks were asked to increase their capital adequacy ratios to 10% by June 2013.

Overall, between 2010 and mid-2012, over €100 billion were lost to the Greek banking system. This liquidity gap was plugged by an €86 billion increase in ECB borrowing – thereby avoiding violent deleveraging in the private sector. The bailout loans, together with Eurosystem lending to banks, bought the country time. But that time had now run out. For the banking system to be saved, consolidation and recapitalization with private capital participation had to be the order of the day.

The big bang in the Greek banking sector occurred after the twin elections of 2012. There had already been attempts at consolidation between some of the larger banks – National Bank of Greece (NBG) with Alpha in 2010, and Alpha with Eurobank in 2011. Both had failed; in the first case the egos of those involved got in the way, and in the second the Troika blocked the merger, fearing the new bank would be too big for its own or anyone else's good. Now the grand design involved consolidating the smaller banks into the larger ones, a process already started in 2011.

When the dust settled, there were four "systemic" banks standing: NBG, Alpha, Eurobank and Piraeus Bank; by absorbing several smaller banks, the latter had managed to rise from a weak fourth place to become the largest Greek bank. A fragmented banking sector had suddenly become one of the most concentrated; the four banks now accounted for over 90% of the market.

Next came recapitalization. The decision to recapitalize the systemic banks was taken in May 2012 and executed in the first half of 2013. The estimated bill was just over €40 billion, of which €27.5 billion was for the systemic banks (the remaining was to cover the losses of the smaller banks which had been absorbed – in the form of "bad banks"). By contributing €3 billion in three of the four (NBG, Alpha and Piraeus), private shareholders retained the right to manage them; the remaining was covered by the Hellenic Financial Stability Fund, which kept a say over strategic decisions. Eurobank did not attract the required private investment; it was recapitalized fully by the HFSF.

Stability in the banking system had been restored – until the next crisis, which would come earlier and be worse than expected.

Throughout the first half of 2013, there was progress in Greece. In February, the Eurogroup expressed its satisfaction and two months later the Troika completed its periodic programme review in Athens. The thumbs-up came just as Greece had several bits of good news: its first large privatization, with the sale of the state gaming monopoly OPAP to a Czech-led consortium; a repatriation of over €10 billion in deposits to Greek banks since mid-2012; and positive growth predicted for 2014.

And then, on June 19th, the government of Antonis Samaras decided to show its reformist zeal by suddenly shutting down the public broadcasting service, ERT.

The history of state broadcasting in Greece is chequered. Rather than a source of independent news and public service, it has for decades been beholden to the government in power and its communication requirements. Funded lavishly by a compulsory levy on electricity bills, with 3,000 staff (more than practically in all private broadcasters combined), excessive salaries and crony appointments, it was a clear example of waste of public funds and an obvious case for reform.

Since 2010, there had been some attempts to rein in expenditure and slim the organisation down, with limited success. Rather than continue down that difficult road, the government decided to shut ERT down altogether. And in doing so, Samaras was hoping to find 3,000 public sector layoffs that he had committed to in the negotiations with the troika.

It was a huge miscalculation. Samaras believed ERT's well-known excesses would produce a surge of support for the government that finally dared to take drastic action. It did the opposite. The empty screens of the state channels stunned the nation, and public sentiment rallied behind the fired journalists and staff. Abroad the government came up against the strong tradition of European public broadcasting. It was hard to make the distinction between ERT and the BBC.

Soon, things got worse. The sacked journalists started broadcasting illegally from the occupied ERT building, in a move reminiscent of illegal broadcasting during the dictatorship in the 1970s. DIMAR, which had been looking for a way to leave the governing coalition, found in ERT the perfect excuse and withdrew its support. PASOK came to Samaras' rescue; a few days later he reshuffled the government, giving a number of cabinet posts to PASOK MPs, and appointed Venizelos minister of foreign affairs and deputy prime minister.

A three-party coalition spanning the political spectrum from right to moderate left had now become a coalition between two parties that had both signed bailouts. Apart from a reduced (though still comfortable) parliamentary majority, the reshuffle had a broader significance. It completely polarized the debate: on the one hand, were the two pro-bailout parties, ND and PASOK; and, on the other, all the other parties, with SYRIZA as the standard-bearer of the anti-bailout campaign.

The next chapter of the ERT saga was written in November when, in a pre-dawn raid, police stormed the occupied building and shut down its clandestine broadcasting. That solved one problem; but only a year after election, the hourglass of the

GAME OVER

Samaras government was emptying fast. I had lived through a similar period during our own tenure – the signs were unmistakable.

As the political climate deteriorated, the government tried to regain public support by avoiding its obligations under the programme. The autumn 2013 review was suspended twice, with the November Eurogroup noting that Greece needed to "urgently deliver" on missed milestones, to outline measures to close the fiscal gap in 2014 and 2015, and to proceed faster with structural reforms and privatizations. "The job is not done", were the words of the Eurogroup president.

What was even more striking was the contrast between this admonishment of Greece and the Eurogroup's warm words for other programme countries.

Spain's financial sector programme was almost complete and the country was due to exit from it in January 2014. In Ireland's case, the government had decided for a "clean exit" without successor financial assistance. Both were proof that adjustment programmes work, "provided there is strong ownership and genuine commitment to reforms", as the Eurogroup noted. In sharp contrast there were already voices suggesting Greece might need additional help at the end of its second programme.

On December 15th, Ireland officially exited its adjustment programme. It had at the time a cash buffer of more than €20 billion, covering more than the sovereign's gross funding need in 2014, so there was no immediate need to access international markets. The Irish programme had lasted three years.

A tale of two countries: Greece's first €110 billion bailout was in May 2010; Ireland got its €85 billion bailout six months later, in December. In March 2012, Greece got a second bailout, this time of €130 billion. Ireland exited its programme in December 2013. Greece was due to exit its second programme in February 2016, with the last IMF loan disbursement.

We had no idea at that point how much longer that would actually take.

Chapter 23

THE "SUCCESS STORY"

The top-floor restaurant at the Grande Bretagne, Athens' most prestigious hotel, was full. It was eight in the morning on a bright winter's day, with a fine view over the rooftops to the Acropolis. Every table was occupied with smartly dressed men – and a few women – speaking English. These were all money people, representing US and European funds, back in Athens after a very long time.

Good times seemed to be here again.

The atmosphere in the room was representative of the financial community's attitude towards Greece in early 2014. Investors were happy that a European-minded coalition government was pursuing the programme. Many were willing to invest as long as the price was right – but without committing for too long and with an eye on the door. We still had a way to go to attract investors who would come to stay.

The new vibe was very much encouraged by the government. The diary of Finance Minister Stournaras was full of meetings with prospective investors; the most notable of them also secured one-on-one meetings with Prime Minister Samaras, who was taking a hands-on approach to attracting international investors. The government was busy building the "success story" of a turnaround of the Greek economy.

That was not completely without merit. By the end of 2013, Greece had attained that holy grail of public finances, a primary surplus. Excluding interest payments, the state was finally managing to spend less than it brought in as revenues. Official figures released in April 2014 would show a 0.8% of GDP primary budget surplus for 2013. Given that the 2009 starting point was a primary deficit of over 10%, this represented a massive correction. Almost all of it took place in 2010 and 2011 under PASOK governments, but that did not stop Samaras claiming credit.

The economy was also showing signs of recovery. After six years of recession, and a cumulative loss of more than a quarter of the nation's output since 2008, GDP was predicted to start expanding in 2014. An astute observer could see the change in the increased numbers of cars circulating in the streets and people in restaurants. Foreign journalists were quick to point that out in their reporting – it was a nice change from the images of burning trashcans that had long dominated international news.

Even unemployment was expected to start falling, though few people of the one-quarter of the population without a job would feel the one or two percentage drop in the jobless rate foreseen for 2014. In the banks, deposits had stabilized and at the end of 2013 were even slightly up; Greek banks had also started to regain access to the international interbank market.

This optimistic feeling was evident as the government hosted the entire European Commission in Athens in January 2014 for the official start of the Greek presidency of the EU. One after another, European Commissioners paraded in front of cameras to express their satisfaction at the progress the country had made.

The "feel-good" factor however was not necessarily shared by Greek society. True, there were fewer demonstrations on the streets, no doubt partly because, since 2012, SYRIZA had shifted its tactics from street protests to parliamentary opposition; it was now, after all, the largest opposition party and government-in-waiting. But beneath the surface there was a sense of fatigue, even resignation. Greeks were muted in their reactions, by no means convinced that the path followed was the right one.

At this point the government overreached, setting the bar too high. With Spain already out of the assistance programme and Portugal about to follow, Samaras told the German newspaper Bild that Greece would not require a third assistance package. And in March, he announced that the government would distribute part of the 2013 primary surplus as a "social dividend". The message was clear: no more Troika; austerity is over; we are back to business as usual.

On April 10ᵗʰ 2014, an important milestone was reached. The Greek sovereign was back in international markets, issuing a bond to borrow €3 billion over 5 years with a yield a little under 5%. This foray was almost four years to the day since the last time in April 2010, and three years behind schedule; in the original May 2010 bailout a partial return to markets was planned for 2012. But the significance was unmistakable: Greece was making one of the fastest returns to markets after a debt restructuring; it could once again access private capital.

It was the kind of news Samaras needed as he was preparing for the June European Parliament elections.

What neither he nor the country needed was the dawn explosion of a terrorist bomb outside the Bank of Greece in downtown Athens. The booby-trapped car blast damaged offices and shattered windows; fortunately there were no casualties. In a country with unfinished business with its recent terrorist past, the explosion struck a raw nerve – and raised security concerns as it occurred one day before Angela Merkel was due to visit Athens for the second time.

However, the chancellor's lightning visit occurred without a hitch. She arrived at lunchtime, saw representatives of Greek start-ups to turn the spotlight on growth, and met with Samaras at the Maximou mansion. In their joint press conference, Merkel congratulated Greece on returning to the markets and addressed unemployed Greeks, promising them a better future once adjustment was complete.

A dinner followed in a traditional *taverna* next to the Acropolis, and the chancellor was on her plane back to Berlin by 10pm. The whole affair had only lasted a few hours, but these were sufficient for her to deliver the message: the German government, and Europe as a whole, trusted Antonis Samaras to get the job done.

The reason for all this support was on that very day speaking at an event in Brussels. Alexis Tsipras, the 40-year old leader of SYRIZA, was busy transforming himself from president of a loose federation of leftist factions in Greece to international icon for change in Europe.

As the chosen candidate of the European left for the job of commission president and leader of the left's campaign in the European Parliament elections, he had a new legitimacy and a whole European stage at his disposal. He used it well: his awkward "Go back, Madame Merkel" phrase, aimed in the recent past at a bailout-weary and angry Greek audience, was now being transformed into an anti-austerity narrative echoing all over Europe to a much larger audience than he had ever hoped to reach.

A new star was being born.

Greece had triple elections in June 2014. Whereas the rest of Europe voted to elect representatives for the European Parliament, we also elected mayors and regional presidents. This made for a more complicated scene, in which broader political messages were intertwined with local issues, personalities and politics.

Samaras entered the elections with a clutch of good news: the primary surplus, return to international markets, clear European support. Even Portugal's exit from its own programme without a safety net in May allowed him to spin his narrative that Greece was turning the corner, that the country would soon leave the bailout behind it and that Samaras was the only one who could be trusted to pursue this road.

During the campaign, Samaras decided to outdo SYRIZA in anti-bailout rhetoric. With Tsipras proclaiming that, once in power, he would "rip up the memorandum, and it will be in broad daylight", the PM upped the ante in his closing campaign speech, telling supporters, "I rip up the memorandum every day, minute by minute, page by page". He had failed to recognize a glaring contradiction: it was impossible to sell a "success story" of exiting the crisis based on implementing the memorandum, while at the same time engaging in a contest on who will rip it up best.

The June elections produced the result most analysts were expecting. In the vote for the European Parliament, New Democracy finished four points behind SYRIZA. Despite the fact that most of its parliamentary group was in jail, Golden Dawn shocked the Greek political system by coming third. PASOK continued its decline with a paltry 8% of the vote. It was followed by To Potami (The River), a new centrist party founded by TV journalist-turned-politician Stavros Theodorakis, in its first attempt to capture the "reasonable vote".

The final results of the regional and mayoral elections held on the same day gave a more nuanced picture. New Democracy captured six of Greece's thirteen regions, with only two going to SYRIZA-backed candidates and the rest to independents. But in taking Attica, Greece's most populous region, by the thinnest of margins, SYRIZA stole the show. The fact that Athens and Thessaloniki re-elected their moderate centre-left mayors could not detract from the overall impression.

SYRIZA had won, notwithstanding the fact that at the European level, the left ticket headed by Tsipras came last, polling just 5% of the vote. SYRIZA's first place in Greece meant that Tsipras really was now prime minister-in-waiting.

Once the elections were over, Samaras reshuffled the cabinet to make a fresh start. Finance Minister Stournaras, who had gained the confidence of our European partners but had become an irritant to New Democracy MPs, became governor of the Bank of Greece. He was replaced by Ghikas Hardouvelis, an academic economist who had served as advisor to Prime Minister Kostas Simitis a decade earlier, as well as more recently to Lucas Papademos in his brief tenure as prime minister. The move was meant to reassure creditors.

However, Samaras was sending mixed signals. In most new cabinet appointments, reformists and technocrats were replaced by populists. The prime minister was trying to do two things at once: reassure our partners and the markets that it was business as usual; and tell Greeks that he was dropping unpopular reforms, promising an end to the bailout and a quick return to "normality" without austerity.

The Greek economy continued to improve over the summer, with a bumper tourist season boosting revenues and GDP. Tourism from Germany, a large market for Greece, was at an all-time high. August and September also saw a sovereign credit rating upgrade by Moody's and Standard and Poor's. Greek bonds continued to languish at the bottom of rating leagues, in junk territory, but from 2013 they had been making a slow comeback. This improvement extended to the banking sector. Following a second wave of bank recapitalizations in 2014, this time by €8 billion of exclusively private capital, Greek banks successfully passed the October Europe-wide stress tests.

By the autumn of 2014, discussion on the "day after" the memorandum was already under way. The European part of the EU/IMF joint bailout was due to expire at the end of 2014, with the IMF's parallel programme running until mid-2016. The last thing the government wanted was to remain exclusively under IMF tutelage. Hence the idea of finding a way to also "send the IMF home" was popular in Athens.

Broadly speaking, there were three options. At one end was the "clean break" of Ireland and Portugal, with Greece funding itself fully from the markets. At the opposite end was a third programme, much smaller this time, but still in the region of €10-€20 billion. And in the middle was the preferred option of the Commission: a precautionary credit line, provided for in the new Eurozone arrangements, for Greece to draw upon if markets turned sour.

The preference of the Greek government was for a "clean break". Buoyed by the successful return to markets a few months earlier, the idea was to forgo the remaining €12 billion of the IMF and, once Eurozone assistance ended, rely only on private funding. The government believed this would also facilitate the IMF, which was experiencing internal criticism of its "Greek adventure" and was looking for a way out.

In mid-October, a Greek delegation headed by Finance Minister Hardouvelis took these ideas to Washington, while the government in Athens was successfully defending a no-confidence vote in parliament. In a short meeting with Christine Lagarde and her staff, it became clear the Fund did not share the government's confidence in Greece covering its financing needs from bond markets. Lagarde insisted on continuing IMF involvement and for Greece to rely on some kind of precautionary support.

The IMF had calculated the Greek financing gap for 2015 and 2016 at €25 billion, excluding Fund support. If Greece withdrew from the IMF programme, its undisbursed loans would have to be added to that number and the bill would rise to €37 billion. Could Greece really find that kind of money at reasonable rates from international markets? Hardly likely.

Rather than demonstrating confidence that it could do the job without further assistance, the government's "clean exit" talk backfired. Everyone could see it was being driven by politics, not economics. European officials expressed scepticism at Greece's ability to go it alone ("way too optimistic" was the more polite reaction), and Germany said once more it wanted the IMF to continue to be involved in the future as well. But the clearest signal came from the markets themselves: Greek debt yields rose sharply.

Facing rejection of its plans, the government abandoned the idea of a clean exit and the discussion moved to the modalities of the credit line. Would it be a simple Precautionary Credit Line or an Enhanced Conditions Credit Line? The former entailed little supervision, while the latter would maintain the intrusive Troika visits to Athens. The government was so desperate to avoid these that it had been scheduling meetings for the fifth programme review in Brussels and Paris.

Final decisions were due at the December Eurogroup, which would also discuss a possible follow-up to the 2012 decision to provide Greece with additional debt relief "if necessary". But already by October it became evident that the Greek side was not willing to comply with Troika demands to complete the review and unlock the €7 billion loan tranche.

By November, the government had thrown in the towel about two of its aims, light supervision and the IMF going home. But it insisted the improved state of the economy meant the Troika's demands for more austerity were excessive.

As the Greek side hardened its stance, so did the Troika. In fact, it is possible at that point both sides decided it was in their best interests not to complete the review. On the Greek side, Samaras was looking at the polls and a possible election. An agreement with yet more austerity would not play well; he wanted to offer voters a clear dilemma on who could best get the country out of the memorandum without however further sacrifices.

As for the EU and the IMF, the thinking seemed to be that Samaras would lose the elections to SYRIZA. Best therefore to wait and negotiate the day after with the new government, committing it to what needed to be done. So while they could have compromised, as in the past, watering down certain demands and pushing others to the future, they chose not to do so. The bar was set high enough for the current government not to be able to pass it.

This jockeying for positions crystallized at the December 8th Eurogroup. It was acknowledged that there was no more time to conclude the review and disburse before the end of the year. As the remaining money would be lost if the programme expired, it was extended by two months. This way the New Year would not find Greece without the protective umbrella of EU/IMF assistance.

The extension gave Samaras time to pursue his political goals.

At the end of November the Greek finance minister had sent to the Troika final proposals to bridge the remaining differences, notably fiscal – what became known as the "Hardouvelis email". The Greek side noted it was "determined to walk the extra mile" but warned its proposals were "a last good faith attempt". This was Hardouvelis saying that it was as far as he was allowed by Samaras to go.

When these proposals were deemed insufficient by the Troika, Samaras decided to fast-forward political developments.

The term of the president of Greece was up in March 2015 and, after two 5-year terms, Karolos Papoulias would not seek re-election. As the president is elected by parliament with an enhanced majority (180 votes out of 300 are required), the opposition can typically use the end of a president's term to force parliamentary elections. If no presidential candidate has enough support, parliament is dissolved and elections are called, after which the new parliament can elect a president with a simple majority.

In the case in point New Democracy and PASOK together were far from the magic 180 number. They could hope to elect a president only with the support of DIMAR or of MPs sitting as independents, given that the remaining political parties (SYRIZA and the communists on the left, the Independent Greeks and Golden Dawn on the right) would vote against any candidate in order to force elections.

Fearing that any delay would work against him and in an attempt to put a stark dilemma in front of parliament and voters, Samaras decided not to wait until March. In a constitutionally questionable move, he announced the start of the process to elect the new president right after the December Eurogroup, months ahead of schedule. He proposed as his candidate Stavros Dimas, a moderate former-EU Commissioner from his own party.

In three consecutive parliamentary votes in December, each spaced five days from the last, the New Democracy candidate failed to reach the necessary number of votes. On the third vote, he was twelve MPs short. Only a handful of independents decided to support him, the rest preferring to lead the country to fresh elections.

As the process yielded no result, parliament was dissolved and a general election was called for January 25th.

Greece was preparing to go to the polls just as the rest of Europe was leaving the crisis behind. In November 2014, the ECB assumed direct supervisory responsibility for all major banks in the Eurozone, marking an important milestone towards a European banking union. And just before Christmas, the European summit gave the green light to a plan by newly installed Commission President Jean-Claude Juncker to mobilize €315 billion of investment in order to relaunch growth and employment in Europe. It was an important initiative which however would have been even more useful at the beginning of the crisis – Papandreou had in fact been arguing for such "Eurobonds for investment" since 2009.

The election period in Greece was short but intense. New Democracy attempted to frame the voters' choice as a contest between light and dark, Europe or chaos, us or them, and ultimately, Samaras or Tsipras. As the campaign advanced, the "success story" message that Samaras had pushed for months faded in favour of a negative message of fear for the country if SYRIZA won.

The spectre of Grexit came back to haunt the pre-election debate. Many of the factions in SYRIZA wanted the country to return to the drachma. Tsipras skilfully managed a balancing act, avoiding to address the issue head-on and instead projecting the image of a party dedicated to preserving Greece's European destiny, but passionately opposed to German austerity policies.

SYRIZA's central election slogan was "hope is coming". And Greek voters were desperate for hope. They were tired of sacrifices, eager to believe in populist promises, angry at the fact that those who first promised an easy way out had changed their tune when faced with the reality of government. The contrast between Alexis Tsipras' youthful and fresh presence, symbolizing the future, and the grey image of Antonis Samaras was stark.

It was a contest between fear and hope and, once the votes were counted on the night of the elections, this time around hope had won.

But it was the triumph of hope over experience.

Chapter 24

GAME THEORY

It was a landslide. Only this time the world had turned upside down.

In October 2009, Papandreou's PASOK had obtained 44% of the vote. Alexis Tsipras and SYRIZA had barely squeezed into parliament with 4%.

It was only five years later, but it seemed like an eternity. In the January 2015 elections, SYRIZA came first with 36%, with New Democracy trailing by eight points. PASOK polled just above 4%, scraping into parliament.

How the mighty had fallen. And what an incredible upset in Greek politics. The parties which had dominated since 1974 were either humiliated or destroyed. Greeks elected to power a leftist party which included in its ranks communists intent on taking Greece out of the Euro and reversing Greece's European orientation. Its prime minister designate was a 40-year-old veteran of the anti-globalization movement, who would become the youngest prime minister in modern Greek history.

For me these elections had a particularly bitter feel. For the first time in fifteen years, I had no role to play. I was not a candidate, I was not a party member any more, and I had other serious things to worry about: a trial. I was down – and out. As I watched the results, I remembered a scene in parliament in 2010.

Alexis Tsipras was criticizing us for having signed the memorandum. I responded on behalf of the government, asking whether he had €50 billion – the kind of sum we needed to keep the country going. If he did, we would be happy to borrow from him. If not, as the international markets would not lend to us, we had no other option than to go to the EU.

For five years, I believed reality was so compelling that it would shape attitudes. Instead, common sense and pragmatism gave way to conspiracy theories and hatred. I watched in disbelief as those chiefly responsible for the situation the country found itself in clawed themselves back into power in 2012. And I was amazed by the power of populism in shaping people's minds, and by the support for parties like SYRIZA which sailed to victory in a ship built of illusions and empty promises.

We had been defeated. Our ideas, our worldview, had been thoroughly rejected.

Decisive as it was, the victory did not give SYRIZA a parliamentary majority. With 149 seats, they were two short. With a speed that betrayed predetermined decisions, they turned to ANEL, the far-right Independent Greeks. To many people in Greece and abroad, this coalition "against nature" was deeply disturbing, especially as SYRIZA could have asked the centre-left PASOK or centrist Potami for support. But the glue was the anti-bailout stance both SYRIZA and ANEL had consistently espoused. It was more powerful than any political differences.

The next shock came when the new finance minister was announced.

I had come to know Yanis Varoufakis, an academic economist specializing in game theory, some ten years earlier. When Kostas Simitis was prime minister we had on a number of occasions made joint appearances in public meetings to talk about Greece's "real convergence" with its European peers after the country's Eurozone entry. He sounded perfectly reasonable at the time. He was later in a broad circle of people around George Papandreou, while after the 2010 bailout, he re-emerged as a critic of our policies and of the EU's handling of the crisis, amassing a dedicated following. In 2011, when protesters started filling Syntagma Square, he spoke to the assembled crowds and publicly invited the prime minister to get on his bicycle and "become one with the demonstrators" (Papandreou was a keen cyclist).

During the 2012 election campaign, I had accepted an

invitation for an online debate with Varoufakis, moderated by journalist Stavros Theodorakis, before he founded his party To Potami. We were both symbols of the era: the "minister of the memorandum" and its chief academic critic. Varoufakis even coined an expression for our policies: the "Papaconstantinou dogma" – doing whatever it takes to receive the next loan tranche. He believed that it was a policy followed not just by myself, but by all subsequent governments – and that it was "criminal". I actually thought it was a pretty reasonable rule to go by in the circumstances.

The main thrust of his argument in that debate, repeated many times since, was that Greece in 2010 should have declared bankruptcy – unilaterally if necessary, and survive by borrowing directly from the Greek public. We should have looked our European partners "straight in the eye", slammed the fist on the table (or perhaps given them the finger), and refused the loan if necessary. They would have buckled and forgiven the debt.

At the end of the debate, I told him that people like him, who held such absolute truths, should have the chance to test them in real life. But I never thought that these views would actually become the official policy of the Greek government.

The day after the new SYRIZA-ANEL government was sworn in, Martin Schulz, the social democrat president of the European Parliament, flew to Athens to get the measure of the new prime minister. He left the meeting really worried, realizing that Tsipras was on a collision course with the rest of Europe.

Schulz was followed by Eurogroup President Jeroen Dijsselbloem, who visited the new finance minister. In a packed press conference after their meeting, Varoufakis asked for an international conference on debt relief for Greece and announced that Greece would no longer work with the Troika. Before hastily leaving the room, a visibly rattled Dijsselbloem awkwardly shook Varoufakis' hand and whispered a few words expressing his extreme displeasure in his ear. "Wow," was Varoufakis' reply – a word which well captured the beginning of his tenure.

In the next few days the world's media was riveted as Tsipras and Varoufakis separately visited European capitals to explain the new Greek government's position. The prime minister was upstaged by his flamboyant finance minister, whose visits attracted comments as much for his dress code (after he met the UK chancellor the Guardian described Varoufakis as "a man wearing a Wetherspoon's-appropriate bright-blue shirt and an early-1990s Madchester drug dealer's coat"), as for what he actually said.

London provided entertainment, but the real drama was in Berlin. Sitting next to Wolfgang Schäuble, Varoufakis launched into a long political tirade in which he did not fail to mention Germany's Nazi past – guaranteed to improve the climate. When the German finance minister tried to keep the press conference within the bounds of diplomatic decorum by saying, "we agreed to disagree", the response from the Greek minister was, "we did not even agree to disagree". The clash was absolute.

In those early days, the Greek government was punch drunk by its success. It was riding on a wave of excitement across Europe. SYRIZA's election victory was seen as the first serious challenge to Germany's austerity stranglehold.

In Athens that positive vibe and encouraging op-eds in influential international newspapers were mistaken for bargaining power. They led the government to believe Europe would simply yield to "the democratic mandate given by the Greek people". They were ignorant of the way power politics works in Europe and oblivious to the institutional mechanics of its decision-making process. Those of us who had gone through the process waited for the other shoe to drop.

What SYRIZA was saying was not totally wrong. Their two main tenets – that Greece needed debt relief and less austerity – were pretty much accepted by most analysts, investors, academic economists and even policy makers. There was a need for some additional debt relief (it was even promised conditionally to the previous government), and the question was whether this would involve a haircut on official loans or instead a lengthening of loan maturities and lower interest rates. There was also a quasi-consensus on the need to lower the primary surplus target, giving the Greek economy some breathing space.

If SYRIZA had stuck to that and attempted to negotiate the best possible package, they would have succeeded. Instead, they chose to throw out the baby with the bathwater and completely reject the bailout programme. But that was who they were: they were elected on a promise to restore wages and pensions to pre-crisis levels, opposed product and labour market reforms, and vowed to block privatizations. Once in power they stuck to their guns.

It didn't take the European institutions long to start striking back. On February 5th, ECB President Mario Draghi met Yanis Varoufakis and explained to him that statements such as "I am the finance minister of a bankrupt country" were not helpful. Taken at face value, that would imply the Eurosystem should no longer be lending to insolvent Greek banks. Right after the meeting, the ECB announced it would no longer accept Greek government bonds as collateral for Greek banks.

The ECB did not close the tap on Greek banks. Rather, it pushed all lending onto the more expensive Emergency Liquidity Assistance (ELA) mechanism. While Europe was celebrating Draghi's €60 billion monthly quantitative easing programme just announced, Greece was put in quarantine, on drip-feed.

The relay to this pressure from the ECB was picked up by finance ministers. With the clock ticking before expiry of the programme's two-month extension, an emergency Eurogroup was called on February 11th, a day before the European summit. Varoufakis showed up accompanied by Deputy Prime Minister Yannis Dragasakis and read out a long statement of the new government's priorities.

He explained that SYRIZA had a mandate to "terminate the cycle of austerity"; hence there was no intention to complete the programme. He asked for a different programme, with a maximum 1.5% of GDP primary surplus objective, additional debt relief and some bridge financing. Already, this last request was a departure from earlier statements that Greece "does not need the €7 billion" – the loan tranche over which negotiations had broken down with Samaras.

The other finance ministers insisted that rules were rules and an electoral result did not mean a country could ignore what had already been agreed. They were ready to discuss changes, but the current programme needed to be completed first. Schäuble was blunter than the rest, telling reporters on the sidelines of the meeting: "The Greek government can do whatever it likes, but I would like to know how it can do it outside the programme."

The meeting adjourned without any decisions being taken. As the Financial Times revealed the next day, the Greek delegation had initially agreed to a statement "to explore the possibilities for extending and successfully concluding the present programme", but withdrew their accord after talking to Athens. Back home it was important to keep up the fantasy that "the memorandum was finished".

At the European summit which was held the day after the Eurogroup, leaders spent only 15 minutes on Greece, surprising the new Greek prime minister, who had come ready to argue that "Europe needs to respect democracy". They indicated that there was nothing to discuss until there was an agreed position from the Eurogroup. More than one leader made the point that they were democratically elected too.

The impasse continued at the scheduled February 16th Eurogroup. Varoufakis insisted the programme was catastrophic. He did however pledge to repay creditors, and promised not to roll back existing measures and to "postpone" implementation of election promises. He suggested he had no problem with 70% of the agreement; all he wanted was to find alternatives for the remaining 30%. Greece was given a few days to formally request an extension to the programme.

Afterwards, Varoufakis released to the press two different

draft Eurogroup statements and claimed he had been duped. He had agreed to sign the first – given to him by Economic Affairs Commissioner Pierre Moscovici, but it was supposedly swapped at the last minute with a different and unacceptable one by Eurogroup President Jeroen Dijsselbloem. The new Greek finance minister was unable to distinguish between a Commission proposal and one agreed by the Eurogroup.

Two days later, the Greek Parliament elected the new president of the republic. Tsipras proposed a New Democracy politician, Prokopis Pavlopoulos. It was a surprise; he had been widely expected to nominate Dimitris Avramopoulos, the recently appointed Greek commissioner in Brussels. Pavlopoulos ran against respected constitutional professor and human rights advocate, Nikos Alivizatos, who was supported by Potami and PASOK; he was easily elected with the votes of SYRIZA, ANEL and New Democracy MPs.

SYRIZA's choice for president said a lot about their politics. By electing a prominent ex-minister of the Karamanlis government to the highest office, a man best known for the increase in public sector rolls during his tenure, they in effect absolved the Karamanlis period of responsibility for the tragedy Greece was living through.

This was consistent with the narrative that dominated public debate: the problem was the bailout and the Troika, not what led to them. The memorandum had brought the crisis, and not the other way round. SYRIZA and New Democracy shared a common enemy – those responsible for revealing the truth in 2009 and then making the difficult choices which saved the country from bankruptcy.

As parliament was electing the new president, the government formally asked for a six-month extension of the loan agreement – but not the programme. The Germans in the Euro Working Group called the proposal a Trojan horse to get a bridging loan without actually agreeing to complete the programme.

There were now less than two weeks left to agree on another

extension; failing that, the remaining €7 billion in the programme would be lost. It was increasingly obvious that the public coffers were empty. The small primary surplus which existed at the end of 2014 had evaporated, the state had stopped paying suppliers to have enough cash to cover wages and pensions, and it was scrounging for any extra cash available.

The Eurogroup met on February 20th for the third time in ten days, with ministers growing increasingly impatient with their Greek colleague. To avoid blow-ups in session, a solution was sought in bilateral meetings. Dijsselbloem, Moscovici and Lagarde alternated between Varoufakis and Schäuble – having those two in the same room did not seem to be helpful. In the end, there was white smoke.

The Eurogroup agreed to extend the programme for four months, until the end of June. But the extension would be granted only upon first receiving an acceptable list of reforms; and the current review needed to be successfully concluded before any money was disbursed. There would be no rollback of measures or changes that impacted fiscal targets – and all financial obligations to creditors needed to be met "fully and timely".

The Greek side hailed the result as a success. "We turned a page" was the sum-up by Varoufakis right after the meeting. In Athens Tsipras went so far as to claim that with the agreement "we cancelled plans to asphyxiate Greece" and "we left behind the austerity, the memoranda and the Troika".

The government was busy spinning whatever it got: discussions on a "possible follow-up arrangement"; a recognition the primary surplus target will "take the economic circumstances in 2015 into account" i.e. be lowered; and the right to present new measures to substitute those deemed unacceptable. But the best was that there would henceforth be no more Troika; everyone would now refer to "the institutions".

Despite attempts to frame the text as an example of "constructive ambiguity" and interpret it at will, it was the first defeat of the new government. They entered negotiations improbably asking for money without a programme. Instead, they got a programme without money. The trap laid in the decision was that there was absolutely no money on the table. As the liquidity crunch was getting worse, all that the institutions – formerly known as the Troika – had to do was wait.

The result was a protracted stand-off. On February 23rd, the Greek government sent a list of reforms. The Eurogroup approved them as a basis for negotiation, but the following weeks were spent on fruitless discussions about where and how the negotiations would take place. It was finally decided that technical teams could go to Athens, but the actual negotiations would be in Brussels. Not a trust-building process.

Nor was the substance of the proposals reassuring. The first letter Varoufakis sent to the Eurogroup elaborating on the government's plans had everyone wondering whether it was part of some elaborate prank. Third on the reform list was an "Onlookers VAT tax-evasion scheme", whereby students, housewives and even tourists would be hired to pose – while wired for sound and video – as customers and catch tax evaders in the act. You couldn't make it up if you tried.

The climate in Europe towards Greece was rapidly deteriorating. But at home seven out of ten people approved the government's tough negotiating stance. They were sold on SYRIZA's narrative that this was the first time a government had actually negotiated and Greece had regained its "dignity". The prime minister's popularity and that of his maverick finance minister were at all-time highs, with SYRIZA 20 points ahead of New Democracy in opinion polls.

In this climate and in an obvious snub to the February 20th pledge to "freeze" any budget-sensitive measures, the government brought to parliament legislation "dealing with the humanitarian crisis". In a defiant speech Tsipras vowed not to give in to creditors' demands and insisted that Greece would pursue the issue of Nazi war reparations from Germany.

That highly symbolic issue was increasingly used in an attempt to capture the moral high ground. A report was produced putting Germany's legally disputed war reparations to Greece at hundreds of billions. This was complemented by the findings of the Committee on the Truth about Debt created by Parliament Speaker Zoi Konstantopoulou. The entire stock of Greece's debt was declared odious, illegal – awful really. Ergo, Greece owed nothing. All this was absurd; but it had a powerful hold on people.

It was clear that Tsipras wanted to make Greece the main topic of the March 20th European summit; it was equally clear no one else wanted that. In order to shield the summit from being hijacked, Council President Donald Tusk, Jean-Claude Juncker, Mario Draghi, Angela Merkel and François Hollande met with Tsipras before the start of the European Council, in a four-hour meeting to which they also invited Jeroen Dijsselbloem.

The Greek prime minister assured them he would soon submit credible reform proposals and they assured him no one wanted a Grexit. However, when he asked for help with Greece's liquidity crisis, he was referred to the Eurogroup. Still, the meeting did succeed in restoring some of the lost trust.

Tsipras then told everyone in Greece that the meeting confirmed there would be no more austerity, the Troika was over, and there was no short-term liquidity problem. In contrast, in a short statement issued jointly, the European Council, the Eurogroup, and the Commission simply reconfirmed the agreement reached on February 20th by Eurogroup.

Next stop, Berlin. Just one day before Tsipras' first official visit on March 23rd, Peter Spiegel of the Financial Times had revealed a letter Tsipras had sent to Merkel where, in dramatic tones, he had warned that without help in dealing with the cash crunch, he would soon face a choice between repaying creditors, or paying salaries and pensions – and he would opt for the latter.

In the meeting with the chancellor and at the joint press conference that followed, Tsipras sounded reasonable enough.

He appealed for dialogue and commonly agreed solutions, and insisted he did not want to wreck what had been built in recent years but just correct mistakes. On the thorny issue of Nazi war reparations he talked of a "moral" issue, not of actual money owed to Greece.

As a public relations exercise the meeting was a success. But the cash crunch was nowhere nearer to being addressed. Tsipras was told once more to take his issues to the Eurogroup. The problem there however had a specific name to it: Yanis Varoufakis. It was by now obvious that a deal at the Eurogroup was impossible with him as finance minister. He was not negotiating, he was simply playing for time.

Varoufakis was fast becoming a liability to Tsipras. His countless interviews, conflicting statements and continuous tweets had made *him* the story rather than the Greek economy. His life-style interview and photo shoot in the glossy French Paris-Match magazine – after exhorting Greeks to "live frugally" – enraged even people in SYRIZA. But it would be hard to replace him; his popularity had skyrocketed together with the exasperation about him at the Eurogroup meetings.

The breaking point came after the informal Ecofin in Riga on April 23rd. Before the meeting, cameras showed the Greek finance minister sitting alone, skipping the usual chit-chat, shunned by his colleagues. In the meeting itself Varoufakis took a hammering, and ministers privately talked of an "amateur" and a "gambler". In the evening, he opted to miss the official dinner and instead "wander in the night", as his collaborators explained, preferring that to boring dinners with other ministers.

At that point Tsipras decided to reshuffle the negotiating team. He kept Varoufakis as finance minister but sidelined him, appointing Deputy Foreign Affairs Minister Euclid Tsakalotos, as chief negotiator. The new team was less into game theory and more results-oriented. Negotiations seemed to advance. On May 12th, Greece managed to make an IMF payment of €767 million, but only by using some creative accounting: it borrowed the IMF insurance account held at the Bank of Greece, in effect using the IMF's money to pay back the IMF. There was hardly any money left in the state's coffers to pay public sector salaries or pensions at the end of the month.

It is tempting to blame solely Varoufakis for the months lost since SYRIZA came to power. The problem was broader. Tsipras and the SYRIZA majority in the government were hamstrung by their election promises, beholden to the activist left of the party and deeply suspicious of Europe. It was a long road for them to travel.

SYRIZA's leftist roots and suspicion of Europe also guided Tsipras' efforts to seek allies and alternatives in places such as Russia. That was another common point with his nationalist right-wing coalition partner, ANEL, for whom "our Christian orthodox brothers" in Russia were more reliable than the West. On April 8th, in a visit to Moscow, Tsipras tried to play the Putin card, signing a trade agreement and declaring that Greece was open to "look towards new horizons".

The statement reverberated across the EU and in the US; the last thing needed was an upset in the delicate geopolitical balance of the region. But the gambit failed on two counts: Russia had no inclination to help and no money to give (as had been proven already in the case of Cyprus); and both the EU and the US were enraged rather than scared by this naked – if naïve – Greek attempt at flexing its geopolitical muscles.

As May turned into June with still no deal in sight, meetings and teleconferences multiplied, always followed by statements that "progress is being made". On June 1st, the government sent a new proposal to the institutions, with a gradual increase in the primary surplus target to 2.5% of GDP by 2018 and specific measures to get there. Thankfully, the camera-wielding tourists exposing VAT fraud which were prominent in the original Varoufakis proposals had disappeared. Privatizations were back, as were reforms. It was a break with previous positions and we were finally in the back-and-forth of real negotiations; but we were not yet close to the kind of agreement the Eurogroup was looking for.

Facing three impossible IMF loan repayment tranches during June totalling close to €1 billion, Tsipras asked the IMF to lump all loan repayment tranches into one, payable at the end of June. The IMF agreed, so the June 5th tranche was not paid. The unusual move showed Greece was having extreme difficulty with its cash reserves. It was also a precursor of things to come.

Intensive negotiations continued until mid-June in Brussels between the Troika and the Greek delegation, supported by technical work done in Athens. Differences remained, notably on plugging the fiscal gap, pension reform and privatizations, but the two sides were getting closer. On June 14th, as remaining differences could not be bridged, the Greek team received instructions from Athens to leave the negotiating table.

Following this break-up of negotiations, there could be no agreement at the June 18th Eurogroup meeting. In the press conference after that meeting, Dijsselbloem stressed the flexibility shown by the Eurogroup towards reaching an agreement – it seemed like the blame game for the failure had already began.

The discussion in the media and policy circles had already shifted to what would happen if there was no deal, the programme expired and Greece was unable to pay the IMF. Would the IMF board give Greece a 30-day grace period? What would the ECB do? Would it pull the plug on Greek banks? Would the ESFS/ESM call in all their loans to Greece? Capital controls were now becoming a real eventuality.

On June 22nd, Greece submitted a new proposal with a whopping €7.9 billion of additional measures. The Eurogroup responded positively in a short meeting held to prepare for the informal Euro summit. It asked the Troika to work out a list of prior actions in order to reach a final agreement later in the week.

Three days later, after yet another extraordinary Eurogroup, there was still no agreement, prompting Dijsselbloem to say there remained a wide gap with the Greek authorities, and adding a take-it-or-leave it ultimatum: "the door is still open for the Greek authorities to accept the proposals tabled by the institutions."

With SYRIZA in Athens up in arms about the austerity measures included in the latest proposal that the government had submitted to Brussels – and was subsequently rejected – Tsipras flew to the Belgian capital for a last-ditch attempt at a compromise in an extraordinary Eurozone summit. His meetings with Tusk, Merkel, Hollande, Lagarde, Draghi, Juncker and Dijsselbloem before the actual summit did not produce a deal.

At that summit meeting, Tsipras was truly alone. It was not just Germany and the Nordics; the other bailout countries – Ireland, Portugal and Spain – were the first to criticise him for requesting special treatment and not accepting what was proposed, which in any case they found too lenient. Exchanges were harsh. Tusk told Tsipras the game was over; Tsipras responded that the millions of unemployed in Greece were not a game. With an eye to broader global effects, Merkel insisted that there had to be a solution before the markets opened on Monday.

Alexis Tsipras flew back to Athens and convened his cabinet. He addressed the nation at one o'clock in the morning and stunned the world by announcing a referendum on the latest Brussels proposal on the table. He called it "an ultimatum towards Greek democracy and the Greek people". And he called on the Greek people to reject it.

Greece had just clutched defeat out of the jaws of victory – and was now staring straight into the abyss.

Chapter 25

THE REFERENDUM

The morning after the late-night announcement, Greeks woke up to realize they had a week to make a decision that could change the country for generations. And they would be making that decision with closed banks and capital controls in place.

Whatever the mistakes made by successive Greek governments since 2009, they all knew one thing: you do not get yourself into a situation where you have to close the banks and impose capital controls. The cost to the economy is huge and cannot be easily undone. If there was any doubt about that, the Cyprus episode in 2013 and its aftermath should have driven it home.

SYRIZA clearly had not got the message. The referendum announcement at 1 a.m. on Saturday June 27th, four days before the bailout was due to expire, immediately unleashed a chain of events. What was unthinkable until a few months ago was now about to happen.

Later on that Saturday, as SYRIZA, ANEL and Golden Dawn were voting in favour of the referendum in parliament, the Eurogroup rejected a Greek demand to extend the programme beyond its June 30th expiration date. It made clear that the Eurozone was in a stronger position than at the beginning of the crisis and intended to use "all the instruments available to preserve the integrity and stability of the euro area".

In other words, they would not be blackmailed.

On Sunday, citing the fact that the assistance programme was about to expire, the ECB "froze" the Emergency Liquidity Assistance provided to Greek banks at its current level. Leaks to the system due to deposit outflows would no longer be replenished. Everyone was now expecting a run on the banks on Monday, so there was no option that weekend but to declare an extended bank holiday and put in place capital controls.

Bank of Greece governor Yannis Stournaras had been warning the government for months that failure to reach a compromise would have terrible consequences. He now handed the government a decree for closing the banks; the government approved it and President Pavlopoulos signed it.

On Monday, long lines started forming in front of ATMs as people rushed to take out the €60 daily allowance set under capital controls. As end-of-month pensions were due to be paid by Tuesday, some bank branches were allowed to open for pensioners without bank cards to take out a small part of their pensions. Scuffles broke out as old people waited for hours under the hot sun. Supermarkets started emptying and long lines formed outside petrol stations.

The blame game started immediately. The Commission published their latest proposal, showing the two sides were very close to a deal when negotiations had broken down. Donald Tusk wrote to Tsipras, explaining that leaders agreed with their finance ministers; the programme would not be extended, as it was the Greek government which had inexplicably and unexpectedly walked out of the negotiations.

Then Juncker, in an emotional press conference, with a huge video wall of the Greek and EU flags as backdrop, urged Greeks to vote "yes", adding, "we should not commit suicide because we are afraid of death".

In Athens the battle lines between referendum camps were quickly drawn. The "yes" camp settled on a simple message, Yes to Europe. It was not about whether one agreed with the latest EU proposal; that proposal was no longer on the table anyway. It was about Greece's European destiny. A "no" vote meant Grexit, a huge loss of wealth for the country and untold suffering for the people.

The "no" camp was more diverse. Tsipras asked for a "no" vote by telling people this would strengthen his negotiating hand. All he wanted was to bring home a better deal – and he would do so within 48 hours. However, for a significant part of his party, a "no" vote meant saying no to Greece's Euro membership. This was also the position of Golden Dawn and of the communists, who both campaigned for a "no" vote.

Both sides held huge rallies in the week leading up to the referendum. The "no" camp was younger, more populous and better organized. SYRIZA supporters turned out en masse. The Yes rallies were supported by the European-minded parties: New Democracy, PASOK and To Potami. They managed to attract people who had never been to such an event before, but wanted simply to defend Greece's place in Europe.

I cannot remember the country ever being so polarized. It was a battle between two very different understandings of the reality in Greece and in Europe, between two very different conceptions of Greece's future, two distinct worldviews.

As the two sides were fighting it out over the Sunday vote, the Greek government announced it would not pay back the three June tranches of the IMF loan. But to show it still remained on the negotiating table, it sent a letter to the Eurogroup with fresh proposals. Rumours circulated that if his counter-proposals were accepted, Tsipras would call off the referendum. The government was told the programme had expired, so there was no basis for discussion.

Tsipras also requested in another letter a new ESM loan, and a prolongation of the existing programme until the new loan was agreed. The Eurogroup responded that it would not examine any such requests before the referendum.

Throughout the week, pollsters were showing the two sides neck-and neck. As we got closer to the vote, "no" seemed to be edging out "yes" by a small margin. So when the results came out on Sunday evening, it was an absolute shock: "no" gained 61% of the vote, against 39% for "yes" – a massive difference nobody had predicted.

We had all missed the strong undercurrents in Greek

society. The "no" vote went beyond the positions of the parties supporting it. It was a deeply emotional reaction – people just wanted to say "hell, no" to everything that had happened in the past five years. It was about the frustration and humiliation that Greeks felt, about wanting to stand up to the whole world – just for a moment, even if deep-down many understood that by voting No, they would make their lives harder. They did not care.

The result shocked Tsipras; he had not expected it, probably had not even wanted it and certainly did not know what to do with it. A victory for "yes" would have allowed for a climb-down in the negotiations; if the people wanted a bad deal, so be it. But such a resounding "no" vote created expectations that he was unable to manage.

He immediately started back-pedalling, addressing the nation in a tone of national unity and telling Greeks "whatever you chose, we are now all one". He fired his finance minister, signalling he actually did want a compromise.

The next day, party leaders issued a joint statement solemnly stating that the result of the vote was not an instruction for rupture with our European partners; rather, for negotiation "for a socially just and economically viable deal for the country".

The reactions from abroad showed Tsipras was going to have a difficult week.

"This result is very regrettable for the future of Greece" was Jeroen Dijsselbloem's immediate statement. A hastily convened Eurogroup and a summit meeting back-to-back on July 7th warily listened as the new finance minister, Euclid Tsakalotos, and Tsipras assured them they would immediately submit new proposals and a new request for an ESM programme.

A tight timetable was set out, culminating in a Eurogroup on Saturday 11th July, followed the next day by a Euro summit. Inability to find an agreement then could mean "the bankruptcy of Greece and the insolvency of its banking system", as Donald Tusk put it; and Mario Draghi made clear that he would not pull the plug on Greek banks until then – with the clear implication he would immediately afterwards.

On July 8th, a visibly destabilized Greek prime minister spoke at the European Parliament, sounding at times defiant and at other times defeated. He was attacked by all the mainstream political groups, finding allies only on the extreme left, the Eurosceptics and the extreme right. How does a leftist party leader feel when he is congratulated and told to stand firm by the likes of Nigel Farage and Marine Le Pen?

The latest Greek proposal arrived in Brussels the next day. It requested a new ESM loan of €53.5 billion for 2015-18, and committed to fiscal measures in excess of €13 billion – substantially more than a week earlier. So much for "tearing up the memorandum in broad daylight" and for using the "no" vote to get a better deal.

On July 11th, after an all night session, Tsipras became the first prime minister of the crisis to secure broad parliament support for an austerity package. In the 4 a.m. vote, 251 MPs from SYRIZA, ANEL, New Democracy, PASOK and To Potami voted in favour. Amongst those who did not were 17 of Tsipras's own MPs, including two cabinet ministers and Parliament Speaker Zoi Konstantopoulou.

Euclid Tsakalotos had barely caught any sleep when he left for the Eurogroup meeting in Brussels. Once there, he was in for a surprise.

The German finance ministry had decided to play hardball. It circulated a one-page non-paper in which it blasted the latest Greek proposal, claiming it could not form the basis of a new 3-year programme. Either Greek proposals were improved – notably by transferring €50 billion of Greek assets to a fund in Luxembourg, or Greece should temporarily leave the Eurozone. It was the first time such a "time-out" proposal had been put down on paper and tabled, let alone by the Eurozone's most powerful country.

Tsipras would finally get the political negotiation he had been asking for all these months. And he was going to regret it.

The Greek prime minister entered the summit with a very weak hand; rather than strengthening him, the referendum gambit had hardened the resolve of his counterparts. His latest proposal had been rejected by Germany and there was no "coalition of the South" to support him; the prime ministers of Spain and Portugal were some of his harshest critics. Apart from Cyprus he could count on only two allies in the room: the French president, who would not entertain the idea of a Grexit and was willing to go to bat for that; and, less actively, Matteo Renzi, the Italian prime minister.

Summit discussions in plenary and bilateral format alternated through the night. A last minute near-collapse of the talks was aborted as Hollande and Tusk literally brought Tsipras and Merkel back into the room for a last compromise over the €50 billion fund. With the "time-out" proposal – part negotiation tactic, part real threat – as an alternative if talks failed, in the end Tsipras capitulated.

He salvaged what he could: the €50 billion fund would be set up in Athens, not abroad; some of the asset proceeds could be used for investments rather than to reduce the debt or recapitalize the banks; and longer grace and payment loan periods to help debt sustainability were promised. But the measures to be taken – spelled out in the summit statement – would be harsh, the reform agenda broad, including hitherto resisted privatizations, and the IMF would remain on board.

Within a week, what had been a resounding "no" turned into a humiliating "yes"; but at least it was a "yes" that managed to avert catastrophe for the country.

Despite the agreement there was no trust in the room. Greece was asked for prior actions before any loan disbursement. With the cash crunch more acute than ever, the first measures were voted into law by the Greek parliament on July 15th. The bill was backed by 229 votes, but SYRIZA dissenters rose to 38, including prominent cabinet members from the party's left faction. They were replaced in a reshuffle.

Taking account of the vote, the Eurogroup released €7 billion of bridge financing to cover Greece's €2 billion arrears to the IMF and its imminent €4 billion ECB payment, and asked for a second set of prior actions. They were voted through on July 22nd, opening the way for negotiations on the conditionality for the third programme with the newly established *quadriga* (the European Stability Mechanism had been added to the EC/ECB/IMF Troika). After it was agreed, the text came to parliament for another all-nighter, this time on August 14-15th, in the middle of the summer vacation. In the final vote 222 MPs backed the agreement, but a third of SYRIZA MPs dissented.

The country had pulled back from the brink, but it was clear that in its current form the government of Alexis Tsipras could not survive for long.

Greece had a third bailout. Was this a better deal than the previous two?

Both the first €110 billion bailout in May 2010 and the second, of €130 billion in March 2012, were criticized for inflicting too much austerity, getting the depth of the recession wrong, and relying too much on internal devaluation. The Troika has been blamed for prescribing "the wrong medicine" and this criticism has found an unexpected ally in the IMF's admission that "fiscal multipliers" – showing the impact of a contractionary fiscal policy on recession in the context of an austerity programme – had been underestimated.

Yet this discussion partly misses the point. Greece's starting point – the huge twin fiscal and external deficits, coupled with an equally large credibility deficit – did not allow at the time of the first programme anything other than a brutal attempt to correct internal and external imbalances up front. Nor did it allow in the beginning for a discussion on debt restructuring, which had to wait until the second programme.

The political environment in the rest of Europe at the time certainly did not help, with extreme scepticism – even initial hostility – to any support mechanism. As for the large multipliers, these can be explained more by the uncertainty in the external environment and the internal political and social uncertainty in Greece than by programme design or implementation flaws. In fact, were fiscal multipliers correctly assessed up front, given the reluctance to increase the money available to Greece, it is likely that even more fiscal measures would have been asked to compensate for the impact of the recession.

It is true that austerity deepened the recession. Deficit reduction is by nature recessionary; it subtracts public resources and private purchasing power from the economy. But the recession had already started in 2008 and got worse in 2009 (it transpired later the economy had contracted by more than 4% that year). Wild spending and a record fiscal deficit had not helped avoid it.

The logic of the programmes was that the recessionary impact would be partly offset by increased investment from a more sustainable fiscal situation and from growth-inducing reforms. The reasoning was not wrong, but it took more time than expected. The fiscal front-loading was dictated by lenders' willingness to fill the "financing gap". Stretching fiscal adjustment over more years would have been the right thing to do, but meant creditors would have to put even more money on the table in 2010.

Both programmes – and especially the first – did succeed in drastically reducing the deficit, but also in completing important reforms and stabilizing the banks. By the end of 2012, most of the lost competitiveness from 2001-2009 had been recouped. Greece was named the fastest reforming OECD economy, though with still much to do.

There are nevertheless a number of valid criticisms that can be levied at the design of the support programmes: there should have been more focus on structural reforms from the beginning; product market reforms should have taken precedence over those in the labour market; the gradual shift of the burden of fiscal consolidation towards tax increases as opposed to expenditure cuts should have been prevented; and it should have been recognized that it is difficult to implement extensive structural reforms together with tough austerity.

Certain initial design problems such as high interest rates and short repayment periods were corrected, starting in 2011. In effect, successive revisions and additional support became necessary less due to design faults and more because of external factors such as the Deauville decision and delays in addressing debt sustainability. And a large part of the problem can be traced to the fact that both programmes were implemented in conditions of extreme international volatility, dominated by expectations of a Grexit.

Implementation problems and a lack of political and social consensus in Greece also did much to undermine efforts. Unlike what happened in other countries where governments in bailout agreements enjoyed opposition support, the Papandreou government in 2010 shouldered alone responsibilities that were not of its own doing, with intense opposition from right and left. It took two years and two elections for some sort of a broader consensus to start emerging – and by that time populism was out of control.

The third bailout, signed in August 2015, was not different in design or substance to its predecessors. In exchange for ESM financial assistance of up to €86 billion over four years (with €25 billion set aside for the recapitalization of banks), it called for extensive fiscal measures, targeted a lower medium-term primary surplus of 3.5% of GDP, and complemented this with product, labour and financial market reforms – as before.

What really differentiates the latest bailout from the previous ones is that this time around, it could have been avoided. It became necessary because of a mix of ideological blindness, lack of understanding of basic Eurozone rules, unforgivable brinkmanship and plain incompetence during the first six months SYRIZA was in power.

After five years of severe economic and social pain, the economy was growing again, with the state spending less than it collected in taxes, excluding interest payments. What lay ahead was a promise of additional debt relief, and economic and social recovery as lower primary surpluses and reforms got the economy going, this time on a sustainable footing. Instead, we got SYRIZA.

The numbers tell a horrific story. After growing in 2014 for the first time in six years, GDP was projected to grow by close to 3% in 2015. Instead, it went back into recession in 2015, with the economy projected to continue contracting in 2016.

It was the same with unemployment. After falling slightly in 2014, it was due to continue dropping in 2015. Instead, the jobless rate rose again. Similarly on the fiscal front: at end 2014, the economy was running a primary surplus close to 2% of GDP, expected to widen to 3% of GDP in 2015. Instead, the surplus turned into another deficit.

The list goes on. Bank deposits at the end of 2014 were €160 billion; they were down by €30 billion after six months. The stock market capitalisation of the four systemic banks went from close to €20 billion to under €4 billion, while the Athens Stock Exchange bank index dropped by an astounding 70%. Overall market capitalisation at the ASE was down by one-third. In those first six months of 2015 the adjustment effort of the Greek people over a number of years went up in smoke.

How did we end up here? Why did Tsipras and SYRIZA choose to inflict this damage by waiting to sign an agreement and perform what Greeks call a *kolotoumba* – a somersault, only in more vulgar language – after having called the referendum and imposed capital controls? Wouldn't it have been better for the country and easier for them to do so earlier, in February for example?

These reasonable questions miss the true nature of the party Tsipras leads. SYRIZA became a winning electoral machine by taking inspiration from the international anti-globalization movement rather than from the moderate European left. It was openly against all constituent elements of the European project: dialogue and compromise, open societies, rule-based institutions.

Its success fed on anger and frustration, and it thrived on divisions: us versus them; traitors versus patriots; foreign occupation versus standing up for your dignity. Words lost their meaning: "junta" – identified with Greece's 7-year military dictatorship – was used to describe a democratically elected government that SYRIZA disagreed with. The Troika visits to Athens became an "invasion". And "humanitarian crisis" became shorthand for Greece's indisputably serious social problems – but also an affront to people living in countries going through wars or suffering from famine.

The party's main tenet was that previous governments never negotiated properly because they were beholden to special interests. SYRIZA would stand up for Greeks; they would face up to Europe, and Europe would blink. After all, governments and the markets were afraid of a Greek collapse. Fearing global mayhem, the Eurozone would end austerity and cut the country's debt. "We will call the tune and the markets will dance" was Tsipras's rallying cry.

This simple but powerful narrative guided SYRIZA's actions even after their election victory. It found support amongst populist parties of the European left, riding the wave of discontent with German-dominated Europe. It also echoed amongst reactionary forces on the right, preaching for a primitive nationalism, with distaste for anything European.

More surprising was the fact that SYRIZA was also encouraged by some leading US academics. Their vantage point was the well-deserved criticism of Germany's fiscal hegemony in Europe. This led them to treat Alexis Tsipras as the champion of their cause and Greece as the playground of the global anti-austerity campaign. They gave ideological cover and respectability to SYRIZA.

At the height of the six-month crisis, this support became increasingly vocal. In eloquent – but inaccurate when it came to facts – op-eds in influential newspapers, some of them urged Greeks to vote "no", and if necessary to be prepared to leave the euro. This at a time when ATMs in Athens were empty, capital controls were in place – with a €60 daily withdrawal limit – and pensions were not being paid.

From afar, these academics failed to recognise the SYRIZA-ANEL government for what it was: a leftist party with statist and authoritarian tendencies in coalition with a party of the extreme right known for its xenophobic, anti-Semitic, conspiracy-theory rhetoric. To their credit, some have since admitted that error of judgment.

Experience of government did not blunt those instincts. After coming to power, SYRIZA and ANEL exhibited clientelist behavior unlike anything seen before, opposed excellence in universities, punished entrepreneurship, attempted to muzzle the press, and engaged in witch-hunts against those who dared to oppose them. In the days leading up to the referendum, Greece was sliding towards Peronist-style totalitarianism.

Populists believe rules of governance – the continuity of the state, international agreements, basic laws of economics, the *pacta sunt servanda* maxim stating that agreements must be observed – are just swept away when the will of the people is expressed in an election. But in that fateful first half of 2015, the whole world saw what happens when populism collides with reality. Reality doesn't budge.

At some point Tsipras realized the bluff would not work any longer and started looking for a way out. When the Eurozone pushed negotiations to breaking point, he decided to pass the buck to the voters and called the referendum. He knew the banks would have to close and capital controls be imposed, but for him overcoming opposition within SYRIZA took precedence over the economy and the good of the country. When the referendum did not produce the result that would allow him to make an about-face, he realized that time was up.

Despite their bravado, the Greek government and its game-theory experts had been badly outplayed. In fact they played straight into the hands of those who were willing to see Greece exit the Eurozone or extract painful concessions to allow this not to happen. Tsipras had painted himself into a corner, ending up with an economy under capital controls and a state unable to pay wages and salaries.

The rest of the Eurozone waited patiently for the game to play itself out. Faced with the abyss, the prime minister capitulated. He understood what it would mean to be branded the prime minister who bankrupted the country and plunged it into economic, social and political chaos. So he signed the kind of agreement he had hitherto called a treacherous crime against the country.

It was perhaps the most expensive lesson in history. The only Greek prime minister in recent memory who had never lived or studied abroad got a crash course in European policy-making – at the expense of a collapsing Greek economy.

However, the story is thick with nuance and subplots. As Tsipras was coming to terms with reality, a dedicated group of people were actively preparing Plan B.

Yanis Varoufakis was the chief architect and theorist of the "make my day" approach. He had been publicly arguing along those lines for years. When he got the job, he rightly assumed the brief included putting his ideas into practice. But he must have realized early on that at least with the Germans the threat of Grexit was an invitation to test the theory of a smaller but more homogeneous Eurozone.

It was at that point that he mentally switched to Plan B. If threats would not move our partners, Greece would have to try and go all the way. That meant preparing to introduce a parallel currency as a precursor to abandoning the euro. Unlike Tsipras, Varoufakis realized full well what failing to reach an agreement and closing the banks meant. He actually relished the opportunity to test his Plan B.

For months, a small group attempted to work out the mechanics of introducing a parallel currency by issuing government bonds to be used as IOUs if the state ran out of cash and the banks were closed. They even explored how to hack into tax codes so that these could be used for IOU transactions in a parallel banking system.

Another group looked into how Greece could weather a "rupture" with the Eurozone. Alternative financing was explored –from Russia, China and even Iran. A loan was sought from Russia as down payment on a gas pipeline to be built through Greece. With China, the goal was debt purchase. Cheap oil and delayed payment, as well as another loan, were sought from Iran. All these efforts failed. None of the countries wanted to endanger their wider geopolitical interests.

Greece's capacity to maintain its energy supply was explored, as well as ways to maintain supply of medicines and even meat. Fanciful solutions were advanced, including procuring energy from Venezuela, and essential medicines from army labs, as well as from Brazil and Argentina. Total madness.

If Tsipras was the last-minute realist and Varoufakis the irresponsible game-theorist, there was a third group: that of the coldly cynical ideologues. Panayiotis Lafazanis, leader of SYRIZA's Left Platform, and his disciples actually wanted a Grexit from the very beginning. A rogue group had looked into the possibility of "commandeering" the cash kept by the Bank of Greece on behalf of the ECB at the old Mint in the outskirts of Athens.

The group had estimated there was €27 billion in ECB cash stashed away, which could become part of national currency reserves if the ECB refused to allow the government to use that cash as a loan. That would buy Greece time as it re-introduced the drachma. And the Greek state would have become both thief and forger.

In the end, none of these unbelievable plans came to pass. Having signed the deal, Tsipras found an ideal opportunity to rid himself of the Left Platform. On the day the first tranche of the new loan was paid (€13 billion, with an additional €10 billion earmarked for bank recapitalization), he resigned and asked the president to call a general election.

In an address to the nation, Tsipras said that his January mandate had run its course. He talked of blackmail and financial strangulation from Greece's partners, and of the difficult decision he had to make under duress. He admitted he had been surprised by the difficulties he had to face. And he talked of the "moral and political obligation" to ask for the people's judgement of the last six months.

And yet he won the election a month later.

SYRIZA captured 35% of the vote, barely losing one percentage point since January. The Greek people were asked by the captain of a sinking ship for a second chance. They gave Tsipras that chance, perhaps feeling that all the others had been given too many second chances. People opted to reward intent and emotion, not actions and results.

New Democracy finished a distant second with 28%, no improvement on its January score despite the economic Armageddon. With 7%, Golden Dawn was now well-implanted as the third force in Greek politics, while the poor results of PASOK and To Potami confirmed the decline of the once all-powerful centre-left.

SYRIZA's populist extreme right coalition partner, ANEL, managed to squeeze back into parliament. Its 10 seats, added to SYRIZA's 145, gave the erstwhile coalition a fresh stab at governing. And public hugs between Tsipras and ANEL's leader Panos Kammenos at SYRIZA's victory rally on election night proved this was more than just a marriage of convenience.

The newly formed government now had to face the consequences of the new economic catastrophe which its own previous short stint in power had created. Added to that were the challenges posed by the uncontrollable refugee crisis destabilizing the whole region; and all this in an increasingly hostile and unstable international political and economic environment. A perfect storm was forming on the horizon.

It was Groundhog Day.

Chapter 26

THE LIST

In every political career, there is a period known as "the crossing of the desert".

It is right after an electoral defeat or dismissal from a government post when the politician discovers that what goes up can come crashing down. The phone stops ringing, invitations become rare, journalists solicit other people's opinions and you end up wondering what exactly went wrong.

Somehow, I had never thought this would happen to me. My rise was swift; from newly elected MP to the second most-powerful job in government in two years. I believed that I had brought to the finance minister's job decent political instincts, and competence rooted in education and experience. I actually thought these were enough to enable me to handle the job – and do so for some time.

I was obviously wrong. Fair enough. I was not the first politician to find that his or her expectations were not met. The period turned out to be the mother of all political battles, not just by Greek standards. But never in my worst nightmares did I believe that "the crossing of the desert" would in my case involve a specially convened tribunal, almost landing me in prison.

It all started in the spring of 2010. The head of our National Intelligence Service (EYP) visited me to share some sensitive information. This was not unusual. The country was under siege, EYP was monitoring economic information, and anything that came our way could be useful, however it came about.

In this case it pertained to information on thousands of accounts held in a Swiss bank, which had been obtained by the French. EYP had asked their French counterparts if we could have access to the data relating to Greek nationals. They were willing, but it would have to be discussed between the respective finance ministers.

The treasure trove in question was the infamous Hervé Falciani information on bank accounts stolen in 2007 from the HSBC bank in Geneva. Falciani, hired by the bank to upgrade security, had instead walked out with the mother lode. He allegedly initially tried to sell the information in the Middle East. When interested parties tipped off the Swiss, he fled to France. The Swiss issued an international arrest warrant; the French seized him *and* his data, but refused to extradite him.

Was I interested in the information on Greek nationals with HSBC accounts? Of course. As austerity hit the Greek population harder and harder, the clamour for social justice increased. Any success in the fight against tax evasion was welcome – obviously more so when it related to rich people with money in Switzerland. It would be the first time the government would have a glimpse of some Swiss accounts belonging to Greek nationals. Legend put the money at hundreds of billions. That was surely an exaggeration, but no one really knew.

At the June 2010 Eurogroup meeting, I asked Christine Lagarde, French finance minister at the time, if they would give us access to the information. She promised to look into it and get back to me. What I did not realize at the time was that I had stepped into a delicate issue: the right to use the information was being hotly debated within the French government.

The finance ministry wanted to use it. The justice ministry was reluctant; this was stolen information and its use was legally prohibited. Finance won, and the French used it to induce French citizens with Swiss accounts to "denounce themselves" and settle. However in 2011, the French *Cour de Cassation* declared that use illegal and voided all investigations based directly or indirectly on the list.

All this became known much later; at the time all I could do was hope for a positive response – and I got one. Lagarde confirmed they would hand over the accounts of Greek citizens to help us fight tax evasion at a difficult juncture; but, given the sensitive nature of the information, it would have to be treated accordingly.

In mid-September I was in Paris for a morning – it was one leg of a quick hop around European capitals to talk to bankers about progress with the programme. After a breakfast meeting with French bankers, I paid a call to my French colleague in her spacious office overlooking the Seine. As Lagarde escorted me out at the end of the meeting, she told me they would soon hand over the data. I asked our ambassador in Paris to collect the information and arrange for it to be sent to Athens quickly and confidentially.

On September 29th, after a long day in parliament and in back-to-back meetings, I was working late at the office. My chief of staff walked in to hand me an envelope delivered by an envoy from our embassy in Paris. Inside was an unmarked CD-ROM, and an accompanying letter. It referred to "the elements asked" without specifics, and emphasized these "should be kept secret" and used only for tax purposes.

In a move that was to haunt me later, I slipped the CD-ROM into my desktop PC. There were over 2,000 Excel files on it, each with a name consisting of a long string of numbers. I opened a few at random. They looked like bank statements, with the name of a beneficiary, amounts and some notes. It occurred to me that I probably should not be doing what I was doing. But I wanted to know what we had: was it an actual list with names and amounts? How many were there? What were the total amounts involved? None of that was clearly discernible and I stopped.

The next day I flew to Brussels for a Eurogroup. When I got back, the weekend was taken up by the visit of the Chinese premier, and after that I flew to New York and Washington for the IMF meetings. Before my trip, I handed the CD-ROM to one of my close aides, asking him to give me a rough idea of the total sums involved and to single out the largest accounts.

When I got back, he handed me a piece of paper with twenty names and the sums involved; the 2,000 odd accounts on the CD-ROM together accounted for a little over $2 billion. Over 1,000 accounts seemed to have a zero balance or to be closed, while the names on the twenty largest accounts alone accounted for about half of the total.

I now had to figure out how to proceed. What we had been handed was illegally obtained information, and I had promised the whole affair would be treated with secrecy, without betraying the trust shown to us by sharing it. At the same time, we had agreed with the prime minister – who was informed of the arrangement with the French – to start negotiations with the Swiss on a bilateral treaty allowing us to reclaim untaxed money by Greek citizens in all Swiss banks.

The UK and Germany were already negotiating such a deal, whereby depositors would be faced with a choice: either have their names given to their countries or – to keep their identity secret – pay a percentage of their capital as tax to the Swiss, who would pass it on to the country concerned. The last thing I wanted was for the Swiss to know we had information stolen from a Swiss bank.

An additional concern was the sieve-like conditions at SDOE, our Economic Crimes Enforcement Agency of the finance ministry. There were already reports in the papers that we were in negotiations to obtain information pertaining to Greeks with Swiss accounts. If I handed over the data, I would soon see it splashed over the papers, embarrassing me in front of the French and the Swiss. More ominously, SDOE's reputation for corruption also meant that people on the list might be blackmailed to pay up and avoid investigation.

In a European country with well-functioning institutions, such concerns would not arise. The information would be handed to the relevant tax people, would be kept confidential, and an investigation would ensue. In Greece the concern was real and that guided my actions. To resolve the dilemma of using the information without it being compromised, I decided to start a pilot project.

I could not be confident that over 2,000 names would not leak. I could however assume that twenty names given to one person would not leak, and also expect results from the investigation. Restricting this pilot to the twenty names with the biggest accounts was justified; they accounted for half the total amount.

I called the special secretary of the SDOE into my office. He was a career tax official chosen for the job because he knew tax administration well. I told him what we had in our possession and handed him the 20 names with the largest accounts. I asked him to investigate: who were these people? Could the sums be justified by their tax declarations? I was struck with the first name on that list: a lady whose account purportedly contained $550 million. Was that even possible?

He came back some weeks later with the first results. Yes, these people filed tax declarations in Greece, and no, their declarations did not seem to justify those kind of sums in Switzerland. I asked him to pursue the investigation – discreetly – with whatever means he had in his disposal, for example the newly legislated ability of tax authorities to look into bank accounts and transfers of money to banks abroad.

In late January 2011, I was to join PM Papandreou for the annual Davos gathering. In Davos we were due to agree with the Swiss to start negotiations on a tax treaty. I was to meet my counterpart, while Papandreou would meet with the current president of the uniquely Swiss Federal Council rotating system of government.

Before leaving, I called a meeting in my office to organize the bilateral negotiations with Switzerland. I also asked for advice on how best to exploit the information we had received from the French. The legal counsel was clear: the information had been illegally obtained; it would not stand up in a Greek court, nor could it be used to directly impute and collect taxes owed. It could however, like an anonymous tip, trigger a broader tax investigation, that would use only information legally at our disposal.

The question remained: how to go about this? One way was to hand all the data to the SDOE, never mind my worries about leaks, inefficiency or even blackmails. A much smaller list with fewer than thirty people, obtained legally from Lichtenstein and handed over to the SDOE almost a year ago, had still yielded no results. The alternative was to set up an ad hoc task force, though this would become widely known. Deciding on the best way would have to wait for the results from investigating the 20 names.

In March, faced with lagging tax receipts in the regular tax administration, I asked for the resignation of the relevant secretary general and moved the SDOE chief to the post. The fight against tax evasion was vitally important; but the state needed to collect about €4 billion in regular tax revenue month-in month-out. Any slippage was disastrous for our finances.

The job of SDOE chief was filled two months later by an ex-prosecutor, Yannis Diotis, who had become a household name in Greece as the man who brought the November 17 terrorists to justice. He was widely praised for his role in putting the members of the longest-acting and notorious Greek terrorist group behind bars. It was responsible for a spate of bombings and assassinations over nearly three decades.

He seemed perfect for the job as head of the tax crimes squad.

I briefed the new SDOE chief on the data we had received from France, my actions until that point and the on-going investigation by his predecessor into the names with the largest amounts. It was now up to him to take forward that investigation and continue with all the names contained in the French data. I had a member of my security detail deliver a USB stick with all the data I had received from France.

About ten days later, I handed over the finance ministry to

Venizelos in the government reshuffle. I believed the chapter of the Greek accounts in the Falciani list had closed for me.

Little did I know.

Months passed, and I never heard any more about the Falciani list and its Greek accounts. I had given all the information to the person whose job it was to investigate, and I assumed this was being done. I never raised the issue with Venizelos; if he had wanted something on this from me, he would no doubt have asked. He never did. There were many issues more important than the Falciani list; he never asked for my input on those either.

The May 2012 elections came and went, as did the June repeat elections. The new Samaras government was formed. Venizelos was now leader of PASOK and PASOK, along with DIMAR, supported the Samaras government. I was no longer a minister and I was not a member of parliament. I was at home, trying to figure out what to do with the rest of my life. I had my first relaxing summer in many years.

Then, in late September, strange things started happening.

Out of the blue, newspapers started running articles about a "list of Greek tax evaders in Switzerland", which – they claimed – had been handed to Greece by French authorities, and had subsequently vanished. My response to initial questions from journalists was evasive; I was no longer in office, but the confidentiality concerns governing the use of the Falciani list were still there.

As the days went by, I realized in astonishment that the increasingly high-pitched newspaper and TV reports were pointing the finger at me as the person who had somehow made the list disappear. And at the end of a week of many such reports, it was announced that the economic prosecutor was opening an investigation.

I could no longer remain silent and issued a statement detailing the main elements of the story. I pointed out that I was the one who had asked for the list; that when it arrived, I gave the names with the largest accounts for a first investigation;

and finally I handed over the complete information for a full tax investigation. But the attacks continued; the biggest-selling Sunday paper carried an article citing unnamed SDOE sources, who had supposedly learned that the list contained "family members of a leading politician".

On October 1st, the largest TV channel led its evening news programme with the disappearance of the "Lagarde list", as the press was calling it by now, accusing me for the fact that it was nowhere to be found. Trembling with rage, I called the channel and asked to respond on-air. A tense exchange followed, which ended with the news anchor asking me, "so who should we ask then about the list if not you?" My answer was, "why don't you ask my successor?"

The next day, an envelope containing a USB stick arrived at the office of PM Samaras. Its sender was the president of PASOK. In a press statement, Venizelos laid out his version of events: he had been given the USB stick by the SDOE chief after he took over as finance minister in the summer of 2011; he was told that the contents had been illegally obtained and could not be used officially; he had concurred; he kept the USB in his office while he was finance minister; he took it with him after he left office and handed it back over a year later once he realized his copy was the only one.

The opposition had a field day. The symbolism was so incredibly powerful. Here was proof that the PASOK government, while imposing austerity on Greeks, was at the same time protecting its powerful friends and helping them hide their tax-dodging money in Switzerland. The political figures involved were emblematic: not only the hated "architect of the Memorandum" (me), but also the current leader of PASOK and coalition partner of the current government under Samaras.

The government was embarrassed. They had no direct involvement in the affair; when asked about the list before its reappearance, Finance Minister Stournaras had responded he had no knowledge of its whereabouts and would ask for it again from the French. Now he vowed to investigate all the people on the list Venizelos had handed over. However, the implication of the party leader of the main coalition partner in the "Lagarde affair" meant trouble for the government. The opposition asked for a parliamentary inquiry. Its hearings took place in a poisonous political environment, with daily articles in the press about "lists" of politicians supposedly being investigated by the tax authorities. Opposition parties smelled blood.

Venizelos was called to testify. He hated the fact that he was being treated like a suspect in an investigation and it showed. There were aggressive exchanges, especially between him and future Parliament Speaker Zoi Konstantopoulou, who had taken the lead in questioning him on behalf of SYRIZA. She thrived on confrontation and had a penchant for conspiracies.

I was called to testify in late October. A few days before my appearance, there was another strange newspaper article: it alleged that the list had been tampered with and encouraged the government to ask for a new copy from the French. From that point forward, suddenly everyone in the media assumed the list at hand was not the same as the original and that someone had doctored it.

I was skewered at the hearing, especially over the fact that while – as I testified – I had received a CD-ROM from France, I had actually handed over a USB stick. I explained that I had the contents of the CD-ROM copied on to a USB for safety reasons. I had kept the USB, which I handed over, while leaving the CD-ROM with my secretaries for safekeeping.

Unfortunately for me it could not be located. The committee assumed I had "lost the original" on purpose. For me the "original" CD-ROM was just an unmarked copy of what the French had sent; what was important was the content – which I had handed over in a USB stick. I resented any insinuation the CD-ROM had been deliberately "lost", and urged the committee to ask for a fresh copy from France to lay to rest any claims of tampering.

A few days after my hearing, journalist Kostas Vaxevanis published all the names on the list – without the deposit amounts. He was promptly arrested for breaching privacy laws and then released. He never divulged his sources, whether in Greece or abroad. To me, this latest episode was yet another proof of strange dealings around the handling of the data; to most people however, the journalist was a hero and his arrest was yet another proof of an attempt at a cover up.

Over the next few months, the Lagarde list dominated political debate. It seemed to be the solution to everything: cuts in wages and salaries, higher taxes – all we needed to do was catch the people on the list and those covering for them.

The whole country seemed to be waiting for the French to resend the information initially provided in 2010. In December 2012, three officials from the Greek finance ministry flew to Paris to take possession. They returned the same day, arriving after midnight, and went straight to the economic prosecutor to officially hand over the new CD-ROM so there would be no doubt it was the real one.

As we did every year, the family spent the Christmas holidays with my wife's family in the Netherlands. Compared with other years when I was a minister, this time there was no reason to rush, so we drove instead of flying, planning to spend a week relaxing in Jacoline's hometown close to Amsterdam. Or so we thought.

On the morning of December 28th, my phone rang. It was a journalist friend calling from Athens. I responded with season's greetings but sensed hesitation in his voice. Finally he got to the point: there were press leaks that the new list was different from the previous one. It had three more names. They belonged to relatives of mine. The conclusion was that I had removed them.

Certain moments in life are kept in the memory forever, in every vivid detail. I still remember the shock and disbelief, the dizziness, the anger. What on earth was this about? How was this possible? Who had set me up? I remember frantically searching the Web for details as the story exploded in the news, in Greece and abroad.

By the afternoon, I had issued a statement, categorically stating there was absolutely no tampering on my part. If there were indeed accounts that belonged to relatives of mine, that was something I had no knowledge of until that day. I added, "I will not be made a scapegoat, nor will I accept the fabrication of guilt when there is none". After all, it was by my initiative that the files came to Greece and I was the one who handed them over to be investigated for possible tax evasion.

I spent much of the following two days glued to my laptop, scanning news sites, and on the phone, trying to make sense of it all. I was shocked by the press coverage. "Guilty" read the headline in Greece's biggest selling newspaper the next day. No question mark, no doubt. This was typical of the coverage; it was an onslaught. In the midst of it, there were calls from concerned friends, who were outraged at what was being done to me. I was immensely grateful to them.

Jacoline and the boys were doing their best to understand what this new twist in a tumultuous life meant for us all. The magnitude of it dawned when even Dutch radio news mentioned that a Greek ex-finance minister had been caught protecting his relatives from investigation.

We cut short the vacation and drove back. On the way, I heard that camera crews were waiting for us at the Greek port of Patras. Jacoline dropped me off at the airport in Milan, from where I caught a flight to Athens and managed to arrive home unnoticed. The rest of the family took the boat from Ancona in Italy to Patras and were faced by a battery of cameras searching for my recognizable face among the drivers of cars exiting the ferry.

We were back home. But the ordeal had only just begun.

Chapter 27

THE TRIAL

"Defendant, approach the dock".

I was the one the presiding judge was addressing. My lawyers nudged me to advance and stand at the proverbial dock. In front of me, perched at a higher level, sat two rows of judges. Thirteen judges, composing the Special Court, along with their six alternates, all drawn from the two highest legal formations – the Council of State and the Supreme Court, the *Areios Pagos*. They had decided to forgo their traditional robes as these differed in each court, but they still looked intimidating.

I listened to the prosecutor outline the accusations: breach of faith and tampering with an official document, both felonies. As they involved potentially high losses to the state, according to a 1950s law still on the books they carried a life sentence. When the prosecutor concluded, the president asked me to plead. "I am innocent your Honour. I categorically deny the charges against me."

How on earth did I end up here?

According to the Greek constitution, serving ministers and ex-ministers cannot be accused for crimes allegedly committed while in office without being indicted by parliament. A special parliamentary investigative committee is set up, which calls witnesses, deliberates, and issues findings that are put then to a vote. An absolute parliamentary majority of all MPs to indict opens the door to a proper judicial inquiry and eventually to a trial by a Special Court. Its decision is final and cannot be appealed.

In my case the kick-off to this process had occurred two and a half years earlier. It was right after that fateful day in late December 2012 when it was announced that the USB handed over by Venizelos had three names missing – those of my relatives. With astounding speed, and during the Christmas break, the government coalition parties set up a parliamentary committee to investigate me – and me alone.

Already, one day after the revelation, Venizelos had summarily expelled me from PASOK – before any inquiry. The wagons of the government coalition convoy were forming a circle. The message sent out and magnified by the media was very clear. "Look no further. *He* is the culprit in the Lagarde "scandal". The *only* culprit. See, he removed the names of his relatives." It was so terribly convenient.

The investigative committee was a sham. At the start of the process, whose deliberations were closed to the public, the president asked committee members to avoid making any public statements or discussing testimonies. Nevertheless, the case dominated the news with daily leaks, suggesting all the evidence pointed to my guilt. To add insult to injury, committee members regularly appeared in the media, expressing judgements about the case, namely my guilt. A mockery of any pretence that this was a fair, objective inquiry process.

Over six months, the committee heard 80 witnesses, and harassed civil servants who dared to give evidence that supported my version of events. They grilled former members of my staff for days and systematically intimidated them to get what they wanted to hear. If their answers did not fit the script, their honesty and integrity were challenged.

The committee also asked for forensics reports on the USB stick Venizelos handed over, and on finance ministry laptops and PCs. And, early in the process, there was a breakthrough: the first forensics report revealed that the stick from which three names were missing was not the one that I had handed over. It was a different one, which had been created later in the SDOE, while mine had been mysteriously destroyed. And nobody could certify that the new USB stick had not been doctored.

I was elated, thinking that would lead to the case being

dropped. I was wrong – the process continued. Too much had already been invested in my guilt.

Fearing the tampering charge would not hold, the committee broadened the investigation to include breach of trust. To be able to sustain felony charges, it exerted pressure on the SDOE to quickly conclude its investigation and issue a report attesting to tax evasion by my relatives.

The SDOE obliged, auditing their Greek tax and bank statements for the last 17(!) years. In a twist of fate, the investigators made use of a legal provision I had put in place as minister, which allowed tax authorities to "reverse the burden of proof" and label as "undeclared income" any bank deposits whose origin could not be explained by taxpayers. Except that now, in a clear abuse of power, the SDOE arbitrarily ignored or dismissed all explanations offered by my relatives.

When the time came for me to testify to the committee, I was handed the 20,000 page judicial file to prepare myself and was given seven days. It was a joke. I refused to appear, and decided instead to use my right to speak at the parliament plenary when the committee findings came to a vote. I knew the committee had already decided. All that remained was for them to formulate the charges.

The final committee report chose to ignore compelling evidence of my innocence. Inconvenient information and testimonies were censored. To make things worse, the report was signed by two MPs who had not participated in the committee's six-month deliberations. They had substituted for two committee members who were given cabinet seats in a government reshuffle a few days earlier. The new MPs had not heard any witnesses, nor read the evidence; that did not stop them from signing a report to indict me.

As I rose to defend myself at the parliament plenary, I was painfully aware of my circumstances. I was no longer the powerful minister rising from his seat on the government benches to deliver a speech. When I entered the chamber to sit at the space reserved for visitors, I sensed hostility or embarrassment, mixed with curiosity. I was an outcast, speaking to convince MPs to vote against indicting me – probably in vain.

And I was absolutely furious. I lashed out at the cold political calculation and cynicism in this affair; at the hypocrisy and deceit of the people hounding me for a crime I did not commit; at a political system which had decided to wash its sins on my back, offering up the architect of the austerity measures as a sacrifice. People were pretending I was being prosecuted for the Lagarde list, when everyone knew perfectly well that this was a trial about the memorandum and its policies in all but name.

I went through the charges one by one and step by step. How could I be accused of dereliction of duty and breach of faith when I had requested the information, brought it to Greece, handed it over to be investigated, held meetings on how the data could be used, and passed the data in full to the appropriate official to investigate before leaving the ministry?

I pointed to testimonies of the president of the Legal Council of State and of the head of the Authority against Money Laundering – the committee had conveniently bypassed them. They both supported my handling of the data with discretion and secrecy, given its illegal origin. I did recognize my responsibility for the fact that the original CD-ROM from France could not be located. But I objected strongly to the idea that I had misplaced it on purpose. Its disappearance hurt me, no-one else.

On the charge that I had removed the names of my relatives, I argued this did not stand up to plain common sense: their accounts were some of the smallest in the list and one of them even had a zero balance. Why would I remove such an account? Plus, I knew very well that the original data in France could be requested again at any time to check if any names had been removed. And – if they really did believe I was the culprit – why would I have incriminated myself by removing only those three names, rather than instead muddying the waters by removing more?

But my strongest arguments were based on the forensics.

I repeated the fact that the USB stick with the three missing names was simply not the one I had handed over. How was it even possible to accuse me of tampering by brandishing another USB stick made at a later stage by someone else, and simply claim without any proof that it was an exact copy of the one I gave him? And all this while the original "forgery" had for some reason been destroyed – indisputably not by me?

I also pointed out that the forensics examination revealed all sorts of strange happenings in the period after I had left the ministry. Many copies of the original USB stick I had handed over were since made. Forensic traces in laptops and PCs showed manipulation of folders and data that pointed to tampering – again clearly and indisputably, not by me. The "chain of custody" principle – being able to follow and ascertain the integrity of the evidence – had clearly been compromised.

It seemed the information was widely disseminated and "handled" in the SDOE. And yet, in this whole process nobody ever actually investigated who else could have removed those names in order to frame me. The findings were based on one single premise: since we have such a nice theory that the tampering was done by Papaconstantinou, why let facts that contradict this get in the way?

I then addressed the obvious issue: if not me, then who? Who else could have done it and what was the motivation? I did not know, but it could certainly have been many people, and at many different moments during the list's "journey" after it had left my hands. Within the SDOE, or outside it. With political intervention, or without it.

It was clear from forensics and witness testimony that many people had both the technical and practical capability to remove the names. As for motive, I pointed to the obsessive nature of attacks against me by some of the media. During my time as finance minister, I had upset the corrupt practices of many in the SDOE, as well as of many business and political people – many would like to see me pay for this.

My speech concluded with an appeal to MPs: do not allow yourselves to be used in such a blatant political game. Here was an obvious attempt to establish a culprit without evidence – because it suited politically. All I asked was to be judged on the basis of real evidence and with a sense of justice.

I did not convince them. Half of the MPs were not even in the chamber to listen. They had made up their mind and were passing the time in the refectory, waiting for the vote to be called. But there was a consolation: while all parties had publicly taken a position in favour of indicting, many MPs broke with party ranks. On the crucial accusation of tampering, only 165 out of 300 bought the story that had been served to them.

But that was enough. I was officially indicted.

During the long period of the parliamentary investigative committee, I also had two interesting meetings. The first one was with investigative journalist Kostas Vaxevanis, who had revealed all the "Lagarde list" names in his magazine. He told me that while he disagreed with my handling of the whole case, he did not actually believe I was the one who had removed the names of my relatives. The second was with certain high-ranking SYRIZA politicians. They asked me to give them evidence which they could use against Venizelos. I responded that I would not enter into such backroom "deals"; whatever I had to say on the case I would say openly in parliament.

Once the case left parliament in June 2013, it took its course in the legal system. A five-member Judicial Council was appointed to examine the case, and one of its members was entrusted with the task to make a recommendation to the Council. Having studied the file in depth (probably the only one of the five to do so), he concluded that there was no case and that all charges against me should be dropped.

In a rare departure from usual practice, his recommendation was not followed. The Judicial Council decided instead to send me for trial on two felony charges, breach of faith and tampering, while clearing me of dereliction of duty.

My relatives, who had been named as co-conspirators (they were supposed to have asked me to take their names off the list), were cleared of any criminal wrong-doing after two years of defamatory press coverage. However, they still had to face a lengthy fight in the civil courts to clear themselves of tax evasion charges.

Politics continued to weigh on the whole process.

After two and a half years of agony, anxiety, and vilification, I was due to face the Special Court set up for me in February 2015. The last time this Court had been constituted was in 1989, to try former prime minister Andreas Papandreou and a number of his ministers. That trial was broadcast live and watched like a soap opera, and it divided the nation. During the proceedings, one of the accused former ministers suffered a seizure and died on live TV. Papandreou was acquitted on a 7 to 6 vote; he went on to win the elections and become prime minister again.

Twenty-five years later, a Special Court was being convened again, but this time it felt like a farce. And I was in a vastly different situation – alone and politically abandoned by almost everyone. Throughout that Kafkaesque period I could only count on my family and friends. My whole life was on hold; there was no sense in planning for the future while I faced the prospect of a long prison sentence.

This was also a period when I met and appreciated that strange breed of people, criminal lawyers. You don't really want to know them or what they do, but when you need them you want the best. And they have their own unique way of working; heavy on verbal and stage presence, with pre-court and courtroom tactics akin to those of chess players. And the gallows humour you would expect.

I was lucky to have three of the best (who took me on practically on a pro bono basis) and learned to work with them, suppressing some of my instincts and going with theirs. I wanted to shout my innocence to the world; they wanted us to keep a low profile and fight only on legal grounds, while recognizing that politics would always be present. Given there was no political party or broad popular movement backing me, they were right. So here we were – the much-awaited trial. With TV vans parked outside, a throng of cameras and photographers besieged a courtroom crammed with journalists, friends and family. The presiding judge found a compromise between the law – which had since been changed and now prohibited cameras or photos in the courtroom – and the need to feed the beast, with pictures and video of me sitting at the defendant's table. They were allowed in for five minutes, then had to leave.

I do not know how to convey the feelings of someone standing at the dock, listening to charges being read out, knowing that he is innocent and yet that at the end of the process the verdict could involve a long prison sentence. It is beyond me. I am generally composed, maintaining a degree of *sang-froid* even in demanding circumstances. That had certainly helped me do the finance minister job. The case had gone on for over two years, so by the trial I was actually relieved we were nearing the end. But it was not an easy moment.

The first witnesses were called to shed light on the breach of faith charge, which rested on whether my relatives had indeed evaded taxes, and to establish the financial loss to the state, if any. A serving SDOE official testified to the unit's findings on tax irregularities based on tax and bank statements over a 17-year period. However, the flagrant inaccuracies and arbitrariness of the report were quickly apparent to the court. It was a botched job, driven by the need to provide the parliamentary committee with fodder against me.

This was made even more clear by the next witness – head of the "high net worth individuals" tax office, whose job was to calculate the actual taxes owed using the SDOE report. They had not done so – despite having received the report two years earlier. Could it be that they disagreed with the SDOE findings, but did not dare overturn that report? "But we could bring our report tomorrow", he said to incredulous judges. And he did.

It showed that using their own "net worth" method – different from the one applied by the SDOE – there was absolutely no tax owed by my relatives. No wonder they had not made the report public all this time.

It was about this point that the breach of faith charge crumbled. If two parts of the tax administration came to opposite conclusions and the one whose job was to calculate the taxes owed stated that none were due, there was no basis for the accusation that my actions had caused harm to the state; especially when even the SDOE's findings had to be confirmed by a competent tax court and, as the SDOE witness himself admitted, "it could be that in the end there was no tax evasion".

The judges were amazed, and irate at the way the tax people did their job. "How many people on the list have you examined?" "About thirty," was the answer. "Of the 2,062? In three years?" asked an incredulous judge. So much for my actions having stopped the tax authorities from going after the treasure trove.

This left the charge of tampering. The forensics expert's testimony lasted two days, the highlight being the display of the files on a viewing screen ("it's like in the US Supreme Court in here," quipped the court president). Perhaps the most telling part was when one of the judges asked the witness bluntly, "This technical stuff is interesting, but I am a criminal judge. Do your reports show the tampering occurred while the information was in the hands of the accused?" The response was clear: "If it did, we would have said so."

On the fourth week of the trial, after the court had heard almost twenty witnesses, including three who testified eloquently on my character, I took the stand. The courtroom was even more packed than usual; in addition to the court journalists and daily presence of my family, I was gratified to see dozens of friends show up. During the trial I was humbled by the presence of a steady number of friends, as well as by people I did not know, who simply wanted to show their support.

I spoke for two hours. You could hear a pin drop in the

courtroom. I went over the case from the beginning; how I requested the data, how it came to Greece, how I handled it. I described the prejudiced proceedings in parliament, what I had gone through. I spoke of the total lack of evidence for a crime I had not committed, the dark aspects of the case no-one had bothered investigate, the need to find a scapegoat. I was angry, lucid, coherent and completely exhausted by the end.

My statement was followed by a four-hour interrogation in which I tried to cover all details, answer questions and dispel doubts. Given the lack of real evidence against me, the questions focused on whether my general behaviour at the time pointed to the act of removing the names. In my answers I tried to describe accurately the circumstances of the period in question, which explained why I had acted as I did.

With hindsight it was easy to see how certain things could have been handled differently; if they had, I would not be standing in court. But this was now; back then, I was working under extreme pressure, dealing with one of the biggest crises the country had known; the "list" which now was the centre of the universe was then only one of the numerous issues I juggled with every day.

The next day belonged to the prosecutor. It took her a good five hours to explain why she wanted me convicted on two felony counts, with no mitigating circumstances. Her proposal meant a life sentence. This was by far the worse time in the trial. However I tried to rationalize it, I just could not understand how someone who had heard all the evidence could still make such a damning statement.

Finally, the defence. One by one my three lawyers addressed the substantive and legal points of the case: the complete lack of any proof on tampering on my part, the many indications of tampering by others while the data was no longer in my custody, the lack of any damage to the state by my handling of this illegally obtained data; on the contrary, efforts by me to bring the information to Greece and have it used against tax evasion, without excluding or protecting anyone, especially my relatives.

The court adjourned and I had to wait a few difficult days to hear the verdict. I believed in my gut the worst-case scenario could not come true. But it was such a politically loaded case. Were the thirteen judges above that? Would they follow the evidence and their consciences, would they instead be influenced by the public mood for lynching, or would they try to find a middle way?

On the day of the verdict, I took a bag of clothes and toiletries with me. I was calm – hoping for the best, but preparing for the worst. In the previous weeks and months, to keep going, Jacoline and I had run through all the scenarios, faced all the possibilities. If justice ended up being absent from the building on the day and I was sentenced to go to prison, she would keep the family going, making sure the kids were ok. We would cope.

In the end, we did not have to test that scenario.

I was unanimously cleared of the breach of faith charge. And five out of thirteen judges, including the court president, voted to acquit me of the tampering charge as well, and clear me completely. An eight-to-five majority handed down a misdemeanour sentence on the tampering charge. They ruled that I had removed my relatives' names to protect myself and my reputation, not to circumvent any tax obligations on their part.

Once the verdict was announced, the judges retired to decide on the sentence. There were more hours of waiting, but at least now I knew I was not going to prison. It was a misdemeanour conviction. They handed down the minimum – a one-year suspended sentence. After announcing it, the president's parting words to me were from the Bible: "now go, and do not sin."

While the reporters rushed out for live TV feeds, I was hugged and kissed by my relieved relatives and friends, many with tears in their eyes. My lawyers were being congratulated – everyone was treating the verdict as an acquittal in all but name. This is also how it was portrayed in the Greek media – seasoned court reporters could see through the decision and interpreted it accordingly.

The verdict the judges handed down proved that by its very nature the Special Court renders judgment based on legal reasoning, but also takes politics into account. If there was any doubt about this, the passionate speech of the prosecutor should have made it clear. "This is not a trial of Mr. Papaconstantinou," she said. "It is a trial for the Greek people who have been humiliated and made to pay so much money."

Solid legal reasoning led the judges to throw out – unanimously – the breach of faith charge. But the majority could not bring themselves to clear me completely. They used their prerogative to pass judgment based on their "freely formed conscience" – even in the absence of evidence proving guilt beyond reasonable doubt.

Taking into account both the verdict and the sentence, the end result was as close as it could have been to a full acquittal. It allowed the court to claim justice had been served, without bowing to populist pressure for punishment; but it did not allow me to feel vindicated. Too much political capital had been invested in the case for that; in the case of full acquittal, questions would have been raised about parliament's actions, as well about what really happened.

I woke up the next morning realizing the heavy weight on my chest was no longer there. My feelings were mixed and confused. I was angry about what I had been subjected to; bitter that I had not been completely cleared; grateful for the hard work and dedication of my lawyers, and a close group of friends; humbled by the love and support from so many; and relieved it was over.

I could now press the "play" button and get on with my life.

EPILOGUE

Back in 2010, at the time of the first bailout, I used to tell people that our job would be done when Greece no longer featured on the front page of the Financial Times. Three bailouts, four elections, six prime ministers, nine finance ministers and one referendum later, we still have some way to go.

This is not to say nothing has been achieved – quite the contrary. Both Greece and Europe have changed dramatically since that fateful spring in 2010, when the huge Greek fiscal deficit and the big lie told by the previous government about its size became the spark which lit a fire under the shaky Eurozone construction.

For a start, the euro has been saved. There were times when the project could have disintegrated – it did not. Europe initially misunderstood the problem, dithered in its response, and then brought in makeshift fire-fighters. As the crisis engulfed Ireland, Portugal, Spain and Cyprus, and threatened Italy and even France, what started as a one-off bailout turned into a permanent mechanism to help countries in trouble.

Money on the table to be used when necessary is one thing; ensuring it will not be needed is another. The latter involves changes in the EU institutional architecture that have only just started. Stronger mechanisms for surveillance, coordination and crisis prevention are now in place. The same goes for steps towards creating a banking union in Europe, such as common supervision and resolution mechanisms.

But the hard work has just begun; we are still far from facing up to issues such as taxation at the supra-national level, a common budget with permanent transfer mechanisms, joint debt issuance, a monetary policy run by a true "lender of last resort", or a seamless Europe-wide deposit guarantee scheme. They remain a gleam in the eye of those of us who believe passionately that the only way forward involves deeper economic and political integration.

The same holds for growth and jobs. It is not just a case of less austerity; that will not magically bring growth back. Nor will unemployment fall automatically just because fiscal consolidation and structural reforms bring investor confidence back. Reforms increase a country's growth potential, but they are not a short-term fix, nor do they alone tackle unemployment, poverty and social exclusion. As yet, the collective response to these issues has been more rhetoric than action.

At the end of the day, it is not just about policy choices or institutional mechanics. It is about a "new narrative" which builds on the great achievements of the last half century – peace, democracy, prosperity – and fashions a political project for the future. One that reinvents Europe in the new global stage, but also answers today's urgent questions about economic and social justice, democratic participation, prosperity and security for all. We have yet to articulate that narrative. And until we do, the populists of various stripes always win.

Until recently, the forces of nationalism and populism seemed invincible. Following the unexpected result in the US presidential elections, and the UK decision to leave the EU, a kind of existentialist crisis engulfed us. It seemed as if populists would sweep into power in a number of European countries, calling into question the existence of the common currency and even the EU as a whole, together with the values of freedom, tolerance and the open society on which it is built.

Politics however is not linear. The isolationism and ambiguity of the new US administration towards the EU, coupled with the shock caused by the British decision to leave the EU had the opposite effect: pro-European forces rallied in the rest of the

EU. In successive elections in different countries, parties and candidates that openly defended the European idea and destiny of their country in a united Europe prevailed.

These developments open a window of opportunity that actually allows us to address the problems which give rise to populism. The ascendance of the populists is not just a fluke. It is linked to a number of broad economic and social trends which have led many Europeans – and not only Europeans – to question what has been achieved during the last fifty years. Trends such as the onslaught of globalization, which has delivered prosperity and jobs in both the developed and (especially) the developing world, but at the same time also threatens the livelihood and social position of many who see it as a "zero-sum game".

The same holds for ubiquitous technological change; the fourth industrial revolution and the advent of robotics create tremendous opportunities, but also threaten millions of jobs across a number of sectors. Same for new social media; they revolutionize communication, but also give an immense forum to extreme views, obliterate every evaluation filter, blur the lines between fact and fabrication, and can act corrosively on already destabilized societies.

The populist push is finally connected to other great challenges of our era that make western societies question core values such as tolerance, openness and multiculturalism. Recent refugee flows have already led a number of European countries to effectively close their borders and put limits to the transformation of their social mix. And at a completely different level, terrorism has instilled the element of fear into the daily life of European capitals; its obvious goal is the western way of life and the open society itself.

The window of opportunity for a democratic, progressive and convincing response to these challenges exists today, but it will not be there forever. It involves major changes in economic and social policy, in a way that places Europe firmly in the new global competitive environment, but at the same time provides opportunities for those – citizens as well as entire states – most vulnerable to the tectonic changes we are experiencing.

Practically, this implies a "grand bargain" between countries such as Germany, which currently dominate EU economic policy, and those countries struggling to adapt. With one side using existing fiscal space for a more expansionary policy, and agreeing to combine this with resources for more investment at EU level, the adaptation of key European institutions, and greater solidarity to offset "beggar thy neighbor" outcomes of prevailing economic policy effectively favoring the strongest countries. And with the other side agreeing to pursue deep structural reforms in all countries where adjustment has been delayed or hindered. This is the only way to make the common currency work for all.

It is not all about economics, however. Using this window of opportunity also implies finding new ways to remain true to Europe's humanitarian principles and social integration, while also giving society a sense of security. New ways to enhance citizens' participation and transparency in governance. And especially a deepening of European cooperation, with joint actions and policies ranging from the economy to defense and security. Time will show if this opportunity will be used or lost to Europe, but the risks of a failure are all too real.

Just as Europe has evolved since the crisis began, so has Greece.

The past years have been a huge reality check. When the crisis hit, the country was on borrowed time, with an economy living beyond its means, with weak institutions and a self-serving political system. It has since undergone a transformation, but at a huge societal cost.

From the beginning of the crisis in 2008 up to its worst point, the economy had lost one quarter of its GDP, with a full quarter of the working population in unemployment; these are characteristics that can only be found in the US Great Depression of the 1930s. And with real GDP returning to the levels before the country joined EMU in 2001. With widened inequality, an increase in poverty and social exclusion, serious degradation in public services.

The other facet of this grim picture is the budgetary and structural adjustment achieved – the raison d'être of the support programmes since 2010. Most notably, the disappearance of the "twin deficits": the fiscal deficit and that of competitiveness. On the fiscal front, in a remarkable adjustment, a double-digit primary deficit (net expenditures, excluding interest paid on debt) has become a significant primary surplus. Similarly, starting again from a double-digit deficit, the external account has been balanced, although largely due to the collapse of imports in the recession, rather than to an increase in exports.

Regarding structural reforms, the other important part of adjustment programmes, criticism has often focused on a lack of implementation from the Greek side, especially when legislated changes are not followed up. Part of the criticism is rightly placed; spending cuts and tax increases have often seemed easier than facing down special interests opposed to reforms.

At the same time, much has been achieved in a wide range of policies: in controlling public spending, in tax administration and tax evasion, opening up closed professions, facilitating company creation, licensing and operation, labor market flexibility, liberalization of markets. And, taken together, the reforms that have gradually and painfully accumulated since 2010 imply higher productivity and, in the medium term, a higher growth potential.

Nevertheless, Greece today is still an outlier. It is the only one of all "memorandum" countries that has needed not one but three adjustment programmes. While every other country has left behind its own (one and only) memorandum, our country still has difficulty coming out of this support and surveillance framework.

The reasons for this are many. They start from the clearly worse initial conditions; no other country had the kind of twin deficits which Greece had. To that should be added a huge credibility deficit, due to the failure of past governments to deliver promised reforms but also importantly to the fiscal fraud. While some credibility was gradually clawed back after 2010, the credibility deficit came back to haunt us in 2015.

They continue with the uniquely Greek inability to find a political consensus around what actually went wrong in the first place (the prosecution for allegedly "inflating" the 2009 deficit in order "to bring in the IMF" is a case in point); but even more importantly on what should be done once no longer under a support programme. Political parties proved totally unable to find common ground on what were in fact inescapable policy choices. Instead, the opposition continuously claimed it could negotiate a "better deal"; this undermined the implementation of the programme as well as any hope of it being accepted by society.

There have also been serious mistakes in the design of Greek programmes on the part of our EU partners and the IMF, as well as obvious weaknesses in their implementation by successive Greek governments. Domestic criticism focuses on the former, criticism from abroad on the latter. But in addition, it is clear that exiting the programme and returning to markets has remained impossible for as long as EU countries brandished the Grexit threat (in essence cancelling the logic of the programme) and as long as the Greek government (as it did in 2015) attempted to use the threat of Grexit as a negotiating tool.

In the dramatic summer of 2015, we lived through a deeply divisive referendum which proved almost fatal for the country, and with the consequent and unnecessary third memorandum. After then calling snap elections and being re-elected, the SYRIZA-ANEL government had to cover the time lost with its disastrous choices of the first half of 2015, and implement what was perhaps the most onerous of the three support programmes – piling additional austerity measures on those of the two previous programmes.

They did so with equivocation and ambiguity, an eye to their internal party audience, and a total inability to understand basic principles of negotiation. They procrastinated and delayed endlessly every periodic programme evaluation, eventually boxing themselves into a corner, facing conflicting creditors' interests, and with EU countries unable to take politically difficult decisions in view of upcoming elections. Greece paid the price, always ending up with a worse deal than the one available at the beginning of the negotiation.

During this period, the government legislated fiscal measures that the mainstream political parties which have governed Greece for decades, had they been in power now, would have had extreme difficulty convincing their parliamentary groups to support. SYRIZA and ANEL MPs did, no doubt because the alternative of losing power seemed far worse than voting against their stated convictions. In this way, the adjustment that started in 2010 was completed, but at an enormous cost to the economy.

Simultaneously, with the adoption of fiscal measures which will come into effect only after the end of the current parliamentary term, the high primary surpluses required by creditors for debt sustainability have been ensured, at least in part. At the same time, this extraordinary ex ante adoption of measures to be implemented by another government will no doubt undermine politically the government to emerge after the next elections.

On structural reforms, it is clear that the programme's prescriptions to liberalize markets, as well as the entire privatization agenda, are the exact antithesis of what SYRIZA stands for. So everything achieved in this area is due to having been prescribed by creditors as prior actions to loan tranche disbursements. And despite the fact that several interventions have been completed, the negative predisposition of the government to structural reforms has damaged the country's image to outside investors. Despite signing the third programme and adopting its measures, investors have continued to treat SYRIZA very cautiously.

It is nevertheless the case that the SYRIZA-ANEL strategy has gradually shifted from one of conflict with Europe to actually implementing the programme; its narrative resembles increasingly the "success story" developed by the Samaras government in 2014. According to this narrative, SYRIZA, having taken over an impossible job, has actually turned things around, achieved debt relief, and thereby is on course to gain market access, bidding farewell to the "age of the MoU"; and it will eventually be rewarded in elections for this.

Experience suggests that in the Greek crisis, no government is actually rewarded by the voters, even if at some point it has done the right thing (or especially if it has done the right thing...). Disillusionment means that every government is punished in the polls. More so, when as in SYRIZA's case it has came to power riding a wave of anger and false hopes, only to subsequently and spectacularly dash them, unashamedly lying on a daily basis, and exercising power with a cynicism and lack of morality rarely seen in Greek politics.

In the discussion about the day after the support programmes, the Holy Grail is debt relief. It is supposed to be the passport for re-accessing markets, and for sustainable growth. But is that truly the case? No doubt further debt relief, following the 2013 debt haircut – but this time on the debt held not by private investors, but by official EU creditors – will remove uncertainty about the sustainability of the large stock of public debt and the ability to service it (as in effect the national debt is serviced and recycled, not actually repaid).

Greek public debt, however, has particularities. The EU/IMF loans and the haircut on private creditors' holdings means the vast majority of outstanding debt is in official hands. In addition, its average duration is long, the interest burden is low, and for several years redemptions are also small. This does not mean there is no need for relief; but it does mean that debt relief as discussed (in the form of lengthening grace periods and actual redemptions or even pegging today's low interest rates over a long period) is only part of the picture, and perhaps not the most important part.

There are a number of reasons for this. The first can be traced to the lack of trust by our EU partners towards the Greek political system as a whole. As a result, any debt relief decisions at the end of the programme will be incorporated into a new agreement when the current one expires in 2018. Whether we call it an MoU or something else, this agreement will describe a set of policy commitments as a counterbalance to the debt relief measures, which will only be phased in gradually and conditionally; commitments to convince suspicious creditors that the country will continue to pursue reforms.

The second reason has to do with private investors. To them, debt sustainability is a necessary but not sufficient condition for investing in Greece. Yes, opportunistic short-term capital is invested on the fluctuations in Greek government bond yields – and it is often a precursor of investment with a longer-term horizon. But the large-scale, long-term, strategic international capital which is necessary for the country to grow looks at other factors beyond debt (aside from cost). Critical amongst these are the need for stability, predictability and efficiency in institutions ranging from taxation, licensing and the ease of doing business, to the functioning of the political system, the state and the justice system.

At the end of the day, beyond what concerns our EU and international partners and the markets, the key question us Greeks need to answer is whether or how a small, closed economy with weak institutions can have a future in an incomplete economic union with a hard currency. How such an economy can attract investment, generate growth, jobs and prosperity for its citizens. The answer is that it can, but to survive and prosper in this context it needs to change dramatically; there are therefore a number of prerequisites.

The first is political. The current government formation neither wants nor can take the radical decisions required for transforming the state and the economy and ensuring the country's continued participation in the Eurozone. The real turning point for the economy will come after national elections, but only if political change is translated into a real change in outlook. At present, such a new outlook is not evident, nor is there a mood for radical change apparent either in the main opposition or the rest of the political system.

The second condition is correcting the course of economic policy. The shift in the policy mix called for by the Troika – broadening the tax base, tax relief to favor investment, measures for the sustainability of the pension system – is in the right direction. However, the target for the primary surplus in the next years remains too high, dragging down the Greek economy, while debt relief will only come gradually. So here too there is a real danger of being stuck in an environment of weak growth, with little job creation, in turn leading to further disappointment, anger and eventually further feeding populism.

The third condition is a series of courageous structural interventions, starting from a process of quickly resolving or working-out non-performing loans, especially business loans, thereby releasing capital and helping viable businesses get out from under their crushing debt load. The country desperately needs an investment "big bang", with tens of billions of foreign direct investment; there are no sufficient domestic savings to support the investment effort.

The list of required interventions is well known – while much has been achieved since the beginning of the crisis, a lot more remains to be done. But rather than repeating well-worn generalities, let's concentrate on achieving a few practical things, such as improving specific parameters that help the country rise in the international competitiveness rankings investors follow. Or targeted, but transparent, actions to unblock specific investments.

Above all, let us not have yet another debate about the "National Reconstruction Plan" the country needs. We actually have one - it is called the MoU. Let's actually implement its structural policies to open up and modernize the state and the economy. Not everything in the programme is right; but we would be in a vastly better situation had we consistently implemented reforms in product and service markets all these years. And let's complement it with initiatives to create stable, independent and credible institutions, or groundbreaking changes in our political system; no one prevents us from doing so.

It is not easy to be an optimist after all that has happened in the country these past years, nor when looking at the challenges and difficulties ahead; but at the very least measured optimism is justified. The truth is that the country and its political and economic system have been transformed in the last few years. It has been an enforced transformation. That is in fact why it has produced tangible results: little would have happened without the "hated Memorandum". It may have been flawed in design and often badly implemented, but it was the first time the country had a business plan, complete with deliverables, deadlines and sanctions. At the same time, the fact that it was imposed is also why it has not really changed the country. If you don't own the change, it is only skin-deep.

Greece has saved the euro, but not itself – at least not yet.

Attitudes and institutions have lagged behind this transformation. After six years of an artificial divide between people who were pro- and anti-memorandum, 80% of the country has now voted to implement pretty much the same policies. But this signifies much less than what the numbers suggest. It is not a true conversion. It is not a real conviction that change is necessary. We have yet to face what really brought us here.

We continue to view ourselves as the most wronged people in history. We believe that we have found ourselves where we are today not because we happened to be doing the wrong things; but because we were tricked, betrayed, because dark forces conspired against us. But you cannot cure a disease you don't admit exists.

We still see rights as being disconnected from responsibilities. Reforms are as fine as long as they relate to someone else. We protect vested interests and "established rights", in effect shielding rentier minorities; but we are reluctant to go after the major sources of our troubles – the large, inefficient and clientelist state and the corporatist private sector that feeds off it.

We love grand ideas, but we dismiss the possibility that they may not actually meet the test of reality; and we refuse to do the hard work to figure out the difference.

We are still afraid of genuine consensus and compromise. Pragmatism is a dirty word. We are still attracted by the heroism of the useless sacrifice. We prefer those who reluctantly implement difficult policies, claiming they have been blackmailed, over those who understand the necessity of such policies and defend them.

We will choose populists over realists any time – the former are visionary, the latter cold technocrats. We admire those tilting at windmills and when they fail, as they inevitably do, we think, "at least they tried".

Well, I am tired of losing after having fought the good fight. I am tired of pleading for "a conspiracy of common sense" to replace all the conspiracies that have infected people's minds and collectively held us back.

I want my country to win.

AUTHOR'S NOTE

I started writing *Game Over* during the summer of 2012 and finished it in the first months of 2016, with a pause of about a year during the period leading up to the Special Court. To put my thoughts onto paper, I mainly used my personal notes from the period of the Papandreou and Papademos governments, and drew on discussions with protagonists of the crisis period, as well as on publicly available material. I avoided footnotes and bibliographic references in the text; this book is not an academic or historical treatise. It is a testimonial. And it was originally written in English – partly because of my need to keep some emotional distance from the subject matter; I subsequently translated it myself to Greek and reworked it slightly.

I am indebted to a wide circle of friends, journalists, politicians and academics in Greece and abroad who provided feedback and advice in the early stages, and helped me shape my ideas: Michalis Bletsas, Julian Borger, Fotini Christia, Fred Kaufman, Robert Kuttner, Alexander Macridis, Paschos Mandravelis, Stilpon Nestor, Martin Neild, George Pagoulatos, Vassilis Papadimitriou, Andreas Papandreou, Richard Parker, Jean Pisanny-Ferry, Dante Roscini, Jeff Sachs, Dimitris Stefanou, Nikos Stylianidis, Lucas Tsoukalis, Martin Wolf.

Others were kind enough to read and comment on specific chapters or drafts of the entire book as it advanced: Alexandra Dellis, Natasha Fairweather, Costas Karagiannis, Natalie Kedikoglou, Elna Kleopa, Yannis Manuelides, Ted Margelos, Costas Meghir, Yannis Michos, Robert Power, Nick Papaconstantinou, Claus Sorensen, Martijn Vinke, Andrew Wyckoff. I owe much to all of them. I am humbled that Game

Over was the last book my brother-in-law Martijn Vinke read before he passed away so much too soon.

A number of colleagues from the Papandreou and Papademos governments helped me reconstruct and bring to life various instances from this extraordinary period: Maria Assimakopoulou, Petros Christodoulou, Chrysa Hatzi, Eftychia Mihailidou, Tasos Banos, Mona Papadakou, Sofia Ritsou, George Zanias. The diaries of Filio Lanara, George Petroulakis and Nelly Stergidi have been invaluable in helping me organize the book's narrative. Together with Philippos Sachinidis and Kostas Theos, they carefully read every chapter, making suggestions and critical comments. I am very grateful to them all. The book is better as a result of their work.

My publisher Yannis Papadopoulos believed in the book from the minute he read the manuscript; together with Katerina Triantafyllou and their team they supported its publication in both the Greek and English editions with professionalism and enthusiasm. Paul Johnston edited the English edition with care and a critical eye. And I am particularly grateful to my agent Catherine Clarke for her encouragement and support and for introducing me to the mysteries of the publishing world.

I have dedicated this book to my wife, Jacoline Vinke. From the very early stages of the writing, she read and commented in detail on every chapter, with the critical eye of a writer, but also of the person who shared with me this immensely difficult period and stood by me throughout. She is the rock in my life. Together with our kids, Nick and Stef, and my mother Elna Kleopa, they were the people who have given me all these years their unconditional love, their patience and their absolute trust.

George Papaconstantinou
May 2016

ABBREVIATIONS

ANEL: Independent Greeks (Greek political party)
ASE: Athens Stock Exchange
CACs: Collective Action Clauses
CDS: Credit Default Swaps
CDU: Christian Democratic Union (German political party)
DIMAR: Party of the Democratic Left (Greek political party)
ECB: European Central Bank
Ecofin: Economic and Financial Affairs Council
EFSF: European Financial Stability Facility
ELA: Emergency Liquidity Assistance
ELSTAT: Hellenic Statistical Authority
ERT: Hellenic Broadcasting Corporation
ESM: European Stability Mechanism
EU: European Union
EUROSTAT: Statistical Office of the European Union
EWG: Euro Working Group
EYP: (Greek) National Intelligence Service
GAO: General Accounting Office at the Greek Ministry of Finance
GDP: Gross Domestic Product
IIF: Institute of International Finance
IMF: International Monetary Fund
IOU: "I Owe You", an informal document acknowledging debt
IRS: US Internal Revenue Service
ISDA: International Swaps and Derivatives Association
LAOS: Popular Orthodox Rally (Greek political party)
LTRO: Long-term refinancing operations
MP: Member of Parliament

MEP: Member of European Parliament
MTFS: Medium Term Fiscal Strategy
ND: New Democracy (Greek political party)
NBG: National Bank of Greece
PDMA: Public Debt Management Agency
OECD: Organization for Economic Cooperation and Development
OMT: Outright monetary transactions
OPAP: Greek Organization of Football Prognostics S.A.
OTE: Hellenic Telecommunications Organization
PASOK: Panhellenic Socialist Movement (Greek political party)
PM: Prime Minister
PSI: Private Sector Involvement
SDOE: Economic Crimes Enforcement Agency of the Greek Ministry of Finance
SDRs: Special Drawing Rights
SGP: Stability and Growth Pact
SPV: Special Purpose Vehicle
SSM: Single Supervisory Mechanism
SYRIZA: The Coalition of the Radical Left (Greek political party)
VAT: Value-added tax

Made in the USA
Middletown, DE
18 September 2019